C000072173

In Praise of Permi

Angela's life story is a testimony of inner strength, determination and ultimate empowerment against all odds. A beautiful memoir highlighting the power of resilience. In Permission to Rise, forgiveness sprouts.

Vicky Porto - ChairWoman of the
International Women Group of Tulsa

Permission to Rise provides endless opportunities to cultivate greater intimacy with Angela's mind. Her story describes self-healing, heart-listening, determination and courage to transcend inner obstacles. Each page overspills with compassion, encouragement, wisdom and persistence. I strongly recommend this remarkable journey must be read by each and every growing up woman or anyone looking to rewrite their own story.

Solmaz Bulut, MS, LPC Family and
Children Mental Health

This is a story of courage and strength. It shows never to quit because if we persevere through, we will discover our plan and purpose for our life-the victorious life God intended!

Angela Lindskov - Published Author
The Cutting Edge"

Permission to Rise is an incredible account of the author's journey in pursuit of a new and better life, but most of all inner peace and happiness. By stepping outside her comfort zone, she had to re-write her own story and conquer all obstacles with great strength, determination and integrity. Such an inspiring life story!

Isabel Diefenbach - Business
Development Manager

The writer is very raw in sharing her story which kept me sit on the edge of my seat for awhile.

This book is packed with real life stories and in Permission to Rise, Angela remind us to be patient, to slow down and be brave, giving ourselves permission to write a new story. I like the fact she writes with compassion and humor at the same time. Angela is leaving a legacy of literature to the world.

Marcia Jeanes -
personal friend

PERMISSION TO RISE

A memoir

Angela McCluskey-Moses

www.TotalPublishingAndMedia.com

ISBN 978-1-63302-145-7

The peace of trusting my heart to your hands is because you know everything about it. From an inertia of hopelessness and defiant feelings, from a heart's darkest night, to a soul reemerging. Resilient in Permission to Rise like a Phoenix. The beauty of each experience, is knowing even when you Lord is silent, I can feel your presence in the warm blowing wind across my shoulder

Thank you for today. November 17th, 2014.
Angela McCluskey

Foreword

N o one can better tell this story than the author who lived every minute, hour, day and year of unfathomed circumstances. To see her today and hear of the slings and arrow beset her small frame, it is a miracle she not only survived, but managed to flourish emotionally and psychologically, advocating for victims of child abuse and championing women and women's voices from the Favelas of Brazil to the shores of the country she now calls home.

It is hard to imagine a small child protecting female siblings and other small girls from her own father, a luminary within the church and pedophile in a second floor bedroom at home. Bathed in the limitations a young adolescent has within the realms of a parent's home, she not only protected the girls through intervention, but confronted the man she, as a young child, once looked up to and respected. The letter to her father's victims is not only a discerning confession, but a heroically shrewd acknowledgement, unpacking complicated feelings as she decreed those closest to her.

Side effects associated with child abuse and in-home dysfunctionality led her to search for the potency, vitality and protection her father failed to provide, in men who impulsively played on her unrecognized angst and low self-esteem. Maintaining unhealthy relationships led her down a complicated path, blending the desire to achieve economically and financially through career building, with constantly thrusting herself 'emotionally' into a caregiver / overseer's role.

Permission to Rise is about stepping out of the shadows of emotional self-loathing into an aura of self-realization. Smart, aggressive, a self-drive self-starter, the author struggled to balance successes in her professional /work life with the ongoing fiascos played out in her personal life. Did the sins of her father play a role in her need to remain persistent and unrelenting when in her heart she knew she deserved more? Not everyone who alone navigates outrageous fortunes survives. Through the attributes of Resilience, the author not only survives but flourishes mentally, physically and faithfully, reconnecting with family and with a God upon whom for years she conferred rage, blame and guilt.

Permission to Rise details a crisscrossing of hardships and misfortunes in plain, simple, heart-wrenching language, while telling a story of buoyancy, toughness, faithfulness and love.

Shirley Hall - Author
Embrace, One Day & Listen

Table of Contents

Dedication

This book is dedicated to my sister Marineide,
a warrior since the age of six,
fighting her invisible fights through pains and struggles,
You are my reminder to not let evil win.

Also in loving memory of
Thomas Lance McCluskey, a warrior.

Acknowlegments

To my dear husband James for allowing me the downtime and the peace needed to take this trip down memory lane. His constant support and patient heart brings out the best in me. "Thank you with all my heart."

To my daughter Giovanna, my rock and the teacher who forced me to be stronger than I thought I could be. She taught me to protect and nourish her soul. "I am so very proud of the woman you've become."

To my friend Marcia who makes me feel like a superhero, fertilizing my brain with the craziest ideas and making me believe I can do anything.

To my dear friend Isabel, who motivates me in so many ways, and who believes in my work.

Last but not least, to my angel Elizabeth, for all her support - and for healing my soul during my darkest days. For all the love and constant care, I thank you from the bottom of my heart. I wouldn't be here without you and your 'love circle' – OneBand!"

Statement:

In order to tell my story and maintain the "rawness" of it, I've opted to keep some real names and to change the identities of others. The book is not intended to hurt anyone. I narrate every event with details as I remember them, however I do understand perception changes depending on where you are on our path. I appreciate each and every person who has contributed to my personal growth. You have done so by being the person I needed to teach life lessons and apply lessons learned.

Introduction

I began journaling in 2009 as a way to voice my anguish feelings when life took a wrong turn financially and emotionally. Journaling was supposed to help me organize my thoughts and give me a perspective on how to deal with them.

Looking back, I can clearly understand how much time I wasted simply 'vomiting' feelings without looking for 'what was making me sick'. There was no structure, my emotions and ego were literally riding me wild. I eventually collapsed when my husband passed away in 2014.

Supported by family love, and my daughter's encouragement to get off anti-depressant medication, I forced myself to react and took journaling to the next level. I needed to understand how I got so low. I begin writing what I was feeling and found myself creating a timeline, backtracking on the pain.

Pages and pages later, I found myself facing an eight year old. I recalled all the dreams she had given up in an attempt to escape a childhood filled with abuse.

"This is a lot of information I thought to myself. I have to move this to the computer, it is getting out of control."

When I clicked on the first blank page to begin transferring my written words, I found myself putting it in a book format: "How did I get here? What was the lesson?" I mentioned this to my good friend Marcia who immediately supported the idea.

"Branca she said! I think you should write your story!"

"I don't know about that Preta, right now I need time to figure out how to survive." [Branca means witty in Portuguese. It is a sweet way to say I'm too pale. In response I call her the opposite Preta]

I had to be careful with Marcia's enthusiasm because she literally believes I can do anything. If I told her I wanted to build a rocket ship she would start gathering screws and take me shopping for tools. I call her my super-hero-activation-start-plug.

As I kept writing, I found myself having several a-ha moments: "Aaaa, that's why I made that decision…now I know where things went bad. And the most important one: "Here's what I need to fix!"

While I kept busy reconstructing my new mindset with a better reality, Marcia would remind me about the book: "How's the book going?" I would keep it short "it's going." I was writing a little bit here and there and, "Eventually it's gonna be done" I kept telling myself.

Truth is I was having a hard time facing my pains. Sometimes I would need a couple of days to recover after being scared by monsters I had hid under my bed. Once I let them out writing became easier and I was excited. Maybe I could help others face their monsters.

I constantly got taps on my shoulders with new topics - ways to make people interpret themselves in a more positive way, bettering their lives.

I think this is the best reason to read this book. You might not want to change yourself right now, yet you should want to change how you make choices which affect your life.

You can have a coach, a mentor or an instructor but everything starts with the desire to change - surrendering can be a good place to start. By the time you finish this book, you will understand why.

> "If you correct your mind, the rest of your life will
> fall into place."
> ~ *Lao Tzu*

Preface

Since he has been gone, time is what I've got the most of.
And now, what do I do with it?
How did I get here – question or statement?

December 1st, 2014.

In the past ten years of my life, from the first month we lived together, my world revolved around him and I stopped making plans for my future. Yes, I did have dreams but they were lost, most rooted deep inside. I knew none of them could come true with the few resources I had, combined with the challenges of his fragile health.

It's a few days after his burial. I find myself with a box full of feelings I do not have the slightest idea how to detangle, or how to pick up. From the bottom of his heart he sincerely loved me, a joyful love I passionately returned. Yet I ask, how can someone be as loved as I have been yet be so damaged on a devastating scale. How could this love move me from heaven to hell in a matter of hours? All I can say is, this loving has been the most challenging experience of my life.

I must write down these feelings because I need to understand what led me to spend so many years with him. There were so many reasons to leave yet I never did. Here I can rebuild the 'crime scene' - what I call my ten years with him. Here I can unravel the tangle so I can come to an understanding and maybe finally get closure to this chapter of my life.

How did this love lead me to have a spiritual experience?
How did this relationship lead me to become unhinged
and transformed from inside out?

I feel these ten years were a test of fire brought from the sky and placed on the palm of my hand making me walk on the darker side of my soul. I navigated over the years because all the experiences were valid. This love and the challenges encountered in it led me to seek different solutions for the bad situation my family was facing. I explored the black side of my soul and signed in blood on the dotted line. I was willing to do absolutely anything and everything to create a passage out of there. I almost got lost.

In the middle of the desert when there was nothing left but my naked soul, I surrendered to the heavens. My experiences and years of searching came to a realization. I discovered a LOVE which I channeled through the master of all masters. I encountered Jesus, an absolute authority on the subject

How did I get here: Question or statement?

Who cares? Is it really important? I just want to tell my story but I wonder, who in this world would be interested in hearing it? Maybe no one or maybe somehow my story will reach someone one day who is going through a similar situation, someone who like me at some point finds themselves in the eye of the hurricane for a second or third time wondering: is this ever going to get easier?

I remember my time inside the cocoon, walking down a dark valley, everything looked dead to me. Everywhere I looked I saw dead bones and no hope. Every time it seemed I had found a thread of light and walked towards it, I fell into another hole before even reaching it. Keeping my head up while my feet were bleeding from the falls was exhausting - physically and emotionally painful because there were so many days I had to work a full time job without sleeping. So many days I had to use the strength of my 4,10" tall 120 pound body to physically hold Tom's 6" tall almost 200 pound body, or move him to a safe place when he was seizing. The nights I wasn't numb I would sit on the floor and ask questions: Will this ever get easier? How many scars will I have to collect in the process?

I was unaware the pains were changing me. Every emotional scar today reminds me of the pain, yet they show me I didn't give up - I survived. Today my scars save me from attracting new ones because I've learned to recognize the battles which really matter. They remind me of the times I had to stand tall and strong like a tree and wait for the winter to pass. I have become fond of winter because when I look at a naked tree, I see a raw beauty in the exposed cracks. There are no leaves to cover them, there are no sunrays to keep them warm yet still like a rock, they stand. They go inside and fortify their roots, waiting for the winter to pass. IT ALWAYS DOES.

I learned so much with my winter! I barely recognize the person I've became. Layers of ego dried out like dead leaves and fell off. I learned not to get attached to the cold but instead to watch it - feel it in my soul and in my bones. Winter taught me to touch the scars and recall the pain, then kiss the experience and let it go. Once you learn this, you allow it to pass and prepare for new growth in the spring. Ready to enjoy the summer because now you know it will come. IT ALWAYS DOES.

My intent in telling my story and how I got here is not to change people. Hell, that would be setting myself up for failure. I am still a work in progress, and you guys have no idea how many times I talked myself out of writing this by simply distracting my consciousness with some cheap prep talking:

"Oh Angela... it is ok to flip on people sometimes! You are only human. You are still learning. Embrace your bad side, hum?"

While it is true I am learning – hopefully, it is not okay to find excuses for bad behavior. I cannot preach something I have not yet mastered. With that said, my intentions with this book is to be a vessel for creativity. To speak and provoke thought for discussion and create a reaction toward soul improvement - allowing people to be curious so they can understand, not so they can judge. Now putting all my immature philosophy aside, let's <u>try</u> to understand this on the practical side.

Chapter 1
How did I get here – question mark.

T his "here" was 2014 to be more accurate.

The reason I mention the year is because it was then that I went down. Deep inside myself, my soul, my head and my heart as I could not find any answers on the outside.

I remember being there like an empty body with nothing left inside. I felt defeated and lost so I had no choice but to surrender. In fact, I feel this was the breaking point which changed everything but I did not come to an understanding until months later.

I do remember the day was October 29th, 2014 in Natal, Brazil. I had moved there because I felt it was the only way I could keep Tom alive. Back in Florida I had absolutely no help and no family. His health was so debilitated he could no longer stay home alone. It was October 12th 2013 when I experienced the most terrifying moment of my life - the moving force which led me to this decision. We had been trying to get his social security disability approved so we could afford his medication and nurse care but he had been denied for the third time.

That night [one of many episodes] I came home from work and he was hurt, this time he was passed out in a pool of blood. He hit his head on the coffee table after a seizure and ended up in a coma for three days. I was horrified and since I was not able to convince any family member to come live with me to help out, I decided to get rid of everything I owned and move back to Brazil. My family offered to help watch over him and I would be able to get his medicines through my Brazilian citizenship. With this in mind I informed my employer I had to move back home to keep my husband alive. I was ready to quit but they agreed to keep me employed working from home as I was responsible for the South American accounts.

The transition was harder than I thought. First, I had to sell everything I owned, then find a place to store the stuff I wanted to keep as memorabilia, however, I had no money. Not enough to ship things to Brazil or to store them in a warehouse until I had the money to bring them home. This is when God sent a good soul, a friend who owned a freight forwarder company, and for whatever reason, he decided to help. He housed them in his warehouse until I was ready to pick them up. The second part was to get the tickets. I remembered Tom had some miles he never used. It was enough to get us a one-way ticket to Brazil. I sent my daughter first with an employee ticket offered by a good friend Sonia Lima from my American Airlines times in Brazil. She was so generous.

It was hard to watch my daughter Gigi leave behind all the hard work she did in school as an A+ student, and her dreams of going to Harvard. I had made so many sacrifices, including paying high rents since moving to the US to keep her in good schools. Although I've been criticized for that decision by everyone around me I don't care. I listened to all the critics but eventually stopped trying to get them to understand my reasons. It would be hard for them to relate to the decisions I had to make, or to understand moving my daughter away from family when she was only six years old, or the need to work three jobs to make sure I could afford the rent in good school districts.

They didn't know my story, what I personally went through, or all the times I cried as a kid. I just wanted to go to school and get a good 'qualification' to get a good job - and avoid the factory's production line. They had no idea but they didn't have to. It was my story and it did not have to make sense to anyone else but me.

Chapter 2
The Cordeiro Family

My father was a factory worker who had finished third grade and my mom never learned to read or write. Their big dreams was for their children to become factory employees. When I turned 12 I was allowed to stop working in local factories where I had been working since the age of 10 and go work in a bigger factory. For this to happen my mom would wake me up at 4am and we would head to the industrial city to be the first in line. They would start calling people at 7am sharp and pick the first ones in line - depending on the number of people to be hired that day. It took months until I got accepted and begin working on the production line. I had to adjust my 6th grade school hours to the late shift, 7pm to 11pm. I was also forced to quit gymnastics, my favorite sport. I worked from 7am to 5pm, got home by 6pm to get ready for school, then had to do homework when I got back home which made bedtime around 1am.

The name of the factory was Atelier Mecanica Morcego, a Brazilian manufacturing auto parts supplier for a number of auto factories like GM, Ford and Easton. My job as a new hire was to put the blades inside a motorcycle's start plugs. The parts would come in a belt and the time to put the blades in was set to a minimum. I had to keep up with the speed of the pieces provided. I was not allowed to sit down or stop except on my breaks - trips to the bathroom were frowned upon. I started at 7am, had a 15 minute break at 9am, one-hour lunch at 12 and dismissed at 5pm.

I hated that job so much, I hated to smell like diesel and have my hands stained black from the grease and my feet always swollen from too much standing. After six months, I was determined to find my way out and that's how my challenge to get an office job started. I learned I had to know how to type, so I started taking typing lessons on Saturdays. Then I learned it would also be good if I had some computer skills, so I got started that class against all my father's attempts to stop me. For every new class I wanted to start I had to face his rage and mean words - making fun of me and telling the neighbors "look at her, she thinks she is tall enough to get an office job." Well, that was like fuel for me to keep going and prove he was wrong.

My father Carlos was the youngest of two brothers and a sister, he also had one half-brother and one half-sister from my grandfather's second marriage. They lived on a farm in Agrestina, a city of the state of Pernambuco on the North side of Brazil.

My father's biological mother's name was Severina. She died when he was only 5 years old from schistosomiasis, also known as snail fever, caused by parasitic flatworms, a common disease in poor countries where no filtered water is provided. His father remarried when he was seven years old to a woman called Josefa, they both were my godparents. I grew up hearing terrifying stories about how violent my grandfather Alexandrino was raising my father and his siblings on their farm. They had to get up in the morning to feed the cows and the cattle, and plant everything they ate, from rice, potatoes, beans and yucca roots to all the fruits. There was no bathroom, installed water or electricity.

My dad attended school until third grade and he was considered 'far ahead' for doing so. One of the stories that marked me the most was how my grandfather handled fights among the siblings. He would tie them face to face together with a rope until they made peace with each other.

The reason this was hard to forget is that he used this method on us over and over again. I experienced how my father lived growing up during my first trip to his hometown when I was seven years old, in 1980.

It was probably the family trip which marked me the most. I remember the preparation for it, my mom was so excited to get to see her family. It had been a long time since she married my father and moved from the farm life in Agrestina to the big city of Sao Paulo. In those ten years married she was now a mother of five. She had some problems getting pregnant in the beginning and had a miscarriage, but after my sister Marineide was born getting pregnant was no longer a problem. I came in next when my sister was two, then came my sister Alzeni when I was two. After three girls, my father was determined to have a boy. The wait paid off. When Alzeni was a little over one year old my brother Roberto was born and due to a little oversight, Carlos was born less than a year later. Their names combined was to honor my father's favorite singer, Roberto Carlos and that was the end of mom's production line of making babies; she got her tubes tied.

Now with the family completed, they were both ready to show off their wild bunch. We were all very pretty babies, Marineide had pink white skin and my parent's black hair with my dad's dark brown eyes. I had yellowish hair and a combination of my dad's brown eyes and my mom's pretty green eyes making them hazel; Alzeni had yellowish hair and brown eyes, Roberto had very dark black hair and also dark brown eyes and Carlos, was the masterpiece born with the yellow hair and my mom's pretty green eyes – not the traditional Brazilian ethnicity.

It was the week of the trip and I got hurt again. That was an ongoing problem as my parents had a hard time keeping me inside the house like the other girls. I was always outside; playing marbles, flying kites on the streets with the boys, climbing roofs and collecting real scars along the way. This time I had the idea of making a fire to keep us warm outside. Me and my next-door neighbors Carlos Augusto, Lucia and Rose were on a hunt to find anything we could to keep the fire going. One of them had the brilliant idea of adding a piece of plastic, which did not do anything good for the fire of course, just melted everything already in there and the fire got lower. I had to get close to the fire to keep warm. Lucia came from behind trying to hug me but instead touched the back of my knee with her knee making me kneel forward into to the fire. I screamed and jumped outside the fire but a piece of plastic was glued to my skin and kept burning. Everyone is screaming now and someone threw water to stop the fire which it did. We had to remove the burnt plastic that had dug into my skin. Every piece of plastic they pulled, the hole in my shin got bigger, making it almost three inches wide. I went home crying and my mom freaked out because I now have to travel with a horrible hole in my leg and make the whole family think she is a bad mother - which is a great offense in the Latin Community. Also, we don't have time to go to the doctor because we are in a hurry packing bags for the three day bus trip to Pernambuco. I was told to wear striped knee-high socks the entire time to cover the wound which did not help the healing process, and of course it got infected during the trip. I remember being in a lot of pain for the three day ride but I was not allowed to complain because it was my fault I got hurt and I didn't want to hear my mom repeating: "That's what you get for running around like a boy."

We arrived in Recife city, spent the night with my father's sister Amara then got on another bus to his father's farm in Agrestina, another three hour trip. As we entered the country side my eyes popped wide opened. I had never seen so many trees, plants, cows, cattle, birds in just one place. My sister Alzeni saw some small coconuts in a tall tree and asked if they were grapes, everyone starts laughing; look at those hillbillies from the city, they say. In the afternoon we went to see my mom's godmother Maria, a very nice and partially blind lady. The front of her house had a lot of bushes covered with big red fruits and I got super excited! Strawberries had always been my favorite fruit but we could never afford them. Bananas and oranges were all we could have back then because they were so cheap. Once every three months or so, we would be treated with strawberries. Here at Maria's house there was an abundance of strawberries so I didn't think twice about filling my small hands with some and putting them in my mouth all at once. As I chew the first pieces something overwhelmingly spicy burns my mouth and my eyes start watering. I didn't swallow but spit everything out! What in the world is wrong with these strawberries?! As usual my first instinct is to play a prank on my siblings. I offer Marineide some of my strawberries. She is the oldest and of course does not fall for it, she smiles and says: those are not strawberries, these are cayenne peppers! Well, at least now I know what is wrong with my super hot spicy strawberries. I tell her not to say anything to the other ones and she doesn't. I give all of them one full cayenne pepper saying they were delicious strawberries. They take a bite a little suspicious and make a disgusting face. Their eyes start burning so they itch their eyes with the hands they have been holding the peppers in. Now their mouth and eyes are burning and they start crying. First I found it funny then I start panicking as they begin crying even louder. "Uh-oh... I think... I'm in trouble now." It is almost night and there is no electricity at Maria's house. Three small children go inside screaming and my mom asks what have I done, I didn't have time to explain as Marineide had already pointed her finger saying I made them eat cayenne pepper saying it was strawberry. Maria tells my mom to help her find some sugar to easy the burn. Everyone crashes inside her kitchen in the dark looking for the can of sugar. Once found the kids had spoons after spoons to easy the burn. That was only day one.

We go back to grandpa's house as Maria's house is too small for an extra seven people. At grandpa's we eat yams and sip on coffee for dinner, they are not used to having big meals at night. The kerosene lamps are blown out and we go to bed at 8pm. There are no extra beds, everyone sleeps in hammocks in a room with a floor made of mud.

At five o'clock my grandpa wakes me up and ask if I want to help him feed the cows. He is a very tall man and has a hole in his throat due to the removal of a cancer on his tonsils. Its covered by a bandana which he wears all the time. His voice is basically a whisper but not too hard to understand. The sun is about to come out so I see rays of light in the horizon. He stops at this cactus tree by the house and chops big chunks of leaves. He has a very big, long knife and begins breaking the thorns. He hands me a small knife and tell me to do the same thing. About a hour later we have a big bucket filled with pieces of cactus and head to the pasture to feed the cows. He asks me for help open the big wooden gate. The hole in my leg had started to heal but still hurt from stretching the leg. I ignore the pain and climb on the top gate to take the handle down -he pushes inside opening it. We are welcomed by a handful of hungry cows waiting for breakfast. I had never seen a cow so close before but I am not afraid, I pet them as they eat.

After that we head to the plantation to get some vegetables for breakfast and lunch. I help him dig in the dirt to collect potatoes, yucca roots and later some corn. We chop some sugar cane stick then finally

7

head off to get some fruits. He introduces me to the cashew tree and ask if I can climb it to get some cashew fruits from the branches. I hug the tree and begin climbing until I get to the branches with nice yellow cashew fruits, they smell so good. I throw a bunch of them on the ground and grandpa collects them. He puts them in his basket with the other vegetables and I follow him home as he pulls the wheelbarrow with all the goodies down the road. When we get home, grandma cooks some yucca roots for breakfast. I tell them about my adventure with grandpa and everyone laughs at my excitement telling the story. Grandpa takes the nuts on the top of the cashew fruit, roasts them in a fire and they become snacks. We are also introduced to the river nearby for bathing and we play with the very tiny black fish in it. Cashew had become my favorite fruit and I took off on a daily basis to climb the tree and bring them home. My first day on my own I removed the nut from the top of the fruit, took a big bite and my whole tongue got numb. I return home crying and tell mom something was wrong with the cashew nuts; they didn't taste good at all and my mouth was now numb from the bitterness. My mom explains to me they need to be roasted first and everyone laughs at the city girl again. My morning runs with grandpa become a daily chore until we left for the next city to visit my mom's side of the family.

My mom Josefa is a very beautiful woman. Her mother Maria was native Brazilian Indian with olive skin and very pretty long black hair. Her father was from a European family, blond and blue eyed. No one can say for sure which country in Europe, some say Portuguese but once investigating the story of that city, the only European people ever known in that area were Dutch from Holland. With that mix, my mom was born with tanned olive skin, very beautiful black hair and green eyes. She had 17 brothers and sisters but only 11 had survived. Unlike my father's family, my mom's family were very poor people. Some of her brothers became alcoholics at a very young age, yet they were all very close and always seemed to have a lot of love for each other. When my mom arrives in her city, the house is filled with people from all over, aunts, uncles, brothers, sisters, nephews and nieces. She is like a celebrity and she loves to show off her pretty kids and share how things are different in the city. After hours and hours of talking over coffee everyone goes to sleeps in hammocks again.

In the morning I wake up to my aunt saying we are going to wash clothes in a lake nearby and bring some potable water to drink. Me, my sister Marineide, and two other cousins, one 14 and the other 12, head toward the water dam, about 5-8 miles walking in a hot sun. It takes hours to get there and I am about to pass out when we finally arrive. Oh, it was so worth it. The place was so beautiful! A fence made of big tall rocks keep the water in like a magic pool. We are told we have to wash the clothes first then we can play. After we get all the clothes hand washed we set them on the top of the rocks to dry and go play. Luckily the water is shallow because I don't know how to swim; we have a lot of fun. The clothes are now dry, we use the bed sheet to make a big sling to carry them back. We fill the ceramic pots with drinkable water from another river close by and the two cousins teach us how to twist the kitchen rags to put on the tops of our heads to carry the pots. We make it home by the end of the afternoon and get cleaned up for supper. After supper we go outside and climb the tree to tell stories, Nina, one of my cousins is very funny and make us laugh. The moon is so bright we don't need a lamp - back in the city we don't get to see stars like that so I get lost admiring the dark sky and brightness of the moon.

When we get down and head to the house I realize frogs are coming to the porch so I get a stick and start killing them. I killed about three or four and then realized they were coming in bunches. I get scared, run into the house and tell mom I was trying to keep the house safe from the frogs but there are now too many of them so I need help. Again, everyone starts laughing and tells me that means rain is on the way and that I need to stop killing them because if I get too close they can squirt some poisoning milk in my eye and make me blind. My cousin Nina takes me outside and shows me frog footprints on the wall saying it means we have been cursed for me killing the frogs, and everyone in the house will be tormented forever. I run inside crying and tell them what I've done, everyone has a good laugh and tells me she is just messing with me. Those weeks in the country created headlights on family gatherings. It remains with me today as it has throughout the years. It also helped me understand how my parents raised me.

It was only recently that I was able to analyze and recognize that it was indeed a brave move for them to leave that simple life behind and head South to Sao Paulo, a megalopolis at supersonic speed. I now see how much pride exists in being a factory worker when all you knew your whole life was to dig holes to plant your food and work on a farm with not much hope for a better living. I am pretty sure however, if I could go back in time and ask my grandfather about his life growing up I would hear about how much worse it was. What was considered simple to my father for my grandfather had been progress.

For both of my parents living in the city was a big move although I heard all kinds of stories about how hard my mom's mother tried to keep her from leaving the farm, up to including some native Indian spells against my father. According to my mom, he lost the only job he had lined up when they made it to the city so when they could not survive their first try, they went back home. My mom was pregnant with her second child, as she had already had a miscarriage. They stayed in Recife for a short period of time until my sister Marineide was born.

My father was determined to succeed in the city so shortly after my sister was born, they went back for a second try. They returned to Sao Paulo to live in one wooden room, about 13x13 inches long. It was our kitchen and bedroom. The bathroom was located outside in the homeowners yard and that's the house they were living in when I was born. Mom was pregnant again and my father had a job as machinery assistant at a glass company in Ermelino Matarazzo. He also had started a correspondence course to become a professional Lathe Operator.

My dad was at work when he got the phone call from the neighbor saying my mom had been rushed to the hospital in labor. He went to get permission from his supervisor to leave and when the guy saw his excitement, he offered to give my dad a ride to the train station. The other boss offered to come along too. They were all excited for my father. But between the distraction of the jokes and a reckless speed trip running a red light, they got in a very bad accident. The two men in the front got hurt but my father just had minor scratches so he tried to help. He asked them what he could do but his boss told him they would be fine and that he needed to leave to be with my mom but asked a small favor; if it was a boy to name it after him, Angelo and if it was a girl, to name her Angela.

I was a chubby baby with yellow hair who became very active way too soon according to my mom. To add to her desperation, I started walking when I was only seven months old and within the little space we lived I was in a constant hunt for distraction. She tells the story of how I managed to find the eggs she kept stored in the bottom of the stove's drawer as we didn't own a refrigerator and how she found me sitting on the floor playing with the eggs saying they were little balls - and breaking every one of them. We had to eat rice and beans for a week as we couldn't afford to buy more eggs to complement the meals. Things did not get easier when my sister Alzeni was born. The five of us shared the one bedroom. My mom said I was always close to her and always trying to get her to stop crying but one day I went the extra mile by sharing my piece of corn cake with my 7 day old sister. My mom says she heard the baby crying and suddenly stop which was not normal so she went to check on the baby and found me feeding chunks of cake to my sister and whispering to her everything was going to be just fine. I told my mom she was hungry and because I fed her cake she stopped crying. She almost chocked and I was not allowed to get close to the baby any longer.

With the family growing my father put money together and bought a piece of land in a city called Vila Verde (Green Village), where they live today. My mom was excited to finally have a kitchen - the whole family shared the only bedroom in the house. The family got bigger again with the two new boys arriving after we moved in and we were now seven people sharing one bedroom. Five of us slept on the bunk bed and my mom and dad on the full size bed. In order for my father to finish building the house we were already living in, and support five kids, we lived with the bare minimum. I don't remember having much to eat, toys to play with or even clothes to wear. I remember one time all we had to eat was bean broth with yucca flower and the few beans in the pot had to be divided by seven people so we had to count how many beans each one of us was going to have for dinner. It was not more than three for sure.

I also remember one day a guy showed up on the street selling family portraits and after a long negotiation because we could not afford the full price, the guy convinced my mom to make several payments for several months until she finally agreed. We all got excited for picture time. I was allowed to wear my only good dress which was kept in plastic out of site. My mom called the neighbor to ask if we could borrow her daughter's shoes for the picture. The problem was she only had one pair of good shoes so me and my sister Alzeni had to share and take turns on the pictures. When we finally had to take a picture with the whole group, I had to wear my old sneakers with holes showing my toes.

Chapter 3
The grass was not green in the Green Village.

T here was actually nothing green about it. Very few trees spread out around the neighborhood, houses were piled up on top of each other, bars on ALL houses doors and windows. People were very 'lousy' about their outside design and up until today it is hard to find a house which is finished with paint on the outside. You will mostly see naked unfinished cement blocks, making the village look more like slums - not counting the amount of ugly spray painted scrawled from the anarchists who insists on voicing their frustrations on people's walls, adding visual pollution to an already polluted air.

Growing up in Vila Verde (Green Village) created many scars, both physically and emotionally. The physical ones were collected due to my tomboy personality. I was always climbing something – either the roof to fly and chase kites or the gates to play marbles with the boys on the street. Threats to keep me away from it were a daily chorus from my mom and dad like a broken record which never seemed to work, not even the many times the threats became real. Climbing the roof was my favorite for many reasons: I could fly kites, I could watch the stars, I felt safe away from my father and later I watched the airplanes landing on the new airport in Guarulhos. I used to tell the stars: one day I will be in one of those airplanes going to the United States. My father knew how much I loved to climb to the top of the roof but just didn't know how I was able to get up there. My secret was climbing the washboard tank, reach to the wood holding the roof tiles then swing up to the top. When he finally figured out my climbing skills he decided to stop my daily trips by putting broken pieces of glass on the wood I had to reach from the tank. My next attempt not only failed but got me a lifetime scar on my right hand from the glass that dug into my skin, I was only eight years old. The pain was so intense it made me lose my balance and instead of going back to the tank I gave in straight to the floor hurting my leg. Crying a lot, I run into the house with my bloody hand and bruised leg and found my dad laughing and asking if I was going to listen to him from then on.

I did – until the next time. He told me I was forbidden to climb the gate when it was closed (which was most of the time) to play outside with the boys and that the curfew to be back inside was 8pm.

We were always playing somewhere else because we did not have any toys in the house, we didn't have our own bedroom either, everyone including my parents shared the same one, or a living room. The house was more like a shelter to eat and sleep. This one day I was playing next door with my sister Alzeni when I asked my neighbor what time it was. She said it was 2 minutes to eight o'clock. I busted out the neighbor's house trying to reach the gate before the 8pm deadline when the gate was going to be closed. The attempt was useless because the gate was already closed. To make matters worse a storm had started, the raindrops were huge and in an attempt to not get wet I climbed the gate to seek shelter inside the house. It seemed my father with his evil mind had planned it and was waiting for me with the belt on the other side of the gate. The minute I reached the floor he started hitting me and my sister with the belt and the buckle attached. The whips were so violent my whole eight year old body was covered in cuts and bruises and I could not attend school for a week.

My dad was a very violent man. Although I never saw him using that violence to hit my mother or defending us from the neighbors who were always threating us for being Christians, he always found it easier to channel his rage through us. My brother Roberto got punched in the ear when he was only 6 months old because his crying was keeping my father from sleeping. From an early age any argument between the siblings was resolved with a spanking with the belt, and if he had to hit us more than three times, the next one included the buckle of the belt. The older we got the hitting became more regular. Little did I know that the physical pains were about to become much easier to take than the emotional ones. It was an accidental discovery.

My mom used to take time away from us once a year going back to her hometown in Pernambuco to spend about 30 days at a time. This one time she only took my two brothers, leaving the three girls with my father. My sister Marineide was only eight years old but she was in charge - clean the house, cook the meals and take care of us until my dad returned from work in the morning as he worked night shifts. He got her ready for school and went to sleep to rest until she was back. I was six and my sister Alzeni was four and not yet attending school so we just hung out in the house until Marineide was back from school, around noon. The school system in Brazil is very different than the USA. Because they cannot accommodate too many kids, there are four different shifts so everyone can attend school. The first one is from 7-11am then 11-3pm, 3p-7pm and 7pm-11pm respectively. The last shift was for 6th grade on, usually for the kids that had a full time job and needed to go to school at night. Not the most productive one, as per my experience, after a full day working it was hard to stay awake and focused to learn anything. When Marineide came back home she would prepare us something to eat and clean the house. We helped a little bit but we were not tall enough to even clean the table.

One day coming back from playing marbles with the boys and busting into the house I found my father on top of my sister on the couch. My six year old mind didn't understand much of what was going on but I saw my sister was crying and my father jumped, scared and closed his zipper. I kept frozen at the door with my heart racing trying to process that scene in my head. From that moment on I got curious to find out what was happening and it was then that I realized my father liked to be around the little girls a lot. He invited them inside the house, offering candies and putting them on his lap. Although I was still not sure what that meant something inside me keep telling me to stay away and I did as much as I could. The older I got, going inside the house became my ultimate fear.

The happy day to be able to go to school had finally arrived. I had to skip kindergarten due to my birthday being in July, according to school rules I was too old for kindergarten and too young for first grade and since schools in Brazil start in January I wasn't accepted in first grade until I was almost 8 years old. I actually already knew how to read and write because of my curiosity in watching my sister Marineide do her homework. She failed first grade two times, the school said she had some sort of difficulty learning and years later we found out why.

I remember my first day of school very clearly, I remember the pledge skirt, the high knee stocks and the plastic bag carrying my notebook and a pencil. I was delighted and curious, I wanted to learn everything. The first day however was very disappointing. My first grade teacher Lenira began giving us lines to draw on the notebook, big line, side lines, circles, squares… what in the world, I thought! This is too easy! I was so frustrated I could not wait until the next day. I went to talk to the teacher and demanded she give me something to write. My mother was called to school the next day and had to hear all about my attitude. I was grounded so I could learn how to keep my mouth shut and respect the teacher. Months went by until the real learning for me began. Reading became my ultimate escapade but we did not have any books in the house and there was no library in school either. My learning book was devoured the same week I got it. It was either my hunger or my curiosity for learning that led me to a secret *parallel universe* hidden inside the books.

One of my neighbors had another baby and it was common in the village for the mother to send the older kids to help the new mother with chores. On my first visit to Celia's house I felt like I was in an amusement park. She had a playroom with toys, it was the very first time I saw a doll, learning games and shelves with books. I got so excited I didn't want to leave anymore. I played with her two girls and read my very first book to them – Frosty the snowman. From that day on taking care of her girls was my favorite thing to do and I was always volunteering to help with any chores she needed.

Reading became my passion and the first real book I read was "My sweet orange tree". The plot was about a very poor boy who created an imaginary world to escape his cruel family reality. He makes the orange tree in the backyard his confident. Just like the main character Zeze in the book, reading took me to a different dimension where I could be whatever I wanted. In my imaginary world, I always had wings and always flew far away from the village. I was very creative in school and my essays were all rated A+. Often my teacher would ask me to go to other classrooms to read my papers.

As I write these lines I travel back in time and see a clear picture of that 8 years old girl in a pledge skirt walking to other classrooms reading those papers. I think, wow, that's odd how I can still remember this with such a clear vision. I am typing as I smile back at that little girl in my mind. Maybe it was back then this book begin being created but it was not until now that I allowed that little girl to come back and explore her curiosity's full potential.

I have spent the past 36 years of my life allowing circumstances and people to clip my wings and make me fit in a box. I did fight back for that girl and I am happy I never gave up on her.

I spent the next years after reading my first book borrowing new ones from anyone I could find. I wanted to read and learn and increase the adventures feeding my starving creative mind.

I was ten years old when my father decided the whole family was going to become protestant and a whole new radical set of rules were implemented effective immediately. No more TV, which was not a big deal for me since we only had three channels working and never liked to be in the house anyway. The girls were no longer allowed to wear pants, or cut their hair, wear earrings, or celebrate any holidays. Trips to the church were mandatory three times a week and no more playing on the streets – at all. The new conversion was supposed to mean peace for the family and that God had forgiven all of our sins. It also meant we were not allowed to make God mad again or He was going to make us all burn in hell. What my parents didn't anticipate was that all that reading had made me think way too much, meaning, I had become more questioning than before.

The preacher repeated every single Sunday about how Jesus was Love and we were all going to live in Heaven when He returned to rescue us. I started questioning if there were no clothes or sins or material possessions there, why He would care about what I wear?

17

Maybe Jesus only cared about our hearts. And what would be the point of going to church every day, not wear anything that wasn't approved by the church, but inside we had a mean heart like my father's? It didn't help that my sister Marineide was now becoming paranoiac, saying Jesus hated her based on the traumas inflicted by my father. Making her believe she was the sinner. I have memories of my sister being very sad all the time. I don't remember her smiling at all and in all the family pictures we have she is always looking down.

I was eleven years old when I got my period and I remember the impacts that came with it. Another neighbor had a kid and as usual one of us was sent to help her out. This time the neighbor asked me to sleep over and while on the couch sleeping I felt her husband hands between my legs. My heart was racing and I tried to get out by turning to the side but he grabbed my thighs making it impossible for me to move. I was afraid of screaming and he hurt me so I just stayed quiet in the dark crying. I started understanding now what was happening with my sister and all the other girls my father allured to his lap. It was terrifying.

Very early on the next day I ran to my house to take a shower. I felt so dirty so humiliated and embarrassed to talk about it with anyone. I was in the shower - our bathroom was located outside of the house and had a missing glass. I see a shadow and turn to the missing window to see what it is and see the same neighbor standing outside watching me shower. I put my clothes back on without even drying myself off and run to my mom. I tell her what happened and she just basically shoo the neighbor away. Never did anything else. Taking in consideration what was going on in the house with my sister and the other girls, I realized nothing else was going to be done. I got very angry and decided that I was going to take care of myself and I was also committed to not let that happen to my young sister Alzeni.

There was not much I could do but I decided I was going to walk in the room every time my father tried to stay alone with any girl. I made a point to stay there until they went away. Looking back now I felt like I was in a twilight zone series. Every Sunday afternoon the family would gather for lunch downstairs and if any girl would come to the house, my father would invite her upstairs saying he had candies and together they would disappear for a long period of time. I remember looking at everyone at that table and they seemed to be in another world or something. No one found it abnormal which made me furious. I had to be the one going upstairs every time this happened for years and no one ever questioned why.

It became hard to hide my rage against my father as years went by. I started confronting him every time he tried to punish me for something stupid as his reasons for hitting me grew bigger and bigger by the day. I knew however, his only reason was due to the fact I was shooing the girls away from his claws. I was punished because I was reading a book, I was punished for not going to church by staying locked inside the house. I was punished for talking back to him and he now called me the black sheep of the family among other insulting names. I fought back saying I was going to reveal his little secret to everyone but he never got intimidated. He only laughed at my face and said nobody would believe me because I had a very bad reputation for being a rebel child and he was a very respected Christian man. His threats always got the best of me, I always felt intimidated and powerless as the anger inside me got bigger and bigger. I felt like a ticking bomb on a daily basis - every other day I would think about either killing myself or running away.

Love came to rescue me when I was almost 12 years old. I fell in love with a boy from church, his name was Andre. He was tall, black hair with hazel eyes and all I knew was I wanted to be around him all the time. He made me laugh, my stomach felt funny around him, my heart always beat very fast and I blushed every time he looked at me so I looked down avoiding his eyes. He was also very religious so before I realized it I had developed an interest to always be in church. I even enrolled myself to learn how to play the trumpet, singing in the choir and even got baptized. Going on the youth trips to other churches was the best part because I got to spend more time around him. I would get all pretty and convinced my mom to buy my first pair of heels. Although they were only 2 inches tall it made me feel like a young lady and not a child anymore. He finally got my signals, asked if I wanted to be his girlfriend and from that point on we would walk around holding hands.

I was so in love with that boy, I would write in my journal about him, made poems about love like I was a pro on the subject and I even picked Bible verses from Proverbs and Songs of Solomon made all about him. It was such a beautiful and innocent love and being close to him was all I wanted. Two hours during church was not enough anymore so I mastered a plan to convince my mom to move me to his school, a twenty minutes walk instead of the regular five minutes to the one by the house. It was not an easy argument to win but I finally convinced her that his school had a better rating on education then mine – which was true. With that I got all the paperwork for the transfer for my mom to sign. That was the best day ever and I took my time getting ready for school like I was going to a party. I don't remember being that excited to go to school since my first day in first grade. I walked the streets almost hopping, everything is going to be perfect now, I thought. I am going to be able to see him during school, we will have lunch together on recess and then we will walk home together holding hands like we did on the church trips. I was so happy.

Andre was from a very religious family and his mom Lourdes was the matriarch that held everything together. She was also very protective of her kids and also my mom's best friend. Once she heard of our 'little dating' situation she was not happy with it. She said we were both too young for dating and told her son to stay away from me.

Against his will he obeyed his mom' and broke the news on my first day at the new school. He waited for me after class and instead of going home holding hands like I had planned, I went home holding my books very close to my face to cover my tears on the longest twenty minutes back home. I was so devastated, it was my very first break up, and it hurt so much I thought I was going to die from a broken heart. I went back to my black thoughts, my days weren't happy anymore and trips to church became a daily struggle again. I had to come up with excuses my parents weren't buying anymore. They started locking me up in the house and putting chain and locks on the doors so I wouldn't go outside. It did work for some time, until I figured out how to remove the screws from the lock and escape to play on the street while they were out. I had to get back inside about 20 minutes before they arrived to put the screws back in place. My mom started suspecting something with my sudden interest to stay home and told my young sister Alzeni to stay with me the next church night. I was so frustrated, now I had to stay locked in the house with absolutely nothing to do… we did not own a TV, I didn't have any new books to read, we never had toys or games, so it would be just three boring hours until they were back, or just go to sleep at seven o'clock pm. After almost one hour of staring at the walls and thinking of a way to tell my sister my great plan I finally asked her:

- Do you hear the kids playing outside? Sounds like they are having lots of fun aren't they? She agreed.
- Wouldn't it be nice if we could be out there playing ball?
- Yes, but we can't, we're locked inside – she answered
- What if I told you I know a way for us to go out and play? Our parents would never find out.

She looked at me puzzled but asked, "how?"
I told her she had to promise not to tell anyone and she agreed. I showed her my trick, we went outside, played ball with the other kids for two straight hours and ran back inside before they were back. We went to bed happy and tired and when everyone came back from church we pretended we were already asleep.
The next church day, my sister didn't want to go either so we both stayed and played like the last time. My mom found that again suspicious, somehow she could always tell when I was lying. This time she told my young brother Carlos to stay too.
- Oh no, not Carlos, please mom! He is a boy and has nothing in common with us to play. The truth was, Carlos had always been the annoying baby in the family, always getting us in trouble and telling on us.
- "He is not to be trusted", I told Alzeni. He is going to blow our cover.

But, it was decided and mother was not going to change her mind. He stayed and instead of protecting our cover up and going to sleep, we couldn't hide our excitement of wanting to go outside to play. We told him about our plans and made him promise he was not going to say anything. He did and we believed him. We got out, played and had a lot of fun and he did too. We went back home like before, making sure we were in bed before they were back.

They barely made it in the house when Carlos jumped out of bed showing them the reason we were not going to church anymore and how we were escaping to play outside. I was dragged out of bed by the arm and hit with the belt getting new marks on my legs while Carlos was laughing in the corner. The next church day I was forced to get ready to go with them - no more staying in the house.

It was the first time I was going to be in church since Andre broke up with me and I was not ready to face him. I sit on the last bench on the back avoiding any eye contact with him sitting on the side benches with the youth group.

It was running away from Andre that I run into Mauricio, sitting on the last bench like me because he was also, forced to go to church by his mom. We started talking and he invited me to his mom's birthday party on the following Saturday night and again I found myself getting all pretty for a party for unknown reasons. We were not boyfriend and girlfriend but subconsciously I was starting to enjoy the attention game of becoming a teenager. That also kept my mind away from my house's monsters who had now found a place to unpack under my bed. All I had to do was not to look there – ever! Maybe one day they will leave, I thought.

Back at the party, Mauricio was staying and showing lots of interest in me. Yes, I did like all that attention and by end of the night he had asked me to become his girlfriend. He lived in a very nice house with a very nice family; his mom Dejanira, his dad Laercio, his two brothers Paulo and Marcio and his sister Marta. Mauricio was the middle child between the two brothers and the same age as I was. Always dressing nice in school and very popular among the girls. People would call him a version of a Don Juan character in a famous novella back then, making him the very opposite of Andre - I had no idea the territory I was getting myself into. My parents of course did not allow us to go out together and was always chasing him away. We would only stay together during the church trips and by 'together' I mean, holding hands and talking About eight months later, when I was almost 13 years old I finally had my first kiss. He had been trying to be alone with me after church but we were always surrounded either by people or our friends Irineu and Miriam. This one Sunday morning after bible school we walked home together, his house was very close to church and we stopped to talk, letting everyone else disappear down the hill. I told him I had to go to catch up with them and when I was about to say goodbye he pulled me closer. He ran his fingers through my hair, gently tucked a strand behind my ears and kissed my lips slow and gently.

- I'll see you later on at church. - He said, releasing my hands. I had to run to catch up with the rest of the group which was a good way to hide my blushing face and racing heart. I was in love again.

It just occurred to me, to think that I was working full time before I even had my very first kiss – interesting.

We dated on and off for over two years. We had very good days filled with lovely memories and we had bad days marked by a lot of arguments. He was jealous of my clothes, jealous of me talking to other boys but he was the one popular with the ladies. One of them even got me into my first fight with an older girl in school because according to her, Mauricio would not hangout with her ever since we started dating. I had never been in a fight before. My family raised us to not even try to defend ourselves from insults from anyone. We were Christians and had to be the good example like the Christ had taught in the bible, offering the other cheek. I was actually doing a good job staying away from Cecilia who was not only taller but also older than me by three years. She would make fun of me because my Christian clothes but so did everyone else in the village. I was just used to it and never reacted as she expected. One night however, I was buying my snack in the candy store cross the street from school and she cornered me:

-   So you're not going to do anything to fight back?
-   I really don't care what you think about me. – I responded.

23

Before I realized her friends had closed a circle around me I found myself in the middle of it with her. My head start spinning and my heart was racing, my parents would kill me if I got in a fight but when she put her finger on my face I lost it. My face turned red.

- Do not put your finger on my face!!! I demanded.
- Or what?... – she asked.

That triggered something in my brain, I had to react! Without too much thinking I twisted her finger and dropped her to the floor.

- Hey! No fighting inside my store! – The candy shop owner yelled from the back.
- No problem! I'm taking her outside. – I answered.

Still holding her finger I dragged her by the hair outside and punched her on the face so hard she passed out. Her friends broke the fight and went to help her. I didn't have any friends with me so I just stayed there lost, not knowing what to do but realized people didn't want to come too close because they were afraid of me. Wow!!! I thought. It was a new feeling I was experiencing at that moment. It felt good to fight back, in fact it felt damn good! For the first time I walked to school with my head high, I felt taller, I felt brave, I felt like I could defend myself and I was very proud of it. The word spread quick and soon enough the whole school heard about the fight. By recess time I had acquired a hand full of new friends and the bullying stopped.

The bigger problem to face was back home, there I had no voice and there was no surprise to arrive and have my father waiting for me with the belt. That time however, I didn't mind the physical pain. I took the whips in silence with a proud face towards myself.

That fight changed everything including how I wanted to dress, I want to impress and add a bad girl's vibe to my look so I got a 'fake leather' jacket. I would walk around swinging my arms and feeling like I owned the whole village. No more bullying for the next years.

My relationship with Mauricio on the other hand was always on the rocks, one week he was nice, the other he disappeared, then we would fight and break up then make up. I kept this vicious circle for years because I was in love... so in love with that boy I would chase after him everywhere, like a little puppy.

Things changed when I begin getting attention from other boys and realized I didn't have to be part of his game. I was now almost 14 years old and had made my first big move from a production line worker to an office job. I had completed my typing lessons and had started computer classes too. One day coming back from my computer lessons I saw an ad for a typist job posted at the subway's newspaper. They were not asking for any experience. I got home very excited and told my mom I had to dress for an office interview and that I needed bus money to go back downtown. I had quit my job at the factory two months earlier and had no money left so I had to ask my father for it. He asked what the money was for and when I told him, he started laughing uncontrollably:

- Who do you think will give you an office job? You're not even tall enough to get a job like that.

I said I wanted to try but he said he was not giving me any money. I started crying, he was always mean and cruel with his words. My mom searched her pockets for some coins and gave me enough for a bus and the subway round trip. I busted out the door as it was almost 3pm and it was going to take me 1 hour and 30 minutes to get there so I had to run. I made it just before 5pm and was one of the last ones in line for the test among 15 girls total. From the 15 girls, three passed the test and I was among them. The office manager came to talk to me and said I was the fastest typist but they were afraid of hiring me because I was too young. I filled my application as I was 14 years old but it was still June so I was actually still only 13 but I didn't say anything. The lady continued saying she was going to give me a chance and I, exhilarating responded, I was not going to disappoint her. I went back home riding the subway like I was in a first class seat of a big airplane. Wow, my very first office job! I did it! I got it and the sense of accomplishment was even sweeter when I pictured myself telling my father that against all his cruel comments and discouragement, I was the best one among 15 girls!!!

When I got home he looked down on me and said:

- "So, will you stop now and go back looking for another factory job? I told you nobody would give you an office job!"
- Well, I don't need another factory job because I am no longer unemployed, I start working tomorrow in the office. - I replied with a sarcastic smile.

I turned my back and went to have supper. He did not know what to say and remained static as he was in shock.

Yes, that office job meant the whole world to me and I can say for sure it was a life changing event not only for myself but for my whole family. The office job meant it was okay to want better, it was okay to dream and it was even more okay to fight hard to get it. Just because I was born on the poor side of town it didn't mean I had to stay there forever if that life did not make me happy. It never felt good, it never felt like I belonged, something was always off. Life shouldn't be that hard and I was on a mission to prove that. I wanted my brothers and sisters to believe this too, there was so much more out there to be explored! So, there I went breaking new ground, yet combating the walls of fear inflicted by my father were going to require assiduous work, and this was just my first step.

I got up the next day and put on my office clothes like it was a hero costume. A nice black skirt, a light yellow silk blouse – yes, I do remember everything about that day – black pantyhose and black heels. I had my lunch packed in a container, put in the purse lent by my mother and headed to the bus stop. It would be a 30 minutes ride to the subway station then another 45 minutes downtown and 10 minutes walk to get to the building. About a one and a half hour commute so I left at 6:30 to start at 8:30 – I didn't want to be late on my first day. I could not make it on the first bus because it was so packed there were people hanging at the bus's door. I didn't make the second or third one either and by the time the fourth packed bus stopped, I just basically forced myself among the giant legs blocking the door – good thing at 13 I was even smaller then I am today. I don't remember much of the 30 minutes ride to the subway station as I could not move at all, squeezed by dozens of people just like me, trying to get to work on time. Once I made it to the subway station I had to bust out toward the train platform because I had run out of time waiting for a bus to get in.

I had only 30 minutes to make it to the office now. This time I could not afford to wait for a less packed subway so I did the same thing, pushing myself inside the doors once they were opened. This time I was squeezed by hundreds of people and I felt my container had bust opened as a rice and beans smell was coming from inside my purse. Great! I thought. Now my wallet and notebook will have stains of food forever! Ugh. The thought of it went away as I kept my eyes up fixed on the train stops so I could not miss mine. I had been squeezed by so many people my face almost glued to the glass door. I kept picturing peeling myself off the door once I made it to the station and that thought make me want to laugh.

I arrived at Republica station minutes before 8am so again I busted out through the streets to get to the office on Barao de Itapetining street, about 10 minutes walking but I didn't have that time left. I ran fast and arrived at the office with my tongue sticking out and shaking. Thankfully the receptionist wasn't in yet and that gave me sometime to put myself back together. Once I sat down I saw a big hole on my pantyhose, my skirt was sideways and I unfortunately confirm my suspicious... my lunch container had opened and my food was all spread inside my purse. I took a deep breath and convinced myself it was going to be ok. When the office manager Maria Agripina arrived, she started explaining how they liked my test, I was the fastest typist out of the three girls but how concern they were because I was only 14. I lowered my head knowing she was about to get even more concerned when she found how old I really was. I handed her my documents and kept my head low until I heard the inevitable: "Oh gosh, you're not even 14 yet, I am not sure I can hire you! I stood up and started my speech: Oh no, please, please don't do that. This job means so much to me, you have no idea. I will be 14 in a month! Let's make a deal, you don't have to register me as an employee right now. I will work for free for a month until I turn 14, if you don't like my work you can dismiss me and you won't owe anything, I can sign whatever you want to make sure I am telling you the truth! She looked at me wondering who in the world would want to work for a whole month without making a penny. She realized I was determined to have that job because I did not make any attempt to leave. She asked me to wait, she was going to talk to her boss Walter. I waited in her office chewing on my nails.

She came back with good news, Walter said it would be ok to register me as an employee now but I was going to be on a three month probation, which was fine. I started my job at Controle Assessoria Empresarial, a CPA company on June 5th 1988 and from that point on my life took a very important turn.

There I met people from very different social classes, older and educated. They were people who were either interns going to college to become a CPA or recently graduated, looking for the proper experience from a big firm like Controle, which was also known as a bad paying company, unless you were a high level executive. My job for instance was paid minimum wage, which in Brazil right now is about $200 a month and for what I knew the recent grads weren't making too much more than that. They had their eyes on the prize which was the experience they were going to acquire working there until they got a much better offer. For me however, it was the absolute victory and I treated that job like it was the best thing that ever happened to me when I was only 13! I typed everything from balance sheets, letters, and even had an extra class to learn how to send telegraphs via telex. I quickly started realizing that most people in the office went out on weekend trips to the beach taking the intercity bus.

My first attempt to be a part of the group did not work. I was under age and needed a parent authorization to purchase the tickets to another city. After I learnt that, I convinced my mom to sign on an authorization and after too many trips to the bus station she agreed to get a permanent one until I turned 18. Those type of things always got me in trouble with my siblings. My mom always trusted me with everything I wanted to do either because she didn't have too much option - she knew I would find a way or because she always thought I did have some maturity to make good choices. Her trust in me though was something I would never want to break. I learned this the hard way when on a couple of occasions she caught me lying. The last one was when I tried to skip class to go see my boyfriend Mauricio. I went to my best friend Patricia's house who lived next door to Mauricio because I was trying to make up after one of our many fights. Patricia was my ears, always listening to my heartbreaks with him and telling me she would never allow a boy to do that to her. She was very strong emotionally and her mom raised her to take no bullshit from anyone. Not me, I was so insecure and always looking for that man figure missing in my life as I did not have any kind of affection from my father. I felt very vulnerable to any attention from the opposite sex. Maybe that was the reason I was chasing boys very early in life.

So, while I was at Patricia's house finding a way to get Mauricio to talk to me, someone knocks at the door and I almost fainted when I saw my mom standing there with fire in her eyes ready to toast me! "How the hell did she find out?" It was very creepy how my mom always knew when something was not right or when I was lying. From that point on, I decided I was going to tell her the truth no matter what and I also never talked back to her. Every time I went out with my friends I would tell her where I was going. Sometimes I would see her passing by on the other side of the street, nodding with her head acknowledging I had told her the truth. I also always respected my curfew.

I was offered all kind of drugs but never accepted anything. I thought about it many times just to disappoint my father. To make him look like a bad father but just the thought of facing my mother and hearing how disappointed she would be was intolerable. I could never face my mom after I've done something wrong. She trusts me, I would think, I cannot do that to her. So that was good enough to make me behave while I was out having fun with friends. My dad never agreed with any of it but he stopped hitting me when I was 12 after I threatened to call the police for an aggression. This time he had punched me on the chest because he caught me reading novels, saying that I was inflicted with evil reading those kind of books. He punched me with such violence I flew across the kitchen and as my breast had just started to develop, the pain almost made me pass out. I told him I could not believe I was being hit for reading and that was going to be the last time he was going to do so. The physical abuse did stop but he found other ways to hurt me with words, calling me all kind of names. He also did a good job creating a bad reputation for me among the neighbors saying how bad of a daughter I was, and a very bad influence too. It was better if they kept their daughters away from me. It worked well since I was the rebel and my father was very respected by everyone on the street because of his religion.

I never cared about what my father or the neighbors thought about me. My mother's opinion was the only one that mattered and with her on my side I was able to go out and travel with my friends. When my siblings asked why I was the only one allowed to go out and travel, she would say that I had a standup character and could say no to things she didn't believe they could. She was right. I once had a boyfriend who tried to drug me to take me to bed when I was 16 but he failed because I saw the drug rolling on the bottom of the cup and threw the whole drink at his face.

All of those experiences served as a compass later on when my daughter became a teenager herself. I did not prohibit my daughter from doing things because I don't believe parents actually have this power, specially when you are a working parent like I was who couldn't control her 24/7. I believed in educating her about the consequences and of course setting limits.

As for my father, I eventually gave up on confronting him. I avoided him as much as I could and started focusing on making enough money to get away from there one day. As my intentions were set, the universe start doing its part and my next breakthrough happened when I was only 15 years old. One of the biggest accounts of the CPA Firm I worked for was Hertz Rent a Car and their staff used our office for administrative support and used the Telex machine in my department as a communication tool to send their daily reservations to their main office in Tulsa, OK. That's how I met Eliana Neves and found she actually lived very close to my house.

When we found that out we started a good friendship and talked all the time when she came down to my office to send her telex files. One of these times she realized I was typing and not looking at the keyboard and asked if I was not afraid I was going to have a bunch of typos. I proudly let her know my typing score in my certificate being 140 words per minute. For me that was only a funny show off in a conversation but when Hertz Rent a Car had a fast grow just months later they had to hire someone with fast typing skills to send out the reservations. Eliana immediately thought of me and sent me a telegram when I was on vacation, as we did not own a phone, saying I needed to call her ASAP. I found the message very odd. What could be so urgent that couldn't wait for my return in a week? I went to the public phone to call her and she told me to come over for a job interview. I arrived at their office with my mom and she asked me to do a test to prove to her boss my typing skills and that was it, I was hired. She explained all I needed to do was to type the reservations at the end of the day, about 80 of them and help around the rest of the day with whatever else they needed. When I heard how much I was going to get paid for it I was speechless! It was almost as much as my dad made at his job. Yes, it was that easy!

If anyone who knows me can say anything about my luck is that I never had problems finding good jobs. It is almost like I have programmed my brain to find good jobs - afraid I would have to work in a factory again. Like a survival skill, I don't know. That kind of mentality earned me a bad reputation later as being snobbish or wanting to be somebody I was not but my desire to leave the Village had nothing to do with poverty or the people. It had to do with memories of a house filled with abuses which my innocent mind thought if I could move away from, it would erase them forever.

My emotional support was my mom and also my mom's best friend and next door neighbor Dalva. She was like a second mother who defended me many times and even hid me from dad and his furies chasing me with the belt. She also knew me better than my mom back then because she listened to my frustration about the religion, cruelty and always tried to ease my mind with positive inputs.

I made friends for life in that Village, and although they never knew the inside horror stories I was too ashamed to share, they welcomed me in their circles. Alessandra for instance was my wild and pretty friend, she was the very opposite of me and every boy's dream. Her self-confidence was the life of the party not only because of her beauty but also for her outrageous humor. Patricia was another childhood friend who I hold dear to my heart until this day and although we don't talk on a regular basis, we know where we left off and where to pick up every time we can meet.

Chapter 4
I was blind but now I see

S o just a year ago before this new chapter, which brings us to 1989, I had my first turning point, a life change event that put me in a pattern which later would lead me to where I am today - but of course, I had no idea!

I met Eliana, a co-worker, and was introduced to the environment of an office. This led me to vision an array of possibilities. The first task I got was to arrange the new cars catalogs into blinds for the phone agents so they could give information to the customers. These cars were brand new models, they had different sizes, colors, air conditioners, steering wheels, etc...etc...etc. Throughout the day I heard the agents asking customers where and at which airport they wanted the cars available. I begin to learn of new places like Miami, Los Angeles, San Francisco, Madrid, and touristic place I had never heard of, but all of my co-workers had. Many had been too these places and some spoke other languages.

My boss Wilson Colocero was an exceptionally nice guy who spoke five languages. Work was like an amusement park for my creative mind. Learning about all these new things, listening to new languages and making daily trips through those catalogs to places I had never seen. I don't remember learning much about International Geography in my school years. My new job however, was introducing me to a whole new world and I was lucky enough to get paid for it.

I asked a thousand questions a day, my co-workers found it funny how young I was, most of them didn't have to work until they were about 18 and they were much older than I was too. They called me Angelinha (little Angela) and treated me like their little sister.

When Celia, one of the girls quit, it opened a position for a new reservations agent and while they were taking the time finding the new person, Eliana decided to train me to help out with the phone calls. She gave me the company's directory and I begin learning International Geography. I learned about the countries, capitals and main airports including the airport codes and their money currency. Throughout the day, all of them would ask me random questions like, what state is Miami at? What's Japan's currency? Back then Europe wasn't part of the European Union so each country had its own currency making the game harder. After a month they decided to put me on the phone during the lunch breaks, which was the slowest part of the day to try out my skills. They gave me a notebook with the questions to ask: what city, what kind of car? Flight information, etc... I get seated and the big green brick analog phone rings. I had to answer professionally: Hertz International how may I help you?

My heart begin racing so fast, I didn't grow up with phones so I was not used to it. The simple task of picking up the phone turned out to a nightmare, my lips were shaking and my voice felt like it was coming from my stomach. I grabbed the 200 pounds phone and before it made it to my ear I hung up. Eliana looked at me confused and said: "What the hell was that?' I answered, "I don't know if I can do this. I don't know how to talk on the phone." Everyone looked confused with my answer but no one made fun of me. It was more like an "aw Angela" kind of look. The nicest thing about that group was how supportive they were. I now acknowledge it is a rare thing to have in a work environment. We were always supporting each other in every shape and form.

So, all the girls, Celia, Eliana and Claudia worked on my phone skills by letting me listen to their conversation on the phone. Later they let me take the reservation but remained on the line guiding me to make sure I didn't forget anything and letting the customer know I was being trained so to bear with me on the answers. When I was ready to fly solo, I became the new agent and they had to hire somebody else for my position.

My new skills as reservation agent opened me up to so many possibilities. I gained so much knowledge and met so many well-travelled people - my mind was filled with adventure. The travel agents who called us to make reservations for their customers would share the experiences of their travelling around the world. Most conversations would begin by looking for a travel destination city somewhere in the world: "My customer wants to pick up or return this car close to Champs Élysées, do you know that street by the Siena River that goes down to the Opera?" No would be my answer ten times out of ten so they would tell me to get the map and help them find a pick up or return store close by and off I would go... travelling inside those maps, walking the streets with my mind. They would share stories about a restaurant or a place they knew there, how the *Hôtel des Invalides* was actually a retirement home built for the war veterans and the Dôme was a large church with tombs of France's war heroes like Napoleon Bonaparte. There was so much knowledge shared, I felt humbled receiving so much information, things I had never heard of. I loved to hear their stories and create mind trips with them. As my geographical line started to expand so did my mind. I decided I wanted to go places. When Eliana let us know she was leaving Hertz to go work for American Airlines who opened in Guarulhos airport back in 1990, I found that would be my next step.

Eliana begin sending post cards from the places she was travelling to. She would write things like: "Angela, if you really want to go travel the world, you need to get a job with the airlines but you must learn how to speak English in order to be hired by an international company."

That's all the information I needed. I was almost 17 years old and still in high school with not much time available for any extra curriculum class. Yet I found a school to learn English fairly close to the office, the challenge was to adjust the time. I asked my boss to do half lunch hour four times a week so I could leave an hour early twice a week for the classes. After the class I had to race to downtown Sao Paulo to the nearest subway station and go straight to school, with no time to stop at home for a shower or dinner. I did this for a year until I graduated high school then I found another school close to home and readjusted the classes to three times a week after work hours.

Managing time however wasn't the hardest thing; sometimes I had time for dinner, sometimes I had time for a shower but never time for both. Sometimes my mom or her friend Dalva would be feeding me some spoons of food while I was changing clothes. My father on the other hand was tormenting me with his array of discouragement on a daily basis. "Why are you doing this for? Why are you taking English classes for? Do you really think you will ever use this? It is clear you can't handle both a full time work and English classes, just quit one already! I suggest you quit school because this lesson is a waste of time."

The struggle with time was only hard because I didn't have a car and had to walk two miles to the bus stop then ride for another 20 minutes. I begged so many times for him to take me, even offering to pay for gas, especially when it was raining because our street flooded from being on the bottom of the hill. He not only refused but tried all he could to make me give up. More than once I put my books in a plastic bag and faced the flooded street with water up to my tights to get to the bus stop and not miss a class – but mainly to confront my father and use his discouragement as an incentive.

I cannot explain why I was always able to find motivation in discouragement. I know it is hard for many people to think that way. I heard over and over how many people just found it easier to give up or to get used to a bad situation - it is indeed easier. I don't know why God built me this way, fearless of new, fearless of trying, fearless of changes. My only fear is inertia. Always been.

The idea of accepting the cards handed to me in life and "folding" has never been an option. I had to try harder to be better and curiosity was my compass.

How do I get there? What else can I do? What else can I learn?. How do I change this situation? Just like that curiosity would be activated. At first it sounded inoffensive and later nearly killed me emotionally however, I would not change any of those traumas for a "safe" shack in the village.

I am not going to deny it, those traumas eventually made me question my decisions - years later when I was forced to learn how to finally use the breaks. I named my break fear, who I just recently had a very serious conversation with because I was forced to acknowledge its presence in my head. I had been in denial since Tom's passing, and had to embark on a new adventure returning to the USA after my failed attempt to save his life – I had to start from scratch, again. Once I found myself comfortable with a job and place to live, I decided I was going to lay low and just be safe for once, but I got bored and curiosity begin taping on my shoulder on a daily basis. I tried to entertain myself with journals, podcasts, books but all it did was keep me busy taking notes of new ideas like a trap. I decided to write a letter to creativity, inspired by Elizabeth Gilbert's "A Letter To Fear". Because I wasn't even close to exposing my creative mind publically like Elizabeth Gilbert, my letter read:

"Dear curiosity, how are you doing today? I understand you've been in my life since forever, whispering in my ears all the adventures you wanted me to embark on, and there is no need to say I have been doing my fair share to keep you alive and entertained. My scars, my financial struggles and regrets are living proof of that as you might well know. Recently I have welcomed a new member to come along on this journey, its name is fear. Its suppose to smack you on the face or hit you in the head if need be every time you decide to jump into something – head first with no parachute to save us both. Don't worry, fear has no authority to shoot you dead. It is just a reality check, so please don't feel intimidated. Your insights are still very important, I am here for you and I want US to do this next thing together. I want you to keep your thirst for creativity unleashed because you're amazing at that and I am here to make your work alive once again. I am here to be your voice and the vessel to make this happen. I feel very honored to be part of your work and I will do my very best to channel you so please feel free to keep whispering. I will pick up the tools available to write it down but you also need to trust me to keep us BOTH safe. Yours truly."

By the time I turned 17, everything seemed to be on autopilot. I had a good paying job, I was taking English classes and I had a group of guy friends - me and my friend Cleuma were the only girls. I spent my limited free time falling in love with the wrong guys. The best part though was hanging out with the boys. They were usually a couple of years older than me and our conversations were always about interesting things, songs, politics, etc. The best part was begin free of the girl's drama. Marcelo and Marcelino were handsome twins and every girl in the Village dreamed of being their girlfriends. Their brothers Manuel Marcos and Rodrigo were also part of the group and had the same handsome genes. All of them were raised to be good gentlemen which explains their popularity among the girls. Denilson, Wilson, Felipe, Carlito, Davi, Anderson, Rogerio, Lucas, Marcelo, Silvio and Ivan were also part of the gang. Unlike me, they were very outgoing and funny on top of being very compassionate. Just plain good people.

The good part was this group met every morning at the 7:10 am bus from Vila Verde (Green Village) to Vila Matilde subway station to go to work. We also took the same subway to the main station downtown, Praca da Se, where we went different ways to get to our jobs. It was my favorite part of the day for years!

Silas was the entertainer of the group and known for his singing skills making people laugh hysterically with tacky and old-fashioned Brazilian songs. The 30 minute bus ride to the station every morning was like a stand-up comedy show. Silas was also the brother of one of my best friends Joab. They were tall and skinny Afro-Brazilians. It was hard not to notice the contrast of us walking around as I was the very opposite of them, with pale skin and only up to their thighs. Joab was like my big brother and I loved him with all my heart. He used to talk like Woody Woodpecker and imitate his horse Sugarfoot's laugh because he knew it was my favorite cartoon. Every time he noticed I was sad he would brighten up my eyes with that silly laugh. Years later I got the news he had drowned on his honeymoon and I was heartbroken; specially from not being able to attend his funeral because I was on bed rest, pregnant with Gigi. Such a beautiful soul the world lost that day.

The brother's house was usually our meeting place and from there every night was an adventure; to a bar, down the canyon to the beaches, or just hanging out and traveling in a philosophical world without ever leaving their yard. More than friendship, the group had a sense of community and personally it was my scape from my house and my father. Whenever he was home I would run away to their house looking for a safe place to hangout.

I was fortunate to find such a good group of friends but as we got older relationships became serious. With girlfriends the group went from being a single gathering to a couple's one. That made me closer to the new girls at the office Andrea Dileo and Alesandra Pergolizzi who were always hanging out at the cool bars downtown [I am lucky to have them in my life through today].

At 17, life was running smooth professionally but emotionally it was a train wreck and it was that way for a little while. I never thought I was good enough, I was insecure so I spent a lot of time trying to prove I had some potential, always overdoing, 'over-loving', always the one doing all the leg work in relationships and when they ended I would use all I had done against them in the most hurtful ways: "after all I've done for you" was my favorite line to make them feel like the smallest person who ever lived for leaving me. Then I would beat myself up and promise I would never love like that again, that I was going to be a real bitch, play hard to catch and guys were going to learn how to respect and treat me better. Well, I never followed through with any of it…next thing I knew there I was falling for the wrong guy and letting him walk all over my dignity, from one short relationship to another. All them were marked by fights – a lot of them – because I did fight back. I was like this little tiny dog who looked so nice and cute until I started barking.

I had a bad reputation for being argumentative and honestly, I never tried to control that. I was never good at setting standards for how I wanted to be treated because I felt I had to do all the work so I let people treat me as they wished until they crossed a line - probably set way over regular limits. Only when that line was crossed, this 8" feet tall wolf would come out looking for blood. It was like my sense of defense and anytime I felt I had to defend myself, my survival mode kicked in. People say I have Napoleon syndrome (maybe) but I also think I start feeding that behavior when I was a kid and the parents who were supposed to be my heroes failed me. I had to learn how to protect myself. If I felt hurt in a argument, I didn't stop until I hurt the other person enough to make her cry and if I was pushed to physical fight (only very few of them) I didn't stop until I saw blood. It took many years to learn how to let things go. Because that was one the most important lessons I had to excel in, in order to become who I am, life started its bootcamp training by putting someone in my life who tested every ounce of self-worthiness in me, trying to prove my value.

Chapter 5
Opposites attract (?)

~ Said people who love to live in conflict.

I t was a Sunday night, the beginning of December 1990, I had quit my job at Hertz rent a car and spent the weekend with my friends Alessandra Pergolizzi and Andrea Dileo Carlos in Guaruja beach, Sao Paulo.

When I returned home my mom was mad at me because I was walking around with the money I had cashed out from my 401k and was on a spending spree. I was wearing sweatpants and had hundred-dollar bills folded in my pocket like those gangsters on TV. My defense was I had worked hard for that money and now I was going to enjoy my time off. After arguing for about one hour I agreed to give her half of it to put away, then left with the other half to a bar.

I went to the Cavalheiro brother's house but as I mentioned, everyone had started dating and Cleuma was the only one still single so she agreed to go out for a drink with me. We walked about five miles to the nearest bar called Little Strawberry by the local university in Vila Jacui and between one beer and another we talked about life and the argument with my mom. Cleuma was a very pretty short girl like me, with light brown skin and wavy black hair. I was wearing shorts with a tank top showing my tanned belly from the weekend at the beach when I realized some eyes turning toward our table.

I left to go to the bathroom and came back to find this guy Roberto flirting with my friend. My plans were to leave so they could be alone but Cleuma told me to stay. Roberto now had his eyes fixed on me and I felt embarrassed because it was way too obvious. We had a good time talking and he offered to give us a ride home, which was nice because we would have to walk almost six miles back. The problem was he only had a bike. After much back and forth we agreed to take the ride – the three of us hopped on his Honda 125. He left Cleuma home first, of course, so he would have time to be with me alone. That alone time didn't last long because my mom heard us talking outside and demanded I get in the house (bikers were her worst nightmare). Before a quick goodbye we set up a time for another date two days later, in front of the school as I was taking my final exams.

Cleuma had made it clear to me from the beginning she had no interest in him so I went to meet him for a second date. That date was on December 5th 1989 and that's when he asked me to be his girlfriend, something according to him had never happened before. For some reason I interpreted that as I was a special one.

Roberto was a very handsome man, white skin, dark hair with even darker eyes and some nice muscled arms. He had been practicing at the police academy for some time to become a cop but his troubled past kept him from passing the neighborhood interview. He was the youngest of four brothers, Reinilson, Reinivaldo, Rubens and he also had two sisters, Rejane and Regina. His father Reinaldo was a bar owner and a butcher on the weekends and his mother, Judite was a housewife. They lived in a very nice house and his family was very loud and very funny people, always making fun of each other.

Our first official date didn't go very well though. We were making out in his car at a park and the police busted us for being out after 10pm when I was under age, 17 at that time. They wanted to take me home but because Roberto had been in the police academy months earlier, they agreed to let me go if he agreed to take me straight home and he did.

I met his family three weeks later on New Year's Eve 1990 and there I started my journey trying to change someone who was the very opposite of me. I don't think there was a single thing we could agree on. He likes samba I like rock, he likes beer I like wine, he hates books I love to read, his friends had nothing in common with mine, his friends wives were stay home moms and I was a career woman. The big red flag I failed to acknowledge though, was he wanted a simple life in a village and I had just started to learn about the infinite possibilities available in the world. The combination of our personalities was a recipe for disaster, all the signs were right there like one of those giant red floating dolls we see in the car dealerships alluring you to go inside and sign on a bad deal, and I did.

Roberto was my first serious relationship. He was three years older than me and according to his family had never kept a relationship for over three months, mostly because it was how long it took for him get the girls in his bed and he never disagreed.

For years I asked myself what was the reason behind my decision of even dreaming of a life with him? We were two different people from the beginning. After five years dating before marriage, the red flags were now intense light beams screaming on a speaker: *make a U-turn!!!*

I had never given too much thought about the bad decisions I've made until years later after endless conversations with Tom, he had the power to provoke "mind search" with his genuine curiosity about my life - without judging even my worst decisions. I have always admired him for that. He always made me feel comfortable talking about my past because he talked about his with no reservations at all. He was true to his core, he never tried to hide behind a saint face. He was a bad guy who made very bad choices in life for the longest time but he took full responsibility for all of it. Sometimes it takes the right questions for you to think about the real reasons for certain decisions. In my case, I came to the conclusion that growing up in a house of abuse with no father figure to teach me the many games men can play, made me believe in pretty much anything they would say. It also made me vulnerable to anything that would offer me a way out- and I would take it.

So the very first time Roberto stood up for me during a fight with my sister, which were many, he touched the core of my vulnerability. That was the first time someone had offered to protect me and God knows how deeply hurt I was in that department. We had been dating for almost a year now and I had lost count of how many times we had broke up and made up. The fights were anywhere from the clothes I was wearing AGAIN and my guy friends but mostly for his sneak outs to go partying with his friends or flirting with other girls. The fact I was still a virgin was always a reason for him to leave me at home after our dates and go back to the bars to look for one-night-stands. For that reason I didn't trust him enough to have my first sexual experience for the longest time. I wanted to be special and told him he would have to wait until I was ready and he did respect my decision. Eventually we had our first special night and I thought that was also going to change everything for the best. He didn't have to sneak out to party anymore.

That was the biggest mistake I'd made. The one believing I could change him by giving more, always more and not realizing the more I gave the more I corrupted my soul - masking how I felt and failing to make decisions which later cost mine and his peace. He wasn't ready to slow down.

Opposites do not attract, we can't change people and that is perfectly fine. The sooner we realize that in life, the lighter the battles we have to fight will become. Back then I didn't have that sorted out so I spent ten years of my life trying to change someone who didn't want to be changed. That was who he was and I should've known from the beginning but instead I kept telling myself stories in denial. I had lost my virginity with him and thought I had to make it work because no other man was going to want to marry me because that's how I was raised.

My mother tried to warn me saying: "Filha, this is not going to work, look at his family base, his father doesn't approve women working, he doesn't even like the fact his mom is trying to get her GED, he has a very strong machista background. That's how he was raised. Are you sure you want to get married?" My high hope always got the best of me: "Mae, he will change once we get married."

I went back to work for Hertz Rent a Car in 1994 and was making very good money again. While my girlfriends were using all their money to go to college, mine was going towards building a big house because instead of college, I decided marriage. My new set of friends at Hertz were career driven women. Silvia was getting her degree in Business, Regina in IT, Isabel and Debora in Linguistics.

My four intellectual friends, with whom I shared so much time commuting home were the biggest part of my days for many years as co-workers and later as sisters for life. We shared many things in common including the desire to improve our English language and to make something better of our lives. Together however, we also had fellowship. Our ride home was marked by soul sharing and sometimes lots of laughs, especially when Silvia got off first and stayed outside the subway window making fish faces like she was inside a fishbowl.

After work they attended college and didn't make it back home until past midnight and I went home to work on construction and wedding party details.

Ignoring all the signs I married Roberto on April 20th 1996. I wonder what would've been if I had waited just another year to get married. On that same week, I was hired by American Airlines in Brazil after applying constantly for almost four years since I've finished English classes. That was another turning point in my life as my world grew a little bit wider with all the flights benefits. My new teammates were well travelled and had both a higher cultural level and education. Of course, I didn't fit in. I never fit in in most of my workplaces; back then, because I was the one from the poorest side of town, most people avoided and looked down on me. I was very young and had not been exposed to the amount of cultural experiences they had, my parents barely knew how to sign their names and my brothers and sisters never worked outside the small village factories.

I stayed quite most of the time because I didn't have much to say so I just listened and learned – a lot. The progression to who I am today is astronomical and yet, I still don't fit in because since I moved to the USA I am the Latino in the office with a very strong accent, who dresses differently and is usually misinterpreted, but I don't intimidate easily. In fact, I am known for breaking new grounds everywhere I go and American Airlines was no different. Ten years after I whispered to the universe my desire in one of my quite times on the top of the roof, that day finally arrived. In September 1996 I was in an airplane flying to Miami, Florida for the very first time. My colleagues were speechless when I told them I was going to use my "welcome on board" ticket to fly to Miami. Those were free round-trip first class tickets to anywhere in the world, and with higher priority on the employee standby list. Those tickets were usually used to go to the Maldives Islands, Tahiti, Europe, Indonesia… places which would cost a fortune. Miami was their weekend quick gateway but for me it was like I had hit the lottery jack pocket. My whole family accompanied me to the airport, through the check in process to the boarding area. We took endless pictures as my coworkers looked at me confused: "aren't you going to be back in four days?" My answer was also confused: "yes, why?" They didn't answer why... I came to understand later the reason. Trips to Miami, just like anywhere else in the world were part of their normal life style.

I flew first class and thanks to my good friend Neusa Perella, who joined me for the trip, I survived without a major embarrassment to scar me for life. In Miami we rented a small car but got double upgrade for being American Airlines employees. It felt like a dream to be in one of those cars of the catalogs I use to rent over the phone. I took pictures of everything, buildings, streets, bridges, etc... and kept thinking of how much more, how many more places and new things there were in the world and now I was going to be able to know it all. It was a very good high... life was good. I was a newly wed, had a beautiful house which I've spent four years building from the bottom up and it was paid off. I had a good paying job working only four hours a day with all kinds of benefits up to and including travelling the world for free. All the hard work had finally paid off and all I had to do was sit back and enjoy the fruits of it, right?

Well, not really. Have you ever felt like you always make it to the silver lining just a couple of minutes late? In this case it was right after my first trip to Miami when Roberto and I had a huge argument and I realized how much he was despising my success, my new friends and my trips. Every time I proposed to go meet my friends he would come up with an excuse until he finally admitted they were too snobbish and he didn't like them. The truth was Roberto felt very intimidated by them. I was too but I had this natural curiosity to learn new things and that's why I wanted to be around them all the time. Roberto wasn't like that. He was used to being the leader among his friends, the funny one and the center of attention. He didn't want new friends and I should've respected that. I started feeling like I was being put in a box and I was not ready to give up my exploring just yet. I knew the marriage was a mistake five months later so I suggested a divorce and he actually agreed but to both of our surprise, I was pregnant.

Oh, that damn silver lining! I almost had it! I can only imagine what my life would be if I had just waited a little longer to get married or if I hadn't got pregnant so soon. Don't take me wrong, I do not regret having my daughter. She is the only and most beautiful heritage from my relationship with Roberto. I was just never able to decide how I feel about getting married so soon. I do wish I had picked a different partner to start a life with, I would have avoided so much unnecessary stress for both of us! If I had picked someone with a little more ambition, someone willing to learn and grow in life or someone that supported me and my dreams. I know together we could've been so much more. It is hard to imagine how far I would have made it if at 23 I already had that job and no mortgage. But Roberto was settled in for life. He was good, living one door down from his parents and a few doors down from all his childhood/ party friends - with a beautiful wife making very good money. He didn't have to worry about getting a steady job, just making some extra money with his side ones.

Well, I must agree, it is easy to get comfortable with all that but the only problem was my creative mind. Ah… that creative mind of mine was way too big for my tiny body and now it was unleashed like a beast. I guess the pregnancy worked like huge emergency parking brakes: "There! Now you calm down and take some time to breath, would you?"

Divorce was now out of the question, an already prohibited word in my family and with child? It was definitely not an option, so we decided to give the marriage thing another chance. I kept all those troubles from my family because I didn't want to get the "I told you so" preaching from my mother. I once again consoled myself with the words I wanted to hear: "he will change once he becomes a father."

It was a not a surprise when I spent my first wedding anniversary six months pregnant - with a candlelight dinner which I spent four hours preparing and he didn't show up until 4am. Back then I barely knew how to cook an egg so cooking a special dinner was a major project. I cried the whole night and finally understood what my mom had tried to warn me about, but it was too late to make any changes now. Sadly enough, that was not going to be the last time.

I found out I was pregnant with a little girl and the news shook up every bone of my body. I had been convinced it was a boy who I had been calling Joao Gabriel in honor or my music teacher back in my church days. I've always been terrified of having a girl because I knew I would never let her spend weekends at my mom's and if my father ever tried to touch her I would have to kill him.

Giovanna was born on Valentine's Day in Brazil, June 12 1997, one month earlier than the predicted date due to lack of space in my uterus for a fast growing baby. She had been positioned to birth when I was six months pregnant but we were able to manage to hold her up for another two months with bed rest.

She was a hairy tiny baby, weighting 6 pounds,17 ounces and she was for sure the most beautiful gift Roberto ever gave me. I promised the minute I saw her to always love and protect her with my own life. Her name was carefully picked to substitute the boy's name Joao, which means, Gift from God so I found an Italian substitution for it: Giovanna. Due to her early birth, she had to spend another week in the hospital to get rid of the jaundice. To go home without her was probably one of the most painful disconnection feeling I ever felt and I cried every night.

I went back to the hospital every day to breastfeed her while she was there and when they finally released her it was the most amazing feeling. I could have her everyday around me. I am not going to lie it was definitely not a walk in the park. Since I decided to only breastfeed her, it became an every 30 minute task keeping me from sleeping for the next seven months of my life. I had post partum depression too and Roberto's lack of involvement combined with my sleep deprived nights made me want to just walk away in the middle of the night more times than I can remember. One night I went outside and set on the stairs and cried for hours thinking how bad of a mother I was for having thoughts of leaving her.

I didn't have any pre-natal classes and no one in my family had every talked about post partum depression so I didn't know this was so common. Today I make an effort to always mention not only this but so many other things I've learned from motherhood with new moms because I know how much I struggled. I made a lot of mistakes until I learned the right way, or at least a better way to adjust to being a new mom. I think sharing wisdom should be broadly spread with no reservations whatsoever, not all learning should be painful and cost scars along the way. Things eventually got easier and when Gigi turned two, I decided it was time for me to start college after so many years putting it off. When I decided to get married, all the money I' made was invested in building our home. I had spent the last four years investing every penny of my salary into building a house from the ground up like I've mentioned.

The college news was received by Roberto and his father like I was going to get a night job in a brothel in Brazil. The first threat was if I registered for college our marriage was over. Then during our Sunday's lunch at his parents I had to hear his father tell him to step up as a man.

"What kind of man would allow his wife to work and go to school?" he asked Roberto.

Roberto did not stand up for me. For the past few years this was no longer on his list. Anytime anything went wrong, he always took the other side and this time was no different. I won the argument saying I would be embarrassed to tell people I ended my marriage because my wife decided to go to college. He then allowed me to register but I was not allowed to go to school at night. I wanted a major in International Business but those classes were only at night so I chose a major in Business Administration instead. With that I also had to change my shift at American Airlines to 7-11pm. It was not a bad set up, I had to drop Giovanna at the day care before classes, at 8am and picked her up when I left school at 12pm. The only setbacks were when I had flights delayed and had to stay over time, which was not rare. There were days I had to go from work straight to school and catch up on my sleep during the day.

Living close to his family finally paid out because they could help me with Gigi. As my schedule got busier, so did Roberto's with his party friends. I had one day off a week and one full weekend a month and those days were never good enough for him to include us in his plans. It was clear we had married way too young and we wanted different things in life. As a consequence, slowly we started to grow apart.

Chapter 6
The Soul Mate – Redefined.

I always thought a soul mate would be someone who is a copycat of yourself which, in my understanding, would give you that happy ever after Cinderella lifestyle. Because it didn't happen to me, I carried angry feelings towards God and His bad timing for the longest time. It was Elizabeth Gilbert's conversation with her friend Richard on Eat, Pray Love about soul mate who helped me make peace with my past: "People think a soul mate is your perfect fit, and that's what everyone wants," Richard tells her. "But a true soul mate is a mirror, the person who shows you everything that's holding you back, the person who brings you to your own attention so you can change your life" I love her so much for sharing this, I have no words to thank their dialog for helping me free from my resentment. However, I had to spend years and make the most stupid mistakes of my life at a very high price, both emotionally and financially to find that out.

I met Paulo in a very ordinary situation but the person I met was anything but ordinary. Definitely a high caliber person with very high standards as a man, a father, a husband and a professional, surely not the kind of man easily found in the hood where I grew up - unless you go on a treasure hunt with a magnifying glass in hand.

Paulo was an Aircraft Mechanic with a bachelor's in architecture who was getting his second major in Mathematics. He overheard me telling a friend I was going to Miami soon and asked me to bring him some vitamins for his daughter and a fax machine. It was not a big deal for me so I agreed and when I got back he wanted to pay me for the inconvenience but I denied. We settled on coffee and he was going to meet me at the end of the shift at the coffee shop next door. That's what I used to do everyday anyway after my shifts so I waited for him. As we set down and started to talk I immediately noticed the difference in the way he talked about his wife, about his daughter, his manners with a very natural tone, something I was not used to. It was a very pleasant conversation and in no way inappropriate or flirty but we lost track of time. I had never had that kind of genuine and undivided attention before from the opposite sex. When I got in my car I was like, wow! What a nice talk! For the next few days all I could think of was how good that attention felt. I realized then the lack of attention and quality time missing in my own marriage. When Roberto wasn't with his friends at the bar or at his family's house, he would stay home watching soccer and our conversations were mostly arguments. He would find something wrong about me, the way I thought, the way I cooked or cleaned, mostly nagging me and just like I did with my father I would attack back. For some reason we always brought out the worst in each other because I was trying to change him to become a more refined man and he was trying to change me to become a housewife. I would call him a caveman and he would call me snobbish and that's how most of our conversations ended. There was no dialogue, ever!

That time with Paulo made me realize how much better my marriage would be if Roberto and I had something in common. "Maybe if I could talk to Roberto and tell him how I feel we can think of a plan to get along better," I thought. I wanted another chance to try to save my marriage. I got a Friday night off and told him I made plans for us to go on a date and talk, his mom had agreed to watch Gigi but like before, he blew it off, and I ended up spending another night on the couch waiting for him. This time I was awake when he got home at 4am. I was furious and I told him he was losing me and it was not going to take much more for me to leave. For the first time, he panicked and said he would do whatever it took to change that. My suggestion was to sell the house and buy another one outside the city. A place where Gigi could grow up safer and he could finally adopt the married lifestyle. Up till then, I was the only one married in that relationship. He agreed to my surprise and I begin buying newspapers with houses for sale. I was happy, there was hope things would be changed for real this time. For the next six months, all the houses I found with the limitations set by him, was denied and I just kept looking and looking, day after day with no success. One day I realized he was just feeding me false hopes expecting me to give-up and forget the subject.

- You are not going to move are you? I asked him straight forward.
- I have no reasons to leave this village. He answered laughing.

That was the final straw and for the first time I decided to give up on the marriage. I had exhausted my options and any desire to make it work.

The next month I came up with a plan to have coffee with Paulo again. The more I got to know him, the more I was amazed by him. I was falling in love and I was falling fast and when he realized it, he begin distancing himself and avoiding me at all cost. Guilt was now a regular feeling, I tried, God knows how much I tried to fight those feelings but his presence was like a drug. It had awakened feelings in me I had never felt before and I was not ready to let these feeling go, I wanted more. My mom had a saying that in a marriage, if you don't provide your spouse with the attention they need, they will find it elsewhere. She was saying it to me, for my role as a wife because that's how she groomed my sisters to be. But I figured this statement could work both ways. Why not?

I had no idea how vulnerable I was until I fell for the little attention Paulo was giving me. I would plan to be working on the aircrafts he was on, I changed all my check in days to be at the gate dispatching aircrafts and I even learned pushback procedures just so I could be down on the ramp mix, but the guilt feeling was consuming me. Good thing I was switched to night shift before school started. I figured that way it would be easier for me to forget about him and it worked, out of sight, out of mind. At home, my feelings for Roberto were completely gone and I didn't care about his 'abouts' anymore so there were no more fights. We had a livable situation and when sex without feelings became too hard for me bare, I kept it to a minimum.

I had never had any physical contact with Paulo while I were married. It was more like a platonic love affair only happening in my head. Raised in a protestant family, I had always been conservative and completely against any sort of extra-marital affairs. That was the main reason I was fighting my feelings for Paulo so much. This changed the morning I got in my car to go to work and found another woman's earing on the passenger's seat. I guess he too, had found the attention he wasn't getting at home any longer. The night before was a Friday night and I had the day off. I asked Roberto to take us out to dinner but he said he had plans with his friends. He asked to use my car as his van was filled with some products from a delivery. I didn't want to create any more fights so I just stayed home with Gigi and he left to meet his friends. This time he didn't make it back until almost 7am, just in time to stay with Gigi while I left to work a double shift. When I found that big hoop earing on the seat I wanted to beat him to death. I felt so hurt, I could not believe he had the nerve to leave me home with his daughter and use my car to take another woman out on my day off. I guess deep inside I knew there were women involved at the parties but my pride never let me believe 100%. He did that when we were still dating, he had an affair with a co-worker called Vanessa when we were engaged, flirted with all kind of women including his own cousins at the family parties and after we separated I learned more and more about his escapades. I just didn't know why I was so surprised. He was young and wanted to have fun and I was the one wanting to get married. There is a famous phrase from Maya Angelou I didn't hear about until 2014 where it says: "When people show you who they are, believe them the first time." It was my own fault I had failed to see that.

I went back upstairs and he was already passed out - we can imagine why. I smacked him in the face and shouted at him "whose earing was that?" He made up a last minute story with the lousiest lie ever but I didn't have time to argue, I had to leave for work.

The drive to work was long, I was crying, I was mad and I wish I could've stayed home to beat the shit out of Roberto or wake him up breaking plates on his head. That bastard! How could he lie to my face like that and use my car to drive other woman around. How many were there? What else didn't I know or pretend I didn't know to keep myself from even more hurt? This time I decided to get a divorce and nothing was going to change my mind.

The morning shifts were the ones where I had a chance to see Paulo, sometimes from a distance, sometimes I was lucky to work in the same aircraft. We didn't engage in conversations anymore - trying to avoid things becoming complicated. Over a year had passed by and I found comfort by just loving him in secret, writing random poems and thinking I was just lucky to know him and that maybe I could one day find someone like him.

That morning however was hard to not engage conversation, my makeup was all smeared, I had to retouch several times but the look in my eyes was from someone in pain. I was never good hiding my feelings – my face always turned me in like a sitting duck. We crossed each other inside the aircraft and he asked if I was ok, I said I was fine and tried to walk away. He asked if I could wait for him at the end of the shift for a coffee. The answer should be NO. I should've gone back home and got things straight with Roberto first, but what did I do? Exactly. I had just been awarded the wild card this time, I could use all the excuses I wanted to justify the stupid reaction of accepting the invitation and I did. The possibility of seeing him again and talking to him placed a "rainbow on my cloud". I told him what happened and when he asked if it was the first time that had happened, I told him about the many other times, including the one from our anniversary just two weeks earlier, where I had prepared him dinner and waited for him wearing my best lingerie but he didn't make it back home until past 2am. By then I had already cried myself to sleep.

From there the conversation took a totally different route, much more personable and I realized the mistake after I had started. He told me he could not believe a man would leave a wife who was willing to dress sexy for him to be partying with his friends. He let slip his wife had never done that for him before and went on, "some guys are just unbelievable lucky!" he said. I was intrigued and wanted to find out what that meant but we ran out of time. I was working a double and still had to go back home to deal with Roberto's lies.

He contacted my friend Alessandra and tried to get her to call me and ask if I had found her earing in my car. Alessandra immediately reminded him she was my friend not his. Then he came up with another lie saying his friend Luciano, who was also married, had asked to use the car to go out with a girl. When I said I was going to call him at that moment to confirm, he made me hang up the phone. Can't blame him for trying, right? The answer was black and white and it was what I needed to give me courage to ask for a divorce.

I started to sleep in the living room because I didn't want to have any more physical contact with him. I was disgusted and he said he was not going to give up his bed so I got the couch. I put a down payment on an apartment but had to wait for it to be built, about 6-8 months before I could move out. I was trying to take one day at the time, going to school, working, being a mom and dreaming about Paulo at night. Three months had passed and it was already the end of July of 2000. I got to work a little earlier for a meeting. As I walk out of my car I see Paulo looking for a parking spot - he asks me to wait for him. My heart was about to jump out of my chest as I waited for him. He asked me how things were at home and I told him I was separated and would soon be filing for divorce. He looked puzzled but also let me know things were not good at his home either and they were thinking about getting divorced too but he wanted to wait until his daughter turned 18 to avoid traumas. I asked if he wanted to talk about it and he asked me to wait for him after the shift so we could talk more.

That night our talks moved from the coffee shop to my car, trying to avoid gossip as we were both still legally married. It was a long and deep conversation, from books, to songs, to physics any subject, we connected in so many levels. I loved to hear him talking, his stories, he was ten years older than me with so much more experience, such an interesting man who kept my curiosity fed all the time. Months went by without a single kiss, he was a very discrete man and had not ever suggested any physical contact until I made the first move. I was done waiting and those talks in the car were getting us both electrocuted from the over pouring chemistry. One night after driving him back to his car, he leaned to say goodbye and I went for his lips. He didn't push me back and it was long enough to show my intentions. He lowered his head: "Why did you do that?" I was not ashamed and told him I wanted to do that for a long time. "You know I am still married, we can't do this."

There I blew it again; he went back to avoiding me. The difference now was he had asked to be transferred to the night shift too and we saw each other every single day. After chasing him again for some time, I got tired and told myself it was enough. I had to have some self respect and maybe it was better to just let him go afterall he wasn't even available yet. I started to flirt with other guys and avoided him at all cost, leaving right after my shift or changing airplanes if we were working together. This one night he asked me to wait for him, he wanted to talk. I said it had to be brief because I had an early exam and he nodded ok.

He said he needed help for an essay about this one book, he was not good at writing and I agreed to read it and help him. I said I had to go and drove away but he was right behind me. When we got to the freeway outside Guarulhos Airport, he gave me high beam to stop at the medium, thinking it was an emergency I did. He walked toward the passenger door and got inside my car. "What happened?" I asked. He just looked me in the eye, took my head with both of his hands and kissed me - a very long kiss. I felt that kiss in every cell of my body, so tender, not an act of lust of passion, but love, sweet and tender love, I felt starts dancing under my feet, I felt my soul had been kissed and our spirits were connected, no hands wondering just lips exploring every corner of each other's mouths. It was beautiful and it felt beautiful. When he stopped he whispered in my ears: "I don't know what to do, I can't stop thinking about you." He then opened the passenger's door and left.

My drive back home was a mix of riding down a roller coaster and dancing in the rain. "What is next?" I was floating with happiness but aware of the challenges coming our way, after all he was still married and I had this guilty feeling that I was responsible for what had happened but I was not strong enough to do the right thing. For the very first time in my life I was being selfish. It might sound like I am looking for approval for all the mistakes it that follow, and maybe it's true because with every decision and at every opportunity I had to stop, I looked the other way. I found excuses and reasons to continue. I blamed it on Roberto and the vulnerable position he put me with his lack of attention and I blamed it on Paulo's wife for taking him for granted not appreciating the kind of man she had by her side, but the truth is obvious and bitter: it was wrong.

Back home as I pushed Roberto out of my life and tried to keep the situation livable for my daughter's sake – at least until our place was ready to move in. But Roberto was trying to work his way back in. It was driving me crazy because I had spent the past 10 years of my life trying to keep him, trying to be the good girlfriend, the good wife and make our relationship work, aside of all his actions to destroy it. Now when there were no feelings and nothing left to be saved and I was ready to give him his official manumission like he always wanted, he wants to stay? Why? What was he expecting anyway? Did he think I was going to just change my mind and live out of crumbs of feelings thrown at me for the rest of my life? How pretentious was that?

Unfortunately, this is the reality and the cause of many unsuccessful relationships and divorces of our era, in my opinion. We expect the other person to put us on a pedestal and worship us on a regular basis. We want the other person to accept who we are and take in consideration every little thing that is important to us but we don't want to walk the other half, we want men to think like a woman and men want us to think like a man. I was highly criticized for spending money on hairdressers, getting my nails done, taking too long to get ready, being emotional and dramatic… well, that's what makes me a woman, I would tell him. If you expect something different maybe you should consider marrying another man.

I was just as bad at criticizing him for not being romantic, being so unconsidered with my feelings, not making one single effort for dates or bringing me flowers, and to have to use sex as a weapon to make him do all those things. Maybe I should've married another woman too, I guess. He also criticized me for not being a role model woman like his sister in laws and my sisters, not knowing how to cook or keep the house impeccably clean like his mom. But in my defense, I had been working since I was 12 and didn't have time to be groomed like the other women because I was either working or studying and most of the time, doing both. I was a career woman but I made the effort to pay for a cleaner and tried many failed recipes, sometimes even had my mom on the phone teaching me how to bake beans the proper way but they never turned out good. I was just not good at.

I guess the main point in all this was we were too young and inexperienced. Maybe some extra help from the mature crowd on guiding us as a couple instead of just pointing out each other's faults could've been a tremendous help. We both had the potential. We were capable of learning, and together we could've worked it out and learned how to compromise. We didn't know any better and like many couples out there, we spent all our energy pointing out what was wrong with each other until one of us gave up, in our case, me.

I was ready to live a relationship where I didn't have to spend all of my energy trying to change anyone or protecting myself from being changed. I wanted someone that had the same personality traits as me, someone more mellow, who likes to talk, read and discuss interesting things in life. Someone who enjoyed my company and more than anything, I didn't have to force any of that. I had found that person but he was not available. I was afraid of losing him forever and missing my chance of a happy ending. So, for the following years I kept myself focused on just enjoying the time I had with him. Living in the moment as much as we could. We found time to meet after work, I travelled to other places when he had training in other countries and just like that, I became the person who I use to judge with my Christian beliefs: the mistress and I didn't stop there.

I made the despicable mistake of making my way into his family by becoming one of his wife's yoga students. Why? I have no idea. Maybe unconsciously I wanted to know if he was telling the truth about their relationship to make myself feel better. She was a unique kind of woman, compared to the Brazilian standards. Not very girly and more focused on her intellect and spiritual knowledge - that's where their differences played to my advantage. He missed a feminine woman.

I improved my cooking skills, brought him sweet treats and spoiled him on a regular basis with simple things. I sent him romantic notes, always reminding him what a wonderful man he was. He always made compliments about how feminine and sensual I was and just like that we were in love with the way we treated each other.

He always coached me on my potential and I loved how he always said I was a hidden jewel that just needed someone who saw that and would invest the time to polish me. He was constantly feeding my curiosity to uncover my intellect and academic talents to support my career growth. Emotionally he played a key role in helping me overcome all my child abuse traumas. He was the only person I ever opened up to about my father's abuses back then. One night during our talks, he asked me why I hated my father so much and when I said "he is just not a good person" he was determined to find out why. He looked me in the eye and said: "you don't have to carry this on your shoulders by yourself. You can trust me." I tried to answer and started: "I…" I…." but I couldn't finish so he just held my hand and stayed in silence with me for almost an hour until I busted in tears and told him my father was a pedophiliac and I had been molested by my neighbor when I was 11 years old.

"Now I understand why you walk around with your head looking down all the time", he answered. We went through all my traumatic years piece by piece and at the end he said: "It's not your fault and you need to stop letting your father's actions own you like that. That's the only thing holding you back. You need to take better care of yourself, you're stronger than you think."

That meant more to me than any other emotional and physical reward I got from our encounters. That night my confidence shifted, my shoulders were lighter and my heart was warmed by the caring of a man I knew so little about.

That transformation became more transparent on the outside as I progressed to applying it on a daily basis. It is a powerful feeling to face your fears.

It is liberating when you look your demons in the eyes and tell them: "it is ok, you can come out of the dark and step with me in the light so we can face this together. Show me where I have to love you."

I had no idea of the damages and the destructive pattern I had created out of the pain of the sexual abuse and trauma or the insecurity of realizing I didn't have anyone to protect me - more so the fact I had no voice as stated by my father. No one would believe me. The outcome had been a marriage to run away from the abuses and now I was about to live a life of a different kind of abuse setting the standard for my daughter to follow– that is until I met Paulo.

I wish from the bottom of my heart I had met him under another circumstance or met someone like him to be my soul mate/ rescuer but it was not. I did not intentionally go out looking for a married man, that is just how it happened. It is hard to try to explain how something so beautiful happened under such wrong circumstances. I gave up a long time ago on spending the rest of my life asking for forgiveness. It was a mistake and we both paid a high price as will be detailed later on however, the transformation in my life could not be ignored.

Paulo was the moving force who brought my attention to my hidden fears: "stop feeding them or they will eat you alive". When we ignore them, they hold us hostage and keep black mailing our thoughts and any plans to move forward with our lives. We feel we will never be good enough because we had that "mark", like a curse. We are doomed to pass it on to our own bloodline like a bad heritage we can't stop, but thankfully, I am given a chance for it to stop with me. Maybe it was the reason I was destined to have the only girl on my family's side. But here's the thing: when you decide to stand up to change the course of something, be ready to fight – hard.

As I kept my decision to go through with the divorce, things got very challenging at home especially when it got closer to the holidays in December.

I had the American Airlines Christmas Party coming up and I told Roberto only me and Gigi would attend for two reasons: the year before I had to hear him complaining the whole time about how much he hated my co-workers and how stuck up they all were. The second reason was, because he didn't blend in, he decided to occupy his time drinking so by the time we left the party he was so drunk he could barely remember his name. I tried to get the car keys to drive but he started yelling, Gigi started crying and I was forced into the car. It is funny how much you can change in a year. A year later, I would've called the police, but at that party he had the power to intimidate and make me cry easily.

61

The 40 miles ride home became a car chase when someone tried to cut in front of him. He was driving like a maniac with both me and Gigi crying terrified inside. When we finally got to a stoplight, about a mile from the house, the guy in the other car stepped out and came in our direction holding a gun. He saw me and Gigi shaking and crying inside the car, shook his head and left. Roberto was shocked maybe realizing what his outrageous behavior almost cost and slowed down till we made it home. The 45 minute drive was hard to shake off. We got in a huge fight and I asked him how he could be so selfish and irresponsible to put our daughter's life in such danger. Instead of apologizing and feeling ashamed, he left to the bar again. For this Christmas party I reminded him of what had happened plus we were separated any away so he was off the hook to spend time with my snobbish friends.

The party was in a ranch and it was a beautiful sunny day, both Gigi and I had a very good time, she played in the pool with the other kids, I took her to the kids park and we had a peaceful and fun Saturday. I had to cut the day short because I had to be at work at 7pm so we headed back to the house around 4pm. I gave her a bath, fed her and put her down to take a nap, as she was exhausted from playing so much. I started to get ready for my shift and called Roberto saying he had to be back by 6pm so I could leave. Gigi was sleep and he let me know he was on his way back - but it was past 6pm and he wasn't home. I called again and he said he was at the bar on the corner of the house and should be home soon. I waited until past 6:30pm and was going to be late if I didn't leave so I got in the car, stopped at the bar and told him to go home because Gigi was about to wake up from her nap and left to work.

It was hot and storming, a typical summer night. Paulo had been out of the country for the past week on training so my nights were going to be long and boring. I worked on the remote position attending a flight and got completely drenched by the rain. As soon as my shift ended at 11pm I went straight home.

As I lift the garage door I see Roberto's van was not there. When I got upstairs I went straight to the shower to get rid of my wet uniform. I put on a robe and went to the other part of the house where his bedroom and Gigi's were and found no one. I panicked and called his mom, she was angry and said Gigi was there sleeping on the couch. The neighbor had called her saying Gigi was crying inside my house's gate. She was all wet from the rain and neither me or Roberto had the decency to let her know the girl was home by herself. I was furious and stormed out to her house to get Gigi. I explained to her what happened and left.

I put Gigi to sleep back in her baby bed and went to the living room to prepare the couch for me to sleep but I couldn't. I was too angry and the more I thought about it the more I realized how the divorce was going to be the best thing for everyone. Whatever reasons he had to hurt me, it was now affecting our daughter. She could not be raised in a house believing this kind of environment was ok. I could not wait for our apartment to get ready so we could move out and have a more peaceful life but little did I know things were going to get even worse before it got any better.

Roberto arrived home around 4am so drunk I have no idea how he made it upstairs. He got in the house and came to the living room where I was sleeping, or pretending I was because I knew I was too angry and it could easily turn into a big fight - I didn't want to wake Gigi. He set on the couch and put his hands under my blanket going up my legs so I jumped to sit down.

- What the hell are you doing? I asked infuriated.
- You're still legally my wife. I want to have sex with you! He answered
- You're drunk! Go get a cold shower and some sleep. I said.
- Come here! He said angrily pulling my legs sideways and forcing me to lay back down.

I kicked and told him to go away trying to keep my voice down. He got on top of me and put his hands around my neck telling me to be quiet like a good wife and started to pull my pajamas down with the other hand. My voice came out between my teeth saying he was going to have to kill me first if he was thinking he was going to have sex with me without consent. He squeezed my neck tighter as I kept trying to kick him but he has holding my legs down with the pressure of his body making it almost impossible for my 100 pounds 4.10" body to move. He hit me in the face telling me to shut up, and I carved my nails on his neck. He put one of his arms on my neck and used the other hand to hold my arms up. He was much taller and stronger. When I finally got one of my legs loose, I used it to push him away so hard that he ended up across the room. I have no idea where I got strength from because my body was shaking from head to toe. I ran behind the bar furniture we had in the living room and grabbed the ice chopper almost breaking all the glasses with my shaking hands. He came closer to chase me and holding the ice chopper in an attack position I said firmly: "I swear I am going to kill you if you get any closer!" He saw I was serious. He stopped and looked at me laughing, but before he headed to his bedroom, he grabbed my car and the house keys with him.

I had told him many times during our relationship if he ever tried to hit me like his father use to do with his mom, to make sure to kill me because if I survived, he was not going to sleep ever again. If he did, I would chop his dick off. I guess he was not that drunk that night because he made sure to double lock the bedroom door after he got in.

I set on the couch holding the ice chopper with my two hands and stayed in that position for a very long time. What I really wanted was to force his door down and keep my promise. I actually walked down that aisle two or three times to do it and each time I could hear him jumping out of the bed. Today this sounds funny but back then I was hurting inside and out, I had bruises on my legs, my tights, my stomach, my wrists and my neck was in a very bad shape.

Gigi's bedroom was right next to his and had no doors so every time I got closer to keep my promise, I looked at Gigi peacefully sleeping and thought: "how am I gonna explain that to her?" I would probably spend a long time in jail and who was going to raise her?"

That was the only reason I walked away back to the couch and watched the dark night end and a new day rise. My anger had passed, the physical pain was tolerable but the emotional pain was unbearable. I felt humiliated and I was going to make a serious decision that very day. I went to take a shower and found he used that window to leave and take Gigi with him to his mom's.

I got ready and went to his mom to get Gigi and go to my mom's. He had already told his mom his version of the story. She asked me if I was ok, I looked at her and showed my neck: "No, I am not ok." She answered: "You know you guys are still legally married so you still have your obligations as a wife." I understood what side she was on and left, after all he was her son. She didn't have to understand my reasons and I didn't make it a point to explain. It was pointless.

When I got to my mom she was horrified with the bruises and I told her what had happened. She said she had no idea our marriage had that kind of problems because I never confided anything with her. Since his mom and I were very good friends up to that date, she was the one I turned on after our fight because I thought it would be fairer to him. If I would've gone to my mom, of course she was going to stay on my side and our marriage would have been over a long time ago. You have no idea how ridiculous this sounds now as I write! What was I thinking, really?

My father had moved up north and was living with his brother in Recife, which was a huge peace of mind giving me courage to tell my mom I had to leave my house. I explained to her if I had to spend another night there, only one of us was going to wake up alive. My mom saw I was serious and told me to come stay with her.

I went back home and told Roberto I was going to leave. He didn't take it serious and went back to his moms. I gathered some clothes for Gigi and myself, she had stayed with my mom and I stopped at his mom to tell him I would come back for the rest. They were having lunch and before I said a word, he looked at his mom with a sarcastic smile and said: "she said she was leaving me, can you believe that?" then looked at me and asked: "where you're going? You have nowhere to go. Go back home." With my eyes looking down I answered: "I am going to live with my mom until my apartment gets ready. I will come back later with my brothers to get the rest of my stuff." I didn't wait to see his reaction, I just left and didn't look back. It was Christmas Eve of 2000.

I came back the next day with my two brothers to pick up some more stuff and found Roberto sitting on the floor of the living room crying and didn't quite get why.

"What is going on, I asked" He was sobbing when he said: "what have I done? I destroyed my family? Where is my daughter?" I answered she was at my moms. He sounded desperate: "please come back, please don't do this to me. I'll do whatever you want, please forgive me." I could not believe what I heard. Where did that came from? I didn't know what to think, I had so many mixed feelings, I felt so sorry for him because for the first time he seemed to be telling the truth. I set down with him on the floor and started crying too. "maybe I can make this work…, I thought." but then I looked at the couch and scenes of the night before started playing as a flashback so instead I said: "Us could never work Roberto. We only bring the worst out in each other. Eventually you're going to find someone else and have another family. Someone who will not want to change you." As my brothers started to carry my bags out, Roberto kept screaming trying to get them to stop: "please stop, don't do that, Angela please stay."

I didn't and I felt horrible about it. Not only for leaving him but also for waiting until things got to that point. Why did things had to be that way? I couldn't go back. How could I trust him to not physically hurt me again? He was not going to change, neither was I and there was not enough love left for either side to compromise.

Once I left, I became the enemy on his side of the family. In their eyes, I was not the wise woman in Proverbs 14:1. I was the foolish one who torn it apart with my own hands. I was a virgin when I met him and he had been the only man in my life for the past ten years. While he was living the wildlife even after we were married, somehow now it is my name that is followed by all sorts of profanities. It is interesting how society sets relationships rules that are only valid for women.

After I moved back with mama Roberto tried one more time to win me back sending a breakfast basket with flowers and a love message. I got very upset with all the show. It was aggravating to know all this time he knew what he needed to do to show he did care and keep our relationship alive. He just didn't want to, expecting I would stay no matter what - and maybe I would have if it wasn't for Paulo. He helped me understand and recognize how I was selling myself short, and how I was setting the standards for people in general to treat me that way because I didn't know any better. "You're a good person Angela and you deserve to be with someone who see the potential you have. It doesn't mean you're perfect, it just means aside your flaws, you have a good heart."

Paulo was so different. He only saw the best in me, he treated me with respect, he admired and supported all my dreams. I felt so loved.

We should never underestimate the power of care and what beautiful things can be transformed into when seen through the eyes of potential. Either it was fate for us to meet or I manifested the help I needed. I felt lucky it happened because it was what triggered the courage and the skills I needed to develop to preparer me for a much bigger battle on future quests. He was a true definition of the soul-mate Richard from Texas described by Elizabeth Gilbert.

Chapter 7
Facing the monsters under my bed

T he peace of living with mama ended when I heard my father was moving back home. He had been living up north with his brother who offered him a job as he had been unemployed for a while. His brother Edval was very successful in the orange business, buying from big producers and selling on the fair market in the city of Recife. According to my father, he had to move back because he got an allergic reaction caused by the intense heat of the city but something just didn't seem right. We were wondering what kind of problems he got himself into. My young sister Alzeni was the first one to bring it up and she hit it right on the head. Right after his arrival we started to get calls from a girl younger than my youngest brother who told us she was having an affair with him and also pregnant with his child. Just like that, there I was dragged into my father's drama again. It was hard to see my mother so hurt as it hadn't been long since she found out about my father's long history of molesting - God knows how many girls from the village.

The story came out when my father tricked one of my neighbor's daughters into the house saying he was going to give her candies and took his clothes off when she got into his bedroom. She ran away and told her father who went to face my father threating to kill him. Shortly after that, the other girls on the street spoke up too, including two of my cousins - daughters of my mom's brother who lived three doors down from us. My uncle was infuriated too and together they were planning on lynching my father on the street but gave up in consideration of the bad shape my mother was in when she found out. My mom came to tell me the news which wasn't news to me. I told her I knew it for years and that was the cause of my constant fights with him. Both my mom and my neighbors started to understand the real reason for my rebel behavior during my teen years.

When the news about the affair followed by pregnancy got to my mom's ears, me and my siblings talked to her and asked if she wanted to leave him. If she did we would stick together to support her but she didn't. He denied everything like he usually does, not only denying all the accusations of the abuses but also the pregnant girl's calls. He said the girl was a prostitute and was only looking for extra child support. He never stood up as a man to take responsibility for any damage he created in so many kids lives' this was not a surprise to me. The surprise was my mother's decision to forgive him for all of it. Her decision made me worried enough to rush and find another place to live. The apartment I had invested in had construction delayed and could take up to another year to be ready. I started panicking at the idea of Gigi being around my father that long, I had to call every hour while working asking where Gigi was and beg my brothers not to let my father get close to her ever. One night I was home and heard my father calling Gigi to go upstairs with him. I stormed out of the kitchen to his bedroom and found Gigi on his lap. I grabbed her and with my finger on his nose told him to never get that close to my daughter again because if he did, I would kill him. Giovanna was only three years old but I set her down and explained to her to never let anyone touch her above her legs and if anyone ever tried, she had to scream very loud. It didn't matter who it was, she had to tell me immediately and to never be afraid even if they threated her.

I realized I had to do something and get out of there before it was too late. I found a way to make extra money going to Miami to pick up merchandise for store owners. About six months later I had enough money saved up to put down on another apartment ready to move in, that put me at peace again.

Facing my father directly face to face made me realize where my mother had failed my sister Marineide and myself. It also made me understand why God had planned for me to bare the only granddaughter my parents ever had - to date. I understood I would be the only one who stood up against him. The monsters inside that house fed off my fear for years every time the lights went out and my mistake was to run away from them by marrying Roberto. I had to go back to understand they were still very alive and would be a threat to my daughter at any visit to my moms even if I was not living there. I made a point to make clear to my father I had instructed my daughter to report to me if he ever tried to get close to her and she was not afraid of doing so.

I don't think a molester can quantify the amount of damage sexual abuse can do to a kid's life. The shock of forcing you to be aware of things your brain is not ready to process steals precious years of our innocence and childhood. It makes you grow up without the proper preparation for being an adult. I stopped being a child when I was 6. When I was eleven I lost all of my teenage dreams, but I believe my books kept me strong. My sister Marineide was not this lucky. Of all my father's victims, the damage done to her life is beyond repair. She failed first grade twice like I said before, she attempted suicide many times and in 2007 she had a nervous breakdown. She told me the only reason she never got pregnant from him was because it took longer for her to develop and have her first period. My sister's life is damaged forever, she has an eating disorder, anxiety, deep depression and takes several anti-psychotic medications. She has focus problems and has never been able to keep a job.

One of my cousins lives with severe depression locked in the house. Another had problems consummating her marriage, and her sister has panic attacks on a regular basis. It is hurtful to me every time I hear stories of my father's victims and I am unaware of how many there are. I wish I had had the courage back then to speak up. It probably would have avoided the spread of more pain but I was too scared fighting my own monsters and trying to not lose myself.

I feel embarrassed and sometimes even guilty but I can't explain why. It was not my fault I know that. Somehow the victims are the only ones who suffer the consequences of their molester's actions. We suffer with shame, we suffer from guilt believing it is our fault, we suffer with insecurities, anxiety and a lack of worthiness paying for a crime we did not commit. We carry our perpetrator's cross with weights so heavy it sinks our souls, our dreams and any potential. We become easy targets and susceptible to other kinds of abuse due to our lack of confidence.

When I begin writing this book, I did not know exactly what direction I was going to take or which chapter was going to be the highlight with the most meaning. I did not plan to write about my father's victims but as I started this page I realized how much more fortunate I was to have met Paulo, who broke down the walls where I was hiding and helped me to stand tall.

Before I started this page, July 18th 2018 I got a call from my sister Marineide who shared some disturbing news from one of my mother's cousins. (I know, another cousin but remember, she had 11 brothers and sisters). My sister let me know this particular cousin had her two daughters open up about my father's attack when they were little. She had invited my mom to her house to ask how she was able to live with that man after knowing everything he put my sister through, her own daughter? And how devastated she was for learning he did the same to her daughters, a man who she always respected had betrayed her with despicable actions. She wanted justice and she had asked her son, who is a cop, to start a process to make this happen. My mother told my sister she left her cousin's house ashamed and that she was tired of being embarrassed for my father's actions.

I begin questioning how's that so? Why it is the victims who always feel responsible for the molesters actions. It is the victims who have to suffer it all? I am not talking about my mother in this case. It is hard to make a decision from a daughter's perspective, believe me I tried. I held so much resentment towards her for most of my life that it was hard for me to admit I love her. I love my mother more than anything and I use to reprimand myself every time I thought of how wrong she was for allowing this to happen under her nose. It was confusing and a big struggle to deal with this feeling until I finally opened up with a counselor who helped me understand this dueling inside my heart. He said: "It is ok for you to love your mother and not love the fact she failed to protect you."

Today my struggle is to understand "why" she never left after she learned all that? I had so many conversations with her where she asked me for details of what I had witnessed and when - I did, she cried so hard. "I can't believe I let this happen to my own daughter and other girls". Yet, it just does not explain why she decided to stay.

Divine justice however showed up to claim my father's dues a couple of years ago following a stroke he suffered while I was living with them after my divorce, I saved his life. His poor eating habits begin affecting his back which was already damaged from the stroke sequel. Today he no longer walks and lives depending on my mother's help even for trips to the bathroom.

You would think this situation would make him humble enough to take responsibilities for his actions and to ask for forgiveness right? No, it does not. He denies everything and I don't know how to feel about it anymore. I used to get so angry before but throughout the years I have decided his actions were no longer controlling me and it was God's responsibility to judge his case. I could however decide how I was going to react and I have chosen to deliver myself from his chain of abuse.

It is when I hear about his victim's fallout. I question what is the unfinished business I still have to work on? How do I go back to pick up the pieces of peoples' lives affected by him? Is it my responsibility? The easy answer would be: They have to find a way like I had to – but things are not black and white like we wish. Sometimes it is just a gray shadow fogging our judgment.

I understood then, they were not "lucky" enough to get involved in a wrong relationship to find the right answers like I did. So, if I had to pay the price for the sin, they might just as well take advantage of some good advice which was very helpful to me:

Chapter 8
Letter to my father's victims

I know for sure most of you were his victims, others I suspect, and there might be some I never knew. What I want to say to all of you is, I am deeply sorry for what has happened to all of us. It is not ok and no matter what anyone says, nothing will be able to fix it. It might sound like there is no justice to be served. The sad news is: there isn't.

We cannot change what happened to us but we can change how it changes us. We can change by talking about it, and talking a lot, until it doesn't hurt as bad. There is no shame in assuming we were victims. I know from experience how sensitive this subject is because we make trips back to the crime scene. We relive the feelings, we relive the shame and we feel unsafe again. I know those painful hours will be very hard to erase from our memory but ignoring them won't make them disappear. Believe me, I tried. I ran away and I thought building a life that didn't include seeing my abusers on a regular basis was going to make all the difference. Yet, here I am forty years later living 5,000 miles away from them but forced to face those feelings again on a different scale with the need to reach out to each one of you.

What I want to share is there is something magical that happens when we acknowledge the feelings, when we allow them to speak and when we tell our pain: "I hear you. I know we didn't do anything to deserve this and we will never have the answer why God or anyone else allowed this to happen, but I hear you."

We must take a "good look" at our pain and hold the broken pieces on our arms like a hurting child and say: "hey, I am here for you and I am going to help you heal. Let's do this together ok?

Let's allow our inner mother/father conscious to rise. To have something, to be stronger, it's what we need within us to be present.

Then invite the strength of THAT conscious to walk along with us on this journey, to build the future we deserve. A strong conscious will help us feel safe - for the next time we cry out in pain it will caress our chest and say, "'it's ok child, it's just a bad dream, you're safe", and the pain can go to sleep.

That is truly what helped me cope through all the years of abuse. Years which insisted on haunting me - but I was lucky. I found someone who helped me expose my monsters and face them. That's why I feel I need to share this with all of you. You can't rip the bad experience from your past and forget it completely.

I had to be stronger than I thought I was to protect myself and not allow my divine spirit to be consumed by pain and anger.

I learned how to release the sad life my abusers set me up with. Filled with sorrow, I reclaimed the life I believed I deserved, a life filled with grace. I stepped outside the bad experience and blessed it so it could be healed. I felt I didn't have to sentence myself with suffering for life. It was way too heavy to keep on carrying on my shoulders.

Does that mean my abusers are off the hook and get the easy way out? Absolutely not. It is not okay and never will be but I cannot spend precious time forcing them to confess to a crime they don't believe they committed. I will leave it to Divine Justice to judge their sentence and I know it will because our actions are like a boomerang in the universe. That's the beauty of God's work.

You might be thinking: "Right, but this is much easier said than done." You are absolutely right! It is not easy at all. It is not going to happen overnight with one prayer on your knees surrendering all to God. It is a long process.

The first time I decided to surrender this pain was back in December of 2004. I was living in Grapevine, Texas and decided to call my father after an attempt to pray but bad memories kept flooding my mind as a form of distraction. I got him on the phone and said I was forgiving him for all the pain he had created in me. I called my ex husband and did the same. For whatever reason, something shifted inside of me, I could feel things were changing all around me. The year 2005 - one of the best years, changed my life forever. I will explain later.

The anger didn't end when I surrendered the pain. I have found myself angry again over those same memories, more times than I can count. I even came unglued and had bad arguments with God. The next day I found myself apologizing for my behavior and we made up again. I guess he can take it, he is God after all, right?

"His love never ceases and his mercies never come to an end.
They are new every morning."
Lamentations 3:22

As the years passed I realized I stopped using that card so often. My angry episodes went from being a weeklong, to a day and now it is reduced to hours. I hope to get down to minutes in the future as I progress on my path to total surrender to grace.

What I am trying to say is it is important to release the past so we can create another path of energy for our bloodline, one not intoxicated by our abuser's sins and the sooner we do that, the sooner we can start living in the present and breathe the purity of a fresh life with endless possibilities.

God has a purpose for your life and for my life; we don't get to leave it up to our abusers to decide how we live it. They should not have that power over you or me and that's how we take our life back. Whether we go out preaching to the world helping other victims, or look inside our own hearts and help ourselves, it is one step at a time - putting one foot in front of the other. Choose you, not your past, not your pain; then hug that person in front of the mirror every single day and say: I choose you. You are the only person who matters right now and the one who needs to be loved the most by your inner power. Allow yourself this gift.

It was not my plans to write about my father's victims because I always thought it would be too much exposure and I didn't know how they would feel about it but in doing so I uncovered feelings I thought I had resolved. It was overwhelming and emotionally painful to write about them. I felt like I was talking to all of their pains at once, I stopped to remember each one of them as a little girl and their visits to my house with their parents either for a Sunday lunch or a church gathering. It is hard not to blame everyone in the adult chain – starting with the main abuser of course.

As parents, we all must be aware and understand we are responsible for the children we bare. We are responsible to teach them how to be emotionally strong to face the monsters under their beds and out in the world because there are so many. We live in an Era where people will try to overpower us in different areas of our lives just so they can feel better about themselves.

By raising an emotionally strong child, they will be able to identify an abuser and not feel intimidated by them. They will be confident enough to speak up and expose the abuser and that way they can be prevented from hurting someone else.

Chapter 9
Relax!, NOTHING is in control.

I eventually bought a very small apartment for me to move into with my daughter at the end of 2001. "Everything is going to be different now". I thought.

It was a two bedrooms apartment located in a very nice area of Guarulhos, close to work and a safe distance from my parent's house. I wanted that place to be the very opposite of the house I lived with Roberto. Half of the square footage and isolated from family meant no people walking into my home while I was still asleep.

Another thing I wanted to make sure was different was the color. Every single room at my house was plain white, so for my new apartment every room got a different color. "Boy! This place is going to look like so much fun!" I thought. The living room was yellow with one red wall, the tiles in the kitchen were painted green in a chess board like style. My bedroom was yellowish and Gigi's room was purple and white.

I was about to embark on a new life and needed colors to make fun memories.

Little did I know this next chapter would scare the life out of me – literally.

Roberto kept the house with the agreement he would pay my apartment's mortgage. I trusted him just like I did to purchase the apartment while we were still legally married. That way he could keep my health insurance and travel benefits. I wanted everything to end on good terms for my daughter's sake. It was not her fault we didn't get along as a couple, he was still her father and I wanted him to be involved and part of her life. We did not have anything written believing we were on the same page, but I learned later he was more interested in hurting me for leaving than using the chance to be close to his daughter. I remember my brother-in-law saying:

"I would purchase this apartment in your mom's name to be safe as you are still legally married."

"I don't think it will be a problem. I don't believe he would try to take the only place I have to live with his daughter." – I responded. "Plus he has the house."

I was impressed on how cooperative he was at getting all the papers signed. A "too good to be true" behavior - probably because he had an agenda my innocent mind failed to see. He made the first and only payment on time and after that his plans became very clear. He wanted me to lose everything and come back to him looking for help and give the marriage another try. As Roberto failed to comply with our verbal agreement, it become harder and harder for me to keep the place as my income wasn't enough to cover the mortgage, car payments, insurances and house expenses.

I tried to make trips to Miami bringing products for store owners like before but after September 11th this became a challenge with the dollar exchange rate. I tried to find an extra job but I couldn't afford a full time babysitter. The last resource was to sell my guest tickets but it was embargoed allowing strictly family to fly. Unable to find another solution, I sold it anyway.

The first year living in the apartment which was supposed to mean a new beginning was filled with struggles and I put up quite a show trying to hide it from everyone. I felt embarrassed for not being able to support myself on my own. I made one stupid decision after another trying to pay bills I obviously could not afford but I refused to ask for help. I was in denial and trying to keep my pride intact, determined I was going to make it work.

Paulo had no clue about my struggles and I was too embarrassed to even mention them. He would come over to see me when Gigi was with her dad and I would have a little piece of heaven inside my sandcastle. I would cook his favorite treats, get a nice movie, and we would cuddle up in the living room for a couple of hours – the maximum of time allowed for our promiscuous relationship - at every goodbye I cried. I cried for feeling lonely after he left. I cried for the unfairness of our situation. I cried because I was feeling guilty. I cried because I would never know what it would be like to wake up next to him. I also cried because he had no clue about the amount of financial problems I was hiding under my beautiful living room rug. I knew one day I was going to open the door and trip over that ugly truth.

The financial mess got so big its energy spread to every room of that little apartment, fogging my judgment even more. I became closer to his wife because I was actually a fan of her work as a professional and she was also pleasant company. It was clear though as a couple they were not a fit. I never witnessed any sort of affection when they were together. They looked like very good friends and unlike Roberto, he seemed to care a lot about how her and his daughter were taken care of. I knew that because I heard from him over and over again that our relationship was going to have to wait until his daughter turned 18. He did not want to cause any distress to his family. They came first and I didn't disagree with his decision. I was willing to wait as long as it took until my time arrived and I could have him for the rest of my life. In my eyes, it was worth the wait because what I had found with him was going to be hard to find again.

Common sense almost got me one time after watching the movie "The Bridges of Madison County". I thought the plot was a sign from God telling me to end it. "Let it go filha. If it is meant to be it will come back to you at the proper time with no one getting hurt." – God whispered. I embarked on a guilt trip for a whole week but jumped with the car still moving before the truth hit me. I told him we had to put an end to it because it was not right and I could not live the mistress life any longer. It was painful, it was wrong and it was not fair to his family to have me infiltrated in their lives like a friend when I was nothing but a big liar who had taken advantage of the situation. And, that was the ugly truth.

When I told him we were done it hurt more than I expected. It felt like I was trying to peel off pieces of him which were impregnated under my skin and some big ass hands were squeezing my heart to a point I could barely breath. I cried myself to sleep for a week withdrawing my feelings for him. Gosh, I loved that man so much. Why it had to be this way?

My common sense was hit hard in the head by lust and left unconscious with a long list of reason to maintain the affair: "Why not take time to decide if this is right or wrong?' Hell, why not? So, I called him and we met to talk. He told me he knew it was unfair for me to live like that, unable to even go on a date because we couldn't be seen in public, but it was all he could offer at the moment so he was going to respect my decision. Well, maybe one last time together… and later that week, maybe another time, then just one last time. Deep inside I knew I was lying. With us, there was never going to be a last time.

I arrived to work and got called by one of my supervisors saying they were going to need proof for the last passengers who traveled with my guest tickets listed as relatives. The suspicions were raised because the guest was complaining her luggage got lost and as a guest traveller you are not allowed to make such complains because you are travelling with a reduced price ticket. A standby trip can become very stressful very quick and because you're not paying full price, some agents can take it very personal. They started an investigation and took my travel card until it was resolved. I was not the only one selling the guest passes but the rules were the same ones applied by the IRS when you are filing your taxes: "don't get caught."

Let's take a little break here to recap how this investigation tied the rope a little tighter around my neck: Roberto refused to pay child support and his agreement on the mortgage, I was having an affair with a married man and with the embargo on the guest passes and trips I didn't have enough money to pay my bills. I was about to face foreclosure and that meant I would have to go back to my parent's house and have my daughter living under the roof of a pedophiliac.

To make matters worse I had asked Roberto to sign the divorce papers and on the first meeting with the lawyer he said he wanted to claim half of the apartment. He wanted it included on the divorce decree since the purchase was made while we were still legally married. I tried to convince him to reconsider as it was the only place I had to live with his daughter, but I was unable to succeed. Everything was falling apart and falling fast and there was not much I could do but wait for my downfall in silence. I knew it was coming and it did - emotionally, financially, and with physical pain – again.

October 3rd, 2002 – Election Day in Brazil.

The vote in Brazil is mandatory and you are only allowed to vote at the place you first registered as a voter. Election Day usually is a day where you meet everyone from your childhood as everyone flocks to their hometown school to vote. I dropped Gigi at her father's and went to have lunch with my family after voting. I would also be seeing people from my childhood. I had to be at work at 7pm so I picked Gigi up and headed back to my apartment around 4pm. The babysitter was supposed to arrive at 5pm but she called saying she had a family emergency and didn't arrive until past 6:30pm. I was already panicking, worried I was going to be late for work. I didn't want to aggravate the situation with the ongoing investigation so my trip to work became a run against time, fast and furious under a dangerous thunderstorm and not wearing a seatbelt. (I know what you're thinking and I agree).

I only made it two miles down the road before I drove my car under a bus in an intersection where the stop sign had been covered by tree branches broken from the storm. I tried to stop but without ABS break systems on a wet cobblestone it was nearly impossible. The road felt like soapy tile when I tried, leading me directly under the bus. Without the seatbelt I flew into the windshield breaking it with my head. I didn't have any cuts or blood except a huge bump on my head.

There is no 911 in Brazil and people simply don't stop to help. I didn't have a cell phone but a kind soul let me go inside her house to make a phone call. I called my supervisor and told him I had been in an accident and also called Paulo since he was closer to the location than my family, hoping he would come to my rescue. He asked his wife to go help me instead as he was at work and their house was only a couple of miles away. She drove me to the nearest hospital and called my sister. I felt a huge pressure inside my head and the pain was almost making me pass out, but I keep forcing my eyes to stay opened. They put me in a wheelchair when we got to the hospital and like all the hospitals in Brazil, they treated me like I was there for a touristic visit. There were police officers asking me for a statement because the bus is city property. I keep telling him I need to see the doctors first but they ignore me. I keep trying hard to stay awake and am asking the nurses for help, I probably have a concussion, I thought. One of the doctors came outside stressed and loud, it was probably her overtime shift.

- I am the only doctor working tonight and if you're not happy you can come do my job! – She yells.
- If you don't like what you do, maybe you should considered being a vet instead because obviously you're not prepared to deal with humans! – I yell back.

I stand up from the wheelchair and ask his wife to drive me to another hospital, ignoring the pain and holding on to the walls so I won't fall. We get to a private hospital covered by my insurance and I am taken right in for a head MRI, then taken to a room where later my family showed up and Paulo joins his wife. I look at the gathering bunch in my room and think: "This is so fucked up!!!.

My sister seemed to have read my mind as she was one of the very few who knew of my affair with him. She looks at me with disapproving eyes and nods her head. Thankfully I didn't have a head injury and was sent home after the results came in. My mom came to stay with me while I was recovering for a week and when I went back to work there was a story going around that I had caused the accident to stop the investigation.

It is really alarming to learn how people can lack serious common sense and start gossip saying someone would risk losing their life over a job. Throughout the years working for different corporations I learned people are capable of much more than just evil gossip, they are capable of doing whatever it takes to keep their jobs too. To this date, I haven't figured why some people hold on to positions in companies with a hostile environment, sentencing themselves to survival mode, willing to make a battlefield out of a workspace. Years working for different corporations also taught me no one is irreplaceable and no job is worth selling your soul and your heart for a paycheck. Jobs will come and go. If you stay truthful to the essence of your spirit something better always come along. Choose kindness always.

Today I better understand when a cycle comes to an end; trying to hold on to something when it has reached its time will cause more damage than letting it go. Back then I didn't know this. I went to play the last card I had available and talked to the president of the company in Brazil, telling the truth about my reasons for selling my guest passes. I laid out my heart, I showed him my collection of "you're someone special" given by customers for outstanding service provided and my "Perfect Attendance" coupon stack for being on time and not taking sick days for the seven years I worked there. I mentioned I had sold my guest passes because I was a single mother going through some very bad financial times after my separation. When he heard that, he cringed and told me to leave. I felt like a criminal, ashamed with my head down and went back home, knowing it was the end. I was right. I went to work the following day and before I even got my check-in counter ready to start my shift I got a call from the office. I headed upstairs knowing exactly why and I was informed I had been terminated.

Another round of judgments from people who did not know my reasons started to rise like a wave of rage. They knew I was not the only one selling but I had to be the sacrificial lamb to stop it -they were happy it wasn't them. "Better her than me", was the comments going around.

I remember walking up and down the aisles of that airport like a lost soul. I didn't know what was going to be next. I had one thousand things going on in my mind instead of making an effort to go home, I decided to stay and wait for Paulo's ride back home, like a safety blanket. Some of the employees looked at me like a lunatic, saying: I wouldn't be hanging around here if I had been fired but no one cared to ask if I was ok. I wasn't looking for sympathy. I was just lost and afraid of what was coming next. Brazil was going through a very bad economic situation and I knew jobs were not going to be easy to find.

I did find another job about two months later but they didn't pay enough to cover the bills. I quit and tried to start my own business with a friend promoting trip package but just like any business you start, you won't have a paycheck until it succeeds, which wasn't happening fast enough for the bills.

Unable to keep anything together, jiggling through so many things trying to stay alive I started to lose my faith. I wasn't sleeping anymore, I was hiding from my family and friends, and some days I had to search for coins under furniture to buy a piece of bread to feed Gigi because there was no food left in the house. I had to swallow my pride when my electricity got disconnected. I went downstairs to use a friend's phone to call my mom asking for help. She first yelled at me for letting things get to that point before calling her and said she was going to find a way to send me food.

Unable to find someone with a car available at that time of the day, she called Roberto telling him to come over and get some food to bring to his daughter. After throwing a fit and delivering a whole speech about how stupid I was for going to live so far away and was now bothering people for help, he went over to my mom's house. She asked if he knew I was in that much trouble and he admitted I had asked for money to buy food for his daughter but he had declined. He said he didn't want me to have access to his daughter's food. My mom asked if he was ashamed of making such a statement and he said no, I was the one who had decided to leave him so I should be able to deal with the consequences. He finally agreed to bring the grocery box my mom had prepared and I had to hear his humiliating speech with my head down, defeated.

I kept trying to look for jobs with no luck for almost a year. My family was worried and kept checking on me from time to time, but there was no way out at that point. I had to face foreclosure of the apartment and find another place to live. The options were two: back to my parent's house or back to Roberto's house. He had asked to try working things out again. My heart was uneasy with either choice as I couldn't' live with my daughter around my father or live with Roberto being still in love with Paulo. My mistake was to never have shared any of this with Paulo. I was too ashamed and didn't want to make him feel he had to make a decision based on my situation.

I didn't know what to do and my choices sounded more like a death sentence than a way out so maybe death was the answer. I was tired of fighting to survive and I wanted to end it. I waited for the weekend when Gigi was going to be at her father's and planned Friday to be my last day. After he got her, I sat on the couch and started to play my life over in my head. I went back to the Green Village days, I thought about my brothers and sisters, my mother and my friends... then I thought about the boys I met, my dreams, my old house, my former job... I tried to figure out how this happened? I had everything planned, I went to school, I had made so many sacrifices and worked so hard to get out of the village to a safe place... I had what people never had at only 23 years old. I had a big house paid off, I had the most amazing baby girl, a new car and a job which allowed me to travel the world... what went wrong? How did I lose control like that?

Today I understand the people you chose to build your future with should be the most important decision you will ever make, but back then I didn't know the answer. I blamed myself and decided my daughter didn't deserve to have a failure as a mother. I got the scissors to cut the protection screen of my patio and headed to the living room where the access was. There I decided to say one last prayer. There on my knees, I didn't find any final words to say... I was numb and disappointed in myself. I felt stupid for having goals so high it kept me from seeing and accepting my reality. I could never be a winner coming from where I did and I should've never tried. I remembered what my father used to say: "look at yourself, what makes you think people will give an opportunity to someone like you? You're not even tall enough for that." I swallowed those words like they were rocks going down my throat. He was right. My last prayer didn't have any words. Just tears. Lots and lots of silenced tears... I was no longer on my knees, I was face down on the floor when I heard the phone ringing. "Who in hell would be calling me at 3am? Can people respect a girls last pray and leave me the hell alone." I didn't answer and the calls continued. Not that it mattered anymore but I thought maybe it could be something serious about Gigi. No one would be calling at that time if wasn't urgent, I thought, so my mother's instinct made me put suicide on hold and answer the phone. I tried to hide my anguished voice.

"Hello"
My sister Marineide responded:
"Hi Angela it's me, Neide".
"What happened?" – I asked
"You tell me" – she answered
"What do you mean?" – I was puzzled
"God kick me out of the bed and told me I needed to wake up to pray for you. So you tell me, what happened?'
"I am not ok, please pray with me". I answered.
She did while I cried my heart out without saying a word. When I was done, she asked: "Do you feel better?" I said yes and she said: "Now, you go to sleep sister. I will call you tomorrow." And I did.

The next morning I went for a walk and sat down by the beautiful small lake close to the house. I had this weird silence in my mind. I was not thinking or trying to find any answers anymore. I was just there, looking at the ducks swimming and feeling the breeze on my face. I looked up and I saw an airplane flying lower than usual but not too unusual because I lived close by the airport.

I hear this voice loud and clear inside my mind: "How about leaving this country?" Before I could even think about what I had heard, I heard another voice" Doing what?' A whole dialogue started inside my head between me and...myself? "Yes, why not? You have a passport and you have a visa don't you?" You do realize you don't have money to buy a loaf of bread but you want to buy tickets to fly to the United States? A third voice shows up like a mother trying to stop the argument between two kids yelling: "Will you please just drop it? Stop this right now!"

I went back home and for every airplane flying over my head I thought... Hum...

How about that?... I got home and made this simple prayer from the heart:

"Dear God, please have some common sense before planting ideas in my head like that. If you really want me out of here, You're gonna have to do a little more work than small talks in my ears. Tickets to the United States cost a lot of money. Thank you very much."

The next morning, while sipping on coffee and still with the subject in mind, I got a call from the builder of the first apartment I had put a down payment on to leave Roberto two years earlier. He said he was interested in purchasing my share of the apartment and offered $11.000 Brazilian Reals, equivalent to $5000 USD back then. I hung up the phone and looked up. Okay, I got the message.

I could almost hear Him giggling upstairs. "Shut Up!" I said with a disapproving voice".

I begin making plans to break the news to everyone. I knew the worst part would be to convince Roberto to sign the minor authorization so I could bring Gigi with me. First was my mother and as expected, she flipped out. "You can't go to another country with a six year old kid like that. Are you insane?" I tried to get myself off the hook by saying it was all God's idea. He told me to do it. She said she was having a hard time believing God would tell me to do such an irresponsible thing. I explained how it happened and once she realized I was telling the truth, she pushed her glasses down to the tip of her nose, like she usually does when she is saying something serious to look you directly in the eyes: "Then you better take one of your brothers with you because there's no way you're going by yourself."

"Mother – I am a 30 year old woman, what do you mean I need to take a brother with me? What for???"

She said: "To make sure you're not going to get hurt!"

I rolled my eyes to the back of my head and went around twice voicing my frustration but she did not back down. "Ugh!"

Now it was the worst part: Telling Roberto.

Honestly, if I knew for sure Roberto would take good care of our daughter, I would be fine in leaving her until I was sure things were going to work out but I knew in my heart, he was going to keep living the single life, and my daughter was going to be left for his mother to raise. I was also worried my mom would want my daughter to come over from time to time and there was no way I was going to be able to know for sure she wasn't going to become another victim of my father. I had the same concerns when I thought about suicide but I guess the fact I wasn't going to be around lift responsibilities in the most selfish way. Alive I could never forgive myself. The option was clear. Gigi had to come with me. I went on and on and on with Roberto, told him we would try for six months until my tourist visa expired and we would probably be back by July of 2004 so he agreed to sign the travel authorization for Gigi.

I talked to my friend Hortencia, someone I had met while working for American Airlines back in 1999 who was flying with her five-year-old kid with a standby ticket and missed the flight due to a rude agent at the check in. She didn't know anyone in Sao Paulo and didn't know where to spend the night with her kid so I took them home with me. We kept in contact and talked from time to time. When she heard I was planning a move to the USA she immediately offered help and I decided I would go to Dallas, Texas, the city where she lived.

I still had another step to decide, which one of my two brothers was coming with me. Both of them were going through a very bad breakup and my mom would call me almost everyday to talk to both of them as they were both locked in their rooms for days, denying to talk or even to eat. My mom always trusted me to talk to my siblings on situations like that. She said I had good insight to share based on the experiences I had on that department. Roberto my older brother was dating this girl Diane for years but being the wild one, she eventually got tired of his games and broke up with him, which oddly enough left him brokenhearted.

Carlos the youngest one, was always the wise one, the kind of guy you would want your daughter to marry knowing he would do anything in his power to make her happy. Always responsible, sweet, romantic but didn't have the ambition his girlfriend wanted. She worked in a retail store and the son of the owner fell in love with her, leaving her to decide between the rich boy or the blue collar one, my brother. The decision left him devastated and although he tried his best to make her stay, her heart was already somewhere else filled with dreams of a much better life - also away from the village. Based on the current situations, I tried to bring them both but Carlos was the one who finally made the decision to come.

I was a little concerned about him coming because he was the mama's boy. He was the very opposite of me, he never cared about getting away from anyone. Since he was little he was connected to my mom and the whole family. The good one, like everyone used to say and surely the one who was going to be missed in the family the most. I was the wild one, they were used to me exploring different places, always away from the village.

It was now December of 2003 and I was planning to take off in January so I spent the next month getting rid of everything left in my apartment, selling or donating it. You might be wondering how Paulo took the news? Better than I would like to admit, which hurt me and made me question all those years with him believing it was a true love story. The truth was clear, his family was the priority not me and maybe that was the moving force I needed to make a decision for a big change.

Looking back now I see what a bold move it was. Most people get through a breakup, bad times, bad luck and decide to move away… maybe to another city, another state…but not me. I was moving 5,000 miles away to a whole different country not knowing if I would ever see any of my family or friends again and bringing a six-year-old little girl with me. Does that sound sane to you? It didn't sound sane to me either but the gut feeling of giving my daughter a better option living in a house that didn't include any sort of abuse put my indecisions to rest. I needed a change for both of our sakes.

The adrenaline of getting everything packed and ready didn't give me much time to think but when the day of the trip came, it hit me hard. I cried and cried a lot the whole time finishing packing our last bags. I put my luggage in the car and drove to the airport to meet everyone in the family who was going to say goodbye. After we were all checked in, it felt like I was attending my own funeral, everyone was crying, Carlos was sobbing. Roberto and his family were there too, kissing and hugging Gigi like she was departing to be a human sacrifice for her crazy mother's adventure. After the onion party ended we headed to the gate. I left Gigi with Carlos and went to meet Paulo for our final words. Since my decision to leave I had been wondering how that moment was going to be… was he going to ask me to stay? Was he going to say I was the one he loved? That we were soul mates and were meant to stay together forever? Was he going to tell me to wait for him? Was he going to rescue me from the incarcerating sentence to move to another land?

I see my prince charming walking towards me…my heart was about to sneak out between the buttons of my blouse… I was shaking from head to toe, my head was going through a blood rush keeping me from thinking… that is it… he is coming now… what it is going to be?…and the wonder ended right there: he didn't get off his white horse, he gave me a kiss on the front head and told me to have a safe flight. The sword I had dreamed of being pulled to fight the whole world to rescue me was now holding my heart at its tip and I was left bleeding to walk to the gate and catch my flight.

Inside the United Airlines flight taxing to Washington DC, our entrance to the United States I had my daughter sleeping on my lap and I could see the airport parking lot. The place where I had marked my life forever with so many good memories, so many nights of loving and soul confiding was now the final period to the very sad ending of my love story. I sobbed for the next 12 hours, the duration of the flight and I was not even sure what was hurting the most anymore.

Chapter 10
Welcome to the United States of America,
"what is your dream?"

I arrived in Dallas with my brother Carlos on January 30th, 2004, with $700 in my pocket, a 6 year old daughter and a broken heart. I had been in the United States other times but never longer than a week, and never had any intentions of becoming an immigrant either, so I didn't have any big dream planned. I wanted a safe place to raise my daughter and give her the opportunities I never had.

Hortencia accommodated all of us in her house, took me to buy a car which cost $1000, lent me $300 and on day one I was not only penniless but had a $300 negative. I got a job at the Brazilian restaurant in Irving, TX making $3 an hour, but since tipping is not in the Brazilian culture, the money was not enough to pay for rent so I had to take on two extra jobs just to make ends meet.

After 10 days living in her house we moved to live with her sister Ana, who was trying to find a bigger place and would leave the apartment for us to finish the lease for another three months. Carlos and I would have to make enough money to pay rent, utilities and food. Without any family to support us in any shape or form, survival mode kicked right in. You will learn all immigrants in history share similar stories and their main quality is strength – because there is no other option. When you are living as an alien it feels like you live on your own little planet and although you are not green with big glassy eyes, you will always be the outlander. It is hard to blend in when you are trying to understand what people are saying. You quickly realize you wasted every single penny invested in English classes because although you can read it, the fluency of native speaking is a whole other story. Even when you do understand and try to answer questions with your strong accent, the native person will not understand you back so frustration of communication is the first punch you get. Then comes taste and smells, a simple chore of cooking a meal becomes a treasure hunt up and down the grocery store isles looking for the right ingredients. See, in Brazil rice and beans is the base of our nutrition and is sold in every corner – probably two or three brands of each at most. Me and Carlos were about to find another level of rice and beans variety on our first trip to the store. He told me he missed mom's food so I decided to cook us the simplest Brazilian dish: rice, beans, steak fillet and French fries for dinner - we headed to the store. We looked for the rice aisle and found shelves with different types, brands, colors, cooked, uncooked, microwavable… you name it, they had it… Carlos look at me and ask: "Which one should we buy?" Me…. Hummmm… I have absolutely no clue… I guess they're all rice, aren't they? Well… the sad news was, they were not. The same happened with the beans, the fillet steak and the potatoes, so here's what our first dinner preparation looked like:

We ended up with jasmine rice, uncooked beans that took over two hours to prepare as we didn't have a pressure cooker, golden potatoes – not exactly the right one for French fries and the steak fillets were so hard it could be used to knock someone down. The rice got sticky to a point of an arts and craft tool, the beans even after two hours cooking, were making rocks noise at every chew and the French fries were chewy.

The excitement of our first attempt to prepare a dinner tasting like home ended up with tears of frustration at every bite and didn't end there: we finished eating very quickly you can imagine why, and now we had to clean the mess left behind. We were beat and still hungry with no energy left for cleaning so we decided to use the dishwasher for the first time not knowing it required special dish soap. Dishwashers are only normal in rich households in Brazil. By using the regular one, our kitchen was flooded with foam in minutes and we didn't even know why. We thought it was broken so we turned it off and now we have to manually do the dishes – and clean the floor. We accepted it was going to be a while before we try that again. Luckily we had the Brazilian restaurant as an option when we were working and when we were not, pizza and hot dogs became a regular on the menu for a long time.

Far harder than figuring out food, however, was to manage my schedule with Gigi's school. The restaurant closed at 3pm and she was dismissed at 3pm too, which meant I had to cruise town on a 30 minutes' drive to make it home before she was dropped at the bus stop at 3:05pm as our apartment was their first stop. She was only 6 years old with no English to communicate and I had no choice but to give her the apartment keys and instructed her to run straight home and lock herself in until I got there. Every day was torment for me, my heart would get so small and I basically just begged God to not let anything happen to her.

I would arrive home just after 3:40pm, helped her with homework, prepared her something quick to eat and then we got ready to leave to my second job with Carlos cleaning offices and the third job cleaning a gym in Fort Worth, about one hour away from Plano, where we lived. We would leave Gigi sleeping on the reception couch until we were done and she would also sleep on the back seat the whole drive home. We went to sleep around 1am.

About a month later I got a letter from the school raising concerns about Gigi's rest time. According to them she was always tired in class and they wanted me to make sure she got proper rest at night to be more alert for school in the morning. "I know what she needs, "I thought. "How to get that done at this point of my life is the real trick." There was nothing I could do, my main goal was to be able to afford a roof over our heads and food so I had to push the situation until school was over, which meant, another three months.

A month later I got another notice, and another one shortly after that with a threat to have the Children Protection Service looking after the case. I did not know what that meant and when I showed my friend Hortencia, she translated it to me in horror words saying I was about to lose my child. She explained to me how serious this country is about protecting kids and I would be surprised how quick that threat would become a reality.

The very thought of losing my baby panicked me enough to tell my brother I could no longer work with him on the last shifts and of course he agreed. The next challenge would be to make more money to make it up. I heard the owner of the restaurant was looking for someone to watch over the store inside the restaurant and immediately I offered myself for the position. She liked my style and how I offered some marketing insights to sell more products at the store so I was offered the job, which meant more hours and although still low, it was better than multiple locations to work.

It is now April and I heard from Paulo how much he missed me and wanted to come over to visit. I panicked because I lived in an apartment with no furniture, no TV and my car was a beat up 1992 Geo Storm. I had problems just trying to make it work for my job commute. Something was wrong with the tire and that made the car shake very badly. I would joke around saying my car had Parkinson's syndrome but to be honest I always arrived to my destinations with headaches from that shaking.

As I mentioned before, I always tried to make things look better when Paulo was around and this time was no different. I wasn't back on my feet yet, as an immigrant it would take a long time until I would see some progress but wanted to prove to him I was doing just fine. For some reason I thought I had to make him believe I came from a different social level and it was a full time job just trying to hide my upbringing. This time I needed a three day plan to set up stage for his arrival. I booked a hotel near the house because I didn't want my daughter to see us together as a couple, just like I did for years. I always took care to not confuse her head with men entering my life without knowing they were going to stay. I also talked to the manager of the restaurant if she would agree to exchange cars with me for three days, I explained to her the situation and she was kind enough to agree.

I get to DFW airport and waited for Paulo like I was the wife excited to see the husband after a very long trip. My hands are sweating, my heart is happy and my eyes are filled with hope. "Maybe this time he will say he wants to spend the rest of his life with me." He had told me how hard it was for him to realize how much he loved me after I left so maybe this time will be different. He walked out the arrival terminal and I almost lose my breath. We hug for a very long time. He whispers in my ears how much he misses me...Happy tears covers my face.

We head to the parking lot and I lie about the Toyota RAV4. I say I had just purchased it and he tells me how nice of a car it is. We head to the Sheraton hotel I reserved in Plano and he is impressed at how I took care of all the details. Little did he know I would have to work two extra weekends to pay for it. In my heart it was worth it because I could always make more money but not the opportunity to see him again.

When we finally make it to the room, he kisses me for the longest time. There was no rush to get naked and jump in bed... we were just there... like time had stopped... our bodies were enlaced in love... his hands on my waist and mine on his... sometimes he moved his hands to my hair without separating our lips, than holding my head in his hands and kissing me even deeper... and finally siting on the bed. "you don't know how much I missed you", he says, looking me in the eye.

We spend the next twenty-four hours inside the room, Carlos had agreed to watch Gigi for two days which meant I had to go back by the time she left for school on day two. I was happy because this time we would be able to go out as a couple without the worry of someone seeing us together. I had my little fairy tale for two days and that felt like a lifetime. I take him to see the apartment I am living in and introduce him to Carlos and Gigi as a friend. I make excuses for not having too much furniture and he believes in whatever I lie about.

Day three comes and I have to drive him to the airport... my heart aches, it is even more painful than when I saw him for the last night in Brazil. It felt like it was torn apart again while still healing. It is a different type of pain this time.

I don't know how to feel about feeding hope to someone just so they'll hang around until you're ready to make a decision. He wasn't ready to commit, so in his eyes it was better to just mark territory to keep me around, and I was addicted enough to accept what he could offer. I was also too busy trying to survive in another land to know otherwise.

I had two opportunities to change my fate and make life easier on me. A friend married to a rich guy told me her husband had a single friend looking for a Brazilian wife. He wanted someone new to the country, which I joked and said he was probably looking for "fresh meat" and she didn't deny it. I did meet the guy, a businessman from Memphis, TN who kept going on and on about how he had life all planned out for me, like he was hiring a personal maid with benefits. Apparently the line for the position wasn't short but being new to the country put me ahead of the game. I politely told him I was not interested in a second date and the answer shocked both him and my friend.

The other opportunity was a night job offered by one of my regular customers at the restaurant, Bill. He was a very nice Brazilian guy, always dressed in a black suit and usually had his dinner at the bar while talking to me. One night I was closing the restaurant and he saw me counting my tips with a big disappointment sigh. He asked me why I was working so hard for so little money when I was pretty enough to make at least $3k a week. I was intrigued and told him I could only imagine what kind of job would be paying $3k a week for an illegal immigrant. He told me he was a limo driver and he had many customers who would pay good money to have a private waiter serving them cocktails. It got me interested enough to ask for more details and we planned to talk more the next day as I was closing.

He showed up the next day and after too many questions he finally let slip that some customers would ask me to come to their rooms. "Of course they would." I told him. I am not going to deny, I was very tempted. $3k a week could give my daughter a much better life... it was worth the sacrifice, wasn't it? Let's not be a hypocrite about it ok. Much better than having CPS on my door right? I just wish I had the guts to do it but I didn't. My mother was already disappointed when I told her I wasn't a virgin when I married Roberto and that I had an affair with a married man. According to my mom's belief, I was only one straw away from burning forever in hell. Becoming an 'escort girl' would take all the hopes she had to save me and I would not be the one ripping her heart like that. Or maybe that was just another bull crap of lies I told myself trying to prove there was still good left in me - and if

I kept working hard and being a good girl, Paulo would finally see I was worth it.

So, I decided to do the right thing in my opinion – like a good girl. Raise your pride flag and like Scarlett O'Hara would say: "after all, tomorrow is another day". I was going to make it the hard way.

June arrived, and we moved to an apartment closer to work in Grapevine and consoling my desperation, Gigi was out of school. That meant I had no clue what to do with her for the next three months. I could not afford summer camp, I didn't know anyone in town to help me watch her, and I was unsure how I was going to make it until the end of summer employed. Around the same time, to make matters worse, my car decided to give up on me in the middle of the busy 635 freeway on my way to work. I called the Brazilian guy who sold me the car four months earlier and he let me know there was no warranty on the engine but he would gladly buy the car back for $50 dollars.

On top of making extra money to pay summer camp for Gigi, I also needed money to buy a new car. Carlos let me know Almir, another Brazilian guy who he was working for was a car dealer on the side. He said he could finance it one for me. Although the interest rate was almost 20%, it was an option – actually the only one.

I heard from Paulo. He was planning on visiting again in July and I got my hopes up thinking he was planning on spending my birthday with me. It would be wonderful to, after almost four years together, to celebrate with him, maybe a romantic dinner… a nice gift… I was sure he had something in mind.

I was able to get two days off at the restaurant getting two poeple to cover my shift. One of the girls agreed and I was all set to spend some time with Paulo.

A week before his arrival, a group of Brazilian people arrived in Dallas from Virginia for a cable company auditing project. A guy called Joao stopped at the store to transfer some money to Brazil and became a regular trying to make a move on me. He said if I wanted he would help me get a job with them making some good money. "Oh well, I guess every Brazilian here has found an easy way to make money in this land, except me…The American Dream…"

"I wonder what the small letters on the agreement were this time." I thought. I politely declined but he insisted on giving me his number just in case.

Paulo arrived and just like before, I moved heaven and earth to make sure everything was perfect. I got some used furniture to make the apartment look homier. I even had a bed this time although the old spring mattress had some springs popping every once and a while poking my buttocks. Both myself and Gigi had learned the hard way exactly which sides to avoid.

The TV stand was hardly standing and the old TV had two channels working. "Well, at least it looks like a home now" I told myself after arranging everything. The only thing missing was one of those staged family picture frames, with everyone looking happy and pretty but ready to fall apart when no one was looking – just like my staged apartment. But I was excited to show Paulo my progress since his last visit. He broke the news saying he was going to leave on the 10th, two days before my birthday and I got disappointed.

We spent the first day together but the magic and excitement we had in April was no longer there and I wasn't sure why. I guess in April it was more like an unexpected reunion after I left as we were unsure we would ever meet again and now that we found a way back to each other, we've lost that fear.

Day two I took him shopping for gifts for the whole family, his wife and daughter had given him a long list and even his father in law got some goodies but my name was not on the list - I hid my disappointment again. When we returned from the mall I got a call from my boss at the restaurant saying the girl who was supposed to cover me had called saying she was not going to make it and I had to come cover my shift the next day. I panicked and tried to call the other girls begging them to work for me because it was his last day in town and I wanted to spend all the time I could with him but no one was available.

You would think I would do the right thing and tell him I had to go to work right? Especially after he said he wasn't staying for my birthday or even buying a small little birthday card… but what did I do? The same stupid mistake a teenager girl in love would do and didn't show up to work. Go ahead and hit me in the head as you read this… I deserved it. I understand. I have made many irresponsible and impulsive decisions when heart got in the way. He left, I cried and cried and cried. I lost my job and cried and cried and cried a little more. My 31st birthday I spent…well, you know… dehydrated from all the crying. You know what is funny? When I look back now I can clearly see every single time major pains took place in the milestones of life changing events.

I called Joao and asked to meet to learn more about the job offer. He explained the work was to audit homes with cable signature and make sure they were properly connected according to what they were paying for and to disconnect illegal accounts. That meant, driving around Dallas the whole day long and climbing poles where the cable taps were connected. Joao needed a partner with a car and that's where I came along. It should be a good partnership because by myself I would never be able to carry a 30 pound ladder in the Texas summer desert climate.

I got the approval from his boss for us to become partners and we started working the next day, 8am to 8pm, Monday through Saturday. The money was indeed good, in two weeks my paycheck was more than I made at the restaurant but I knew this was a temporary job, the project would only last six months total.

I don't know if I could take it any longer anyway, the job was hard, my face and arms got a dirty brown tan and I had to deal with Joao's sexual harassment day in and day out, but quitting was not an option.

Taking care of Gigi got much easier when Regina, Roberto's sister decided to move to the United States to live with us in August. Me and Carlos made the arrangements. She would not have to pay any rent or bills as long as she got a job to make it back home when Gigi was out of school. We also bought her a car to make her more independent. By October the workload had slowed down and we knew it was going to be over soon.

I heard from Paulo he was planning to visit again. If you made the math now, it seemed he was planning to stop by every three months to "mark his territory, right?" Yep! That was my thought too. He did say this time his wife had started a conversation about getting a divorce. (His wife, not him but I was still blinded by love to make the math). I was fed more hope and I was happy with the possibility we could become a couple one day. Since we had Regina living home now, I decided to get us a hotel close to downtown and made us reservations for a dinner at the Reunion Tower to introduce him to nice places in Dallas.

This time I had to dodge bullets from Joao, who harassed me asking why I was going to miss two days at work, which was allowed since I had PTO to use. He stalked my brother with questions as he was suspecting I was with someone. He was right but it was none of his business as we were only co-workers. I also didn't want Regina to know who Paulo was to avoid drama with Roberto so hiding for two days was quite an ordeal. I didn't mention anything to Paulo, after all, he was the one crossing oceans to come see me. When time came for him to leave, I had questions... (Yes, finally!) I asked what his plans to be with me were.

- Well, I can't promise you anything right now, you know that. I have to wait for my daughter to turn 18 so I get things finalized with the divorce. He answered.

  I begin questioning myself. Why was he making such an effort to make things easier for them when both his daughter and his wife were the ones who, according to him, wanted him out of the house? He let me know he was remodeling his old apartment so he could move out, (pushed by them) but that was not enough for him to give me answers about planning our lives together.

This time, after he left my mind was thinking... trying to show me the truth I had avoided for years: I was never the priority. His family was and I could not blame him for that. It was my fault to let myself fall in love, it was my fault to dive into that relationship heads first, and it was also my fault to nurture feelings for so long knowing he was a married man. The fact I was in love, addicted to someone I believed was my soul mate, did not change the ugly truth. I knew what I was doing and it was wrong. Questions, facts and answers started playing in my mind like a wakeup call... I was ready for a change.

Chapter 11
Tom McCluskey, the American Boy.

No matter how much I write, my feelings for Tom will always sound conflicting.

Thomas Lance McCluskey, the "Spaced Cowboy" as some of his friend called him.

He was heaven or hell and nothing in between.

When I started this chapter a couple of weeks prior to today, I stopped to look at the blank spaces on this page, remembering his silly smile. The way he covered his mouth to release his awkward and sarcastic laugh and most importantly, the things that made him laugh which 80% of the time, were inappropriate.

I mentioned to my friend Elizabeth (my spiritual rock) two weeks ago I had to stop on the first line and take a deep breath because talking about Tom could be as intense as the experiences I lived with him for almost ten years. I had to be prepared for an emotional trip down memory lane -for the past two weeks I've been avoiding the computer.

I wasn't sure I was ready to revive those memories but then last night he came into my dreams and would not leave. I woke up three times and went back to the same dream, so real I can still feel his hug and hear him saying: "they don't allow me to come here very often but I had to see you." His hug pushing my head towards his chest was so strong it made me lose my breath and I spent the whole morning feeling it. First thing I told him was: "I am so sorry I couldn't save you and tears rolled down my face." He smiled and said everything was fine and we talked the whole night long. I woke up in the morning and said out loud: "Fine, I'll get back to your chapter today." Again, I tried to restart this chapter but distractions were far more than expected so I stopped for the third time.

This was very unexpected because the whole reason I wanted to start this book was to speak about Tom and how much he changed my life, forever, growth wise. I was really excited about getting here to finally understand what all those confusing feelings from four years ago were all about. Now I just feel like I am again, lost in all the detangling emotions from the beginning of this book and really, what is that about?

I called Elizabeth to ask why she thought that was, she said: "Angela, maybe you're stuck because you feel there is something unfinished about your relationship with him, what do you think?" My answer was: "Hell yeah! I have so much unfinished business with Tom I don't even know where to start - and he knows that! Do you know how many times I argued with him after his passing? Cussing him for leaving me here hanging high and dry and just checking up on me after all I did to save him? Do you know how many times I cried and asked him for forgiveness for not being there by his side when he passed? Actually both him and God got their ears full with my rage about that night. I had spent over nine years by his side during his seizures in the middle of the night! I showed up to work countless times with less than two hours sleep. I have been peed' on, bit on and hurt in the process so many times but both him and God decided to give me the midnight move! He decided to die the night I decided to sleep in my daughter's room so I could have enough sleep for my morning meeting. How fair was that? So, did I have unfinished business with him? You bet your ass I did!

Elizabeth being the angel she is just told me I had to resolve this in my head and I thought to myself: Well, I knew that!

Back to ignoring the computer for another week and all I could think was that this whole book idea now sounds very stupid. It brings me back to the beginning and I don't actually know how I really feel about Tom's passing.

On my very first date with Tom I returned home with the most physical pain in the brain I ever felt. I had to sit down outside alone and smoke some cigarettes to deflate my head, you know why? I was living in America for almost a year and had found how limited my English was after a date with a natural-born citzen. I use to say I spoke canned English from working at the airport for so many years and repeating the same script day after day: "Hello, what is your final destination? How many bags to check today?".... And so on, so when I went out on a date with a real American person who spoke "Texan" not English, my brain was working overtime every second of that dinner. I remember I had to look deep in his eyes for the two hours the dinner lasted and try to keep blinking to a minimum afraid I was going to miss something. I have no recollection of what we talked about at the dinner but the way he looked at me brought me peace and I felt safe for the first time in a long while. Some years later we were talking about that night and I was joking about how challenging it was at our first meeting. He asked me why I decided to go out with him again when I had not understood a word of what he was talking about on date one? "I know you were trying to impress me as a tough guy but your eyes ratted you out. I knew I could trust you – and I was so right!" – I answered.

Apparently he had his eyes on me for a long time but I had no idea. I was just an illegal immigrant trying to make a living after I lost my job at the restaurant. We were a crew of 100 Brazilian people doing street audits for a cable company. I had to have a man partner working with me as I was not tall or strong enough to throw a ladder up on the street pole to check the cable taps. For 6 months I worked with Joao driving through Dallas from 8am to 8pm and he sexual harassed me every single day of work but because I was an illegal immigrant, I had no voice. One day he tried to touch me while I was driving and I had to push his head against the passenger window for him to stop and made him get out of my car on the middle of a busy freeway. I went back to the office to return my badge and tools, talked to the supervisor about quitting but he promised to find me another partner. Days later he called saying he didn't find anyone but Joao had promised him to behave if I gave him another chance. I was making good money and honestly didn't have much choice but to go back working with Joao. Yes, he was lying, he never changed, the jokes continued in a slower level but they were still there, always making me uncomfortable but he stopped trying to touch me as I told him next time I would not stop the car to push him out.

I can be very mean when pushed to the limit and I guess my face convinced him I was being serious. We worked together until towards the end of the project when he decided to go work in another state and asked me to go with him. Of course that was a solid no but he tried to convince me every single day. Finally on the last day working together he offered me his whole entire paycheck to go out with him for a night (about $5k) – another solid no was the answer and thanks to heaven he left. I do not judge anyone who would take the offer trust me, however, the fear of being forced to do something against my will had been the monsters under my bed since I was a kid. It took me years to look them in the eye and say they didn't own me anymore. It took me years to call my father and tell him I forgave him for turning my childhood into a nightmare and also to "ask him" for forgiveness for carrying hate towards him since I was 6 years old. Looking back today I see Joao was put in my life to test my beliefs. Back then I created scenarios on how I was going to run him over, and make it look like it was an accident and even call 911 to come get the body.

So, when Joao left I started working with my brother Carlos, which was kind of tough too because we were both short people to carry a ladder; plus our religious beliefs made working and living together a daily struggle. We were very different people. Carlos was very organized with everything, including the bills. Since my divorce I had been a train wreck financially and emotionally, trying to raise a daughter on my own with not a dime from child support. When he decided to work with the pastor's wife, I was left with no partner to work and I had no choice but to quit. I brought my tools to the office and told my boss, Tom, I could not work anymore. He offered me help and asked if we could go out for lunch so he could explain how. Little did I know my life was going to change forever after that lunch encounter. Tom said he had the perfect partner to work with me, someone who was strong and young but did not have a car. I politely declined and explained to him the traumatizing months I passed working with Joao and didn't want to go through another experience. I was going back to work at the Brazilian restaurant as a waitress again.

He asked why I didn't report, I told him I did, to my supervisor the Brazilian leader and he didn't do anything. He said had I come to him instead it would've been different. He said David Moore, the guy who he was going to let me work with, was only 18 years old but was like his son. He said he was going to make sure I was safe. I froze, I did not know what to respond, I was now 31 years old and no one ever had said that to me before. I never imagined having someone making you feel safe could change the structure of how you feel about everything else. Peace is a powerful feeling.

I agreed and start working with David the following morning. Tom made sure we had only the best routes and I had the highest paycheck I'd ever seen. I was able to payback some money I owned Carlos and buy Gigi some winter clothes too. I saved some money as it was going to be a while until the next project started and I would get another paycheck. The project ended a month later and they were now moving to Pensacola, FL to help on the aftermath of hurricane Ivan. Tom invited me for dinner that night as friends and started his talk trying to convince me to come with them. I said I was going to pass and just go back to work cleaning houses and waitering tables in the Brazilian restaurant. He asked me how much I was making working on those two jobs and offered to double it if I work as his office manager. I knew I could not pass up the chance of working in an office again. Making that kind of money I could give my daughter a little more comfort too. I accepted and that night during dinner he let me know he was in love with me for the past six months. I was surprised, I had no idea but I told him I didn't know what to think and he said I didn't have to say anything, he just wanted me to know. We had become good friends and he was okay with me not feeling the same way about him.

One day he called saying he was in the neighborhood and asked if he could come over to discuss details of the Pensacola project. I agreed but was a little nervous as my apartment was very simple. We didn't have much furniture and almost nothing to eat. It was the beginning of December and we had been talking for some time. He was explaining details of the project which was going to start in January, then helped himself to get water from the fridge. When he returned to the living room, he asked if I would mind going with him get something to eat because he was diabetic and couldn't go long hours without eating. We headed to the grocery store instead and he filled a cart with groceries, paid for everything but never mentioned a word about my empty fridge.

Back at the house, Gigi had returned from school, she was in first grade. I introduce him as a friend and he start making conversation. I asked him to slow down because she didn't speak much English. He sat down on the floor with her and they played Strawberry Shortcake until dinner was ready. I kept looking at that tall and muscular strange man sitting on the floor of my living room playing with my seven-year-old daughter and couldn't help to think, huh?! Who would say this man had a soft spot like that? How sweet he looked. So, we ate dinner and after that Gigi asked to watch cartoons, we had a broken TV with only two channels working. Tom spent the rest of the night trying to fix it and got four more channels to work.

He became a regular, we went out to eat all the time but I never gave the green light for him to move forward and the reason was only one: Paulo was still standing at the door of my life like he had been for the past four years. Never came in and never went away and I was the only one responsible for it since I never shut the door. I have been in love and believing he was my soul mate since I met him and I always believed one day he was going to show up and invite himself in. When he called that second week of December saying he was coming over for another visit, I decided I was going to have some answers this time. I had everything planed inside my head, I was going to give him an ultimatum. It sounded much easier this time with Tom in the picture. The game was changing, I had options now and it felt good, really good. I was starting to get my confidence back, I lost some weight, died my hair and didn't look like a street worker anymore. I can see now, how Tom's feelings for me were the extra push I needed to take better care of myself.

I picked Paulo up at the DFW airport and he was surprised: "wow, you look gorgeous." He filled me with more and more compliments the whole drive to the hotel and again, there I was lost in his arms, completely vulnerable and voluntarily locking myself inside the castle I had been hoping to be rescued from.

I wasn't ready to let him go, gosh, that man meant so much to me… and for some reason I didn't know how to tell him what was going on. I loved him so much it scared me to death the very thought of hurting his feelings. It felt like I would be betraying my own soul but this time I knew I had to make a choice. If I was going to move to Pensacola with Tom it would be a matter of time before we start a relationship. Tom was the only one offering the one thing I have been missing my whole life, to keep me safe and I wanted that at this point of my life. I actually deserved that and so did my daughter.

The last night with Paulo I asked the same question knowing what the answer would be and just like I expected, it did not change. "You know I can't promise you anything right now." This time I cried myself to sleep and even though I tried to hide my tears like I always did just so he wouldn't feel pressured, he heard me sobbing and hugged me tighter but did not say a word. My crying this time was because I already knew what I was going to do. The game was over and I was about to close the door, leaving him outside where he had been standing for all those years. I deserved better and there was someone waiting for me inside, for a nice cup of warm tea, good talks and a safe heaven.

When Paulo left, my instincts told me to break up with him forever but I didn't because I didn't think I was strong enough to face him with a goodbye being still in love with him. I was afraid I was going to trick myself in letting him stay so I convinced myself I was going to let him off easy and start pushing him back to stay with his wife and everybody was going to be happy.

Days later I called Tom and told him I wanted to meet him. He said he was busy finalizing some details of the project at the office and asked me to meet him there. I spent the day getting ready… I wanted to impress Tom and show him I was ready. Up to that day Tom had only saw me in work jeans and boots but that afternoon I showed up at his office wearing a nice skirt with a sleet on the side, knee high leather boots and a leather jacket. He did not hide his "wow" face, neither did the other guy in the office. He said he was going to take me for a ride, he wasn't too comfortable with all the attention I was getting in an office full of guys. He took me out for dinner than stopped at a hotel bar to show me off to one of his friends from Virginia who was visiting.

It was getting late so I told him to drive me back to the office to get my car and once we got there, he said he needed to drink some water and invited me in. I tried to tell him I knew exactly what was going to happen if I went in with him. He laughed sarcastically and said, he didn't know about me but all he wanted was some water because he was really thirsty. I played along and said I was not going to be responsible for my actions once we were in there so he was not going to be able to play the victim card later, after all he had it coming.

We went in playing and chasing each other having fun and laughing a lot. He got his water and I got him in his office like I've planned. I sat at his desk and asked him to kiss me and he did, like he was waiting for that for the longest time.

Tom was tall and strong, he was addicted to working out since he was 17 and now at 43, his body was nothing but muscles with a very nice six pack. He held my tinny body close to his using only one hand and undressed me with the other one. He was an amazing lover and we spent hours in his office learning about each other in the deepest level of intimacy until the very last minutes when we were getting dressed to leave. He broke the news right before we left the building. "I have something to tell you." I thought he was still joking around so I filled in the blanks with all sorts of stupid things. like: oh no, you're gay! I knew something wasn't right about you! Look at all those muscles... he laughed. "you are so silly!" "what is it then", I asked. He said: "I have a wife". I thought he was still joking, so I said: "oh my gosh you are so dirty... shut up!" but than I realized he wasn't laughing any more. "what the hell, what you mean?! What are you doing?" I said almost crying but also wanting to slap him... I was mad and he saw that... He tried to explain: "It is a very complicated situation, we already talked about divorce months ago but we agreed to wait for the holidays." I didn't want to hear the rest, I left slamming the door.

The drive back home was painful. I felt awful and hurt and mad with God, as usual... so mad I shouted inside my car the whole way home asking Him why he wanted to see me in pain all the time. Why the hell he made me believe someone who cared had come along to play the same trick He did with Paulo? What kind of message was He getting from me that made Him believe I was on a mission to wreck all the homes I've approached? I was so furious!!!

The next day I spent in bed, mad and refusing to give details of the night before to Regina who insisted to know what happened. Tom called and I told him I am going out of town for a week with a friend, avoiding any other encounter or conversation about the subject and the fact I felt betrayed by him making me believe he cared and most important, he was available. There was no ring and he never mentioned anything to indicate he had someone in his life.

He calls me after a week and tells me he needed to talk about the project in Pensacola and also to give me my last paycheck. We were going to be moving soon and I agreed telling him I would meet him at a coffee shop in a mall close to home.

He shows up with his oldest son Lance, Regina and Gigi are with me too as the whole point was to avoid being alone with him.

While the kids were distracted and talking, he explains to me how he ended up married to his ex sister in law. She was previously married to his brother who took off with the babysitter leaving her and three children behind. He agreed to marry her so his nephew could have his insurance for a very expensive surgery. Some years later he was the one getting sick and partially lost his memory when his seizures got out of control. They became a couple for some time but they were more like very good friends taking care of each other and according to him, she knew about me.

One thing I've always admired about Tom was the fact he was never afraid to tell the whole truth about him and I found over the years most people are not comfortable with that. I've lost count of how many times I saw the shock on people's face when Tom spoke about his drug addictions and promiscuous past and he never seemed to care because he would say: "that was who I was and what I did and although I am not that person anymore, I enjoyed my life, actually, every minute of it. I heard from both him and his friends how comfortable he was on approaching girls and making them feel really

111

good about themselves and that was probably the number one reason he was so popular with them. Tom had not one, or two but three girlfriends at the same time at one point and to everyone's shock, they all knew about each other. He sarcastically explained to me it just made it easier for everyone as they all could have a break from each other in between.

I told him innumerous times I would never want anything to do with him if I met him back then because I would never accept sharing my man with anyone else but actually who was I to judge. I told him he was just a male whore and he didn't disagree however, we spent many hours going through every detail of his past crazy life and I never felt in a position to judge his past. I was instead always curious to know more about that man and his authenticity of living life to the fullest, which was the very opposite of me. Yes, I did not agree with that crazy life but the fact he was never afraid to admit anything he did, was something I had never heard of before.

He stopped at my apartment afterwards and while his son, Gigi and Regina found a way to communicate with each other he took me to the kitchen for a talk. He opened up about the fact he was lost with his decision because his kids seemed very happy now as a family, including the fact that they were cousins and now also step-brothers as crazy as that would sound. He says his heart wants to be with me forever but he is afraid of tearing his family apart again and hurting his sons. I told him I couldn't help him with that. He would have to figure it out on his own and I wasn't going to be the other woman again.

A week later after Christmas Tom broke the news to me that he had finalized his marriage, he believed they both deserved to be happy. Back then I thought everything were done amicably because he always kept me out of any details. All I knew was they were very good friends and ready to part ways. Many years later I found out both his ex-wife and his nephew thought I was the reason he destroyed their marriage. He defended himself by saying their marriage was over long before he met me and she knew that but she was not going to admit it. He was okay with taking the blame. He gave me his side of the story and of course she has hers, which I will never debate otherwise because that is her truth, just like he had his truth and that is the only side I can write about.

Tom shared with me his last recovery from traumatic months without a memory. He lost the desire to live and thought about driving his car off the bridge on his way back from work, just a month before we met. He explained how hard it was for him to go from being a Head End engineer for Southwestern Bell (AT&T Today) and Charter Communications in Fort Worth, back to an installer due to his health challenges, and how sick he was of trying to make life work trying to paint the portrait of a healthy person. Shortly after that he got a call to be the manager of the project I was working and that's when we first started working together.

Tom was born in Pittsburgh, PA, and he was the oldest of three brothers. Timothy was the middle one and Terrance the youngest. His parents Carol and big Tom (his father) told me about his first epilepsy episode when he was still a baby and things got worst by time he become a teenager.

He grew up on the Southside of Pittsburgh, I heard countless stories of how poor they grew up and how challenging life was when you lived on the bottom of the hill and boy, I could relate on so many levels…

Tom was a natural storyteller, my very own Forest Gump… I lost count of how many hours we would spend just talking about literally everything. He always had the ability to take me with him on his personal trips into the past. He walked me through every small detail, the oil smells in the city, the cracks on the walls, the pollution of the Pittsburgh River, the fish found dead with only one eye, walks to school on a freezing day with his two brothers and trying to climb the icy hills of the city and sliding right back down. He also me laugh with the silly fights with his brothers during dinner: "Mom, Tim is drawing me ugly in the air!" or his innocent questions to his mom after his first day at bible school in church: "Mom, they said God is everywhere… is he here right now?" "Yes, Tommy, He is." Tommy would get the sugar jar to look inside: "How about inside the sugar jar? Is He here? How about in the refrigerator?"… Carol use to say he always brought justice to his name, Thomas the doubting disciple. Even in the present days he would drive people crazy with his questions. I knew from experience how true that was, and I am pretty sure everyone who was part of his life at one point, would agree with that.

I heard stories from his mom and dad of how exceptionally intelligent he was, playing and winning chess game from adults when he was only five. The stories of how half of his family was dead before he was fifteen. Then there were the stories of his father's mom coming to live with them after his grandfather passed and how that affected the family in so many ways. His grandma according to him was a sweet lady through out the day but at night she let her demons out to scare everyone in the house. He told stories of the police returning her home many times after her escapes and his dad having to nail the doors shut to keep her from running away in the middle of the night. There was also the funniest, and scary story of how she managed to set herself on fire after taking too many valiums and sitting by the fireplace.

Another thing that always amazed me about him was how he found humor in those terrifying stories - I guess that was the McCluskey's trademark: The Irish pride seemed to be normal behavior in the whole family but not everyone got that. You had to hear their stories with a compassionate heart to understand their dark humor and very few people got that, unfortunately.

Tom's dream was to become a professional football player. He had the height and the body for it and he had started to make a lot of progress towards that in school but it was interrupted as quickly as he started when he was only twelve.

He told me the story of how out of nowhere he started to wake up in the middle of the night on a regular basis feeling very thirsty, going downstairs to the kitchen to drink water, than almost immediately peeing it all out and repeating this process the whole day and night for several months. He lost about 40 pounds in a very short period of time and finally collapsed on the yard trying to help his dad with a chore.

He was taken to the hospital and was in a coma for several days, later diagnosed with Diabetes type 1. The nurse tried to explain to him and his mom what that meant, back then it was a very unusual and unknown decease. He said he remembers telling the nurse that whatever they had to do to fix it, to please make sure there would be no needles involved. He said the nurse looked at him with tears in her eyes and said: "Son, I'm afraid you will have to use needles for the rest of your life." The doctors also explained how the decease was not curable and they gave him no more than 10 years to live.

Tom explained learning how to live with diabetes was one of the most challenging experiences in his and his family's lives. From learning how to manage his sugar level, the needles, the limitations…everything was a life changing event. It was then his life took a wrong turn forever.

He was prohibited from playing football by his coach after his first seizure during practice and to me this was when reality hit him in the stomach for the first time. At thirteen he found comfort in drugs and embarked on a wild ride for years to come. He had decided to live those last ten years to the fullest with absolutely no rules.

I was 31 when we met and had never tried drugs in my whole entire life, not even marijuana and there I was hearing stories from someone who became a drug dealer before he turned fifteen. There were drugs – plural – you name it, he did it.

His father found his stash of pot one day and flushed it down the toilet. Tom told me how he almost got kissed by death that night when his dealer took him for a ride to explain where the drug money was.

I listened to every story like he was reciting parts of a movie because up to that moment, I thought those things only happened in movies where Robert De Niro was the main actor.

With the boys becoming teenagers and Tom getting out of control, his parents decided to move to Arlington, TX while the other two boys were attending school.

Tom told me how he and his brother Tim came back from school to an empty house, and how he managed to live on the streets of Pittsburgh at seventeen. He told me his diabetes was actually a lot of help because he could get clean needles legally and use them to exchange for food and drugs. Somewhere in that same time frame he met Ted, a rich boy who became his best friend.

Tom was dating his high school sweetheart Mary, they tried to become a group but according to Tom, Ted and Mary were always fighting and didn't get along well.

He left one week to make some money working as a roofer with Mary's uncle Bill and came back to the news that Ted and Mary were in love. Mary tried to explain she needed someone she could see a future with and Tom didn't fit the role. He said he couldn't blame her and promised himself to make a change in his life.

He went to live with his father's brother Ron who offered to help him get back on his feet. He also met a married woman who was 12 years older than him and was responsible for his emotional rebound, including some free lessons on how to make love to a woman. A card he was very proud to use [often] and one that later made him famous with the ladies - along with his intimacy with words. He was very good at expressing his feeling on papers and honestly that's how he made his way to my heart.

I was able to collect some of his writing along the years and although I don't have any date to prove, I feel I can relate specific pieces to match some of the stories he told.

I found this torn page from a notebook with one of his notes written in pencil. Considering its discoloration, I can firmly say it is at least 40 years old, that time would match his relationship with Melissa:

"A rapidly growing from mere friends to hopefully something stronger
The articulate features engulf wishes into strong desire
Intense competitor with a will to succeed in society
Neat appearance with a nice soft personality to match
Yet, she's chained to a man whose like an animal, a mouse
Any time she needs a hammer to break the chain, just ask
Never would I just assume command for it's not my place
Don't fear a mouse, a mere little kitty cat a mouse will fear
Mixed emotions will end once the mouse has been cornered and trapped
Earlier the relationship stops the happier you will be and so will I."

When I first read his notes years and years ago, I questioned why he never tried to explore his talents because he was very good at it. He said he was just too busy trying to keep himself alive. I think just a little guidance could've made so much difference... it is sad to see how much of his talent got lost in his survival mode between diabetes and drugs.

Tom eventually decided to join his parents in Texas when he was about 24 years old, bringing only a few clothes and a wood duck, which he managed to keep for years. It became the subject of several arguments later trying to match our home decorations.

I also heard about his relationships with Linda and then Jackie, who appeared to be more trouble than love but again...who am I to judge... she was engaged to John but in love with Tom and chose security over love just like Mary. She was also the one who introduced him to Isabella, a very good catholic girl who was brought up with traditional and conservative Mexican roots. According to his side of the story, Jackie wanted Tom to come along with her and John to a concert but didn't want to raise any suspicious of her affair with Tom. She invited Isabella, her friend to be Tom's plus one and to look more like a couple's date. Her plans backfired and Tom started a relationship with Isabella, making Jackie very mad.

He fell in love with Isabella but had to face her family' disapproval, as we all can imagine why. Her father offered her a brand new car to break off the relationship with the bad boy but Isabella was in love with Tom's wild side. He told me he was willing to do anything to easy her arguments with her family and to prove he was sincere about his feelings for her.

They had the big wedding and started a family. Lance was born first and it was then Tom realized the power of the Mexican culture in a family. Their patriarchal structure and costumes, their adoration for their mother and how religion played a strong role in their life.

For a white boy raised in Pittsburgh by a mother who had renegaded her rich family to marry an Irish truck driver and who raised her boys to never accept anyone dictating how you should live your life, I can imagine how shocking that was.

Tom grew up seeing his parents in total devotion for each other. They were partners in crime against the world. They never let anyone come between them, including their own kids and that explains why they left two of them behind in Pittsburgh when they got out of control, trying to protect their marriage.

Their values were different and Tom later recognized he didn't have enough maturity to compromise. He told me how shocking it was for his then wife to choose her mother over him in the room when his first baby was born. Then later how he had to listen to her father letting him know he had a job lined up for him at the post office so he could have a more secure income to support his daughter and grandson… he also had problems with responsibilities imposed on his wife by her mother to drive her young brother back and forth to school across town with his new baby in the back seat. According to Tom, he was under the impression their marriage was going to release the family pressure but it was the very opposite for him. When Tyler was born that pressure reached a higher level and Tom explained to me how it just made him feel like they were in a money power competition all the time and both him and his family would never meet their standards.

Years later talking about this subject with him, I gave him my version of what Latin families are all about and I didn't believe they were trying to imply that. I sincerely believed her parents had good intentions to support their marriage, maybe not for him but for their daughter and grandkids for sure. Cultural differences can be very hard to overcome in any relationship, including friendship and workplaces and I can see how this was a big factor at driving them apart.

Tom's lack of stability didn't help either… they moved from place to place and from job to job until their final stop in El Paso before divorce. He said he remembers the kids crying and screaming because they've got chickenpox, Isabella sounded exhausted and yelling at the kids to stop and that's when he snapped and walked out. He said it was too much for him to handle and he left. He acknowledged how wrong he was for doing so, a little too late.

That night he drove back to Dallas and spent the night at Jackie's house.

Common sense had never been Tom's friend. I told him in my opinion, her house should've been the last place to spend the night. He actually should be looking for someone to help him sort his marriage situation out at that point, like his mother for example.

The divorce process had started and too the war over the kids. Tom realized then how far the Latin family would go to protect their own. He was paying child support but the kids visitation became a big ordeal as Isabella was having a hard time with her boys spending time with Tom's girlfriend (plural) and his crazy lifestyle.

In his defense he said there were many times he had to drive four hours from his job in Austin to go pick up the kids after working non stop 70 hours during the week, but if he made it just minutes after 6pm on Friday, she would not let him see the kids. Other times he said if he had a girl in the car with him, this would be another reason for not having the kids. I told him I could not disagree with Isabella on that, taking in consideration his lifestyle and the wild friends he had, probably not the best environment for children. His health was also a problem because she didn't trust the kids with him in the car - afraid he could have a seizure while driving. He mentioned a number of other episodes of driving to go get the kids and not being allowed to see them so he finally gave up on the fight and decided the boys would be better off away from him anyway.

When he told me that part I shared my opinion on the subject, I think they both should have had in mind the importance of having both parents in the kids life, independently of how they felt about each other. It was not about them. They still could hate each other in the backstage but he needed to get his ass straight when his boys were around. He should be focused on proving to Isabella he could be a good father for the kid's sake. He was only focusing on confronting her and her family, trying to force them to accept his lifestyle but the real win should be the boys by his side on his visitations even if that would cost being right. He agreed but again, it was a little too late. He went back to his lusty lifestyle of drugs, girls and alcohol and didn't have much contact with the kids.

In 1996 Tom was making good money at Southwestern Bell as their Headend Engineer during the day and a drug dealer at night. He mentioned his apartment was the party point and among his guest list were high executives in general. He had three girlfriends and according to him, life couldn't be better. They all knew about each other, he said it worked because when one of them was angry he would give her space and spend time with one of the other two. "Babe" is how he addressed them all to avoid name confusion. He said it was not a cheap lifestyle but he was better at that then trying to be a monogamist with a family and hurting people's feeling.

A couple of years later during a visitation to his mom, he realized his parents were going through a very hard time trying to support his brother's ex-wife and the three kids who lived next door. The youngest kid had serious health problems and needed immediate treatment but without insurance it would cost almost $20k. He suggested to marry his ex sister-in-law so they could have access to his health insurance and get the treatment for his nephew and that's how they became a couple.

According to him, not too long after that, he too got very sick. The number of hours confined in the Headend led to developing endless seizures - to a point he ended up losing his memory completely. I had done some research in the past and had found proof of how electromagnetic field can affect the brain and it is my belief his preexisting epileptic condition got much worse with that environment.

He also shared with me all the time he was using marijuana on a regular basis his seizures were in control for years but when the company start doing drug tests, he was forced to quit and that's when the seizures got worst. Since I had never tried marijuana up to when I was close to 40, I was never able to advocate in his favor and this subject actually led to many arguments about drug addiction as I had a different point of view.

Tom and his new family moved to Surgarland, TX. His new wife was the only one working and Tom was collecting disability. A year later he recovered his memory with the help of a friend he met named Rachel, a South African native and her husband who had been transferred to work on the executive team of an IT company. She would push him to focus and try to remember things like an everyday exercise and it finally worked. Shortly after that Tom and his new family moved back to DFW, [the beginning of 2003] and he says his mom was giving him advice to settle down somewhere. He said although he wasn't happy, he thought maybe she was right. It was time to slow down.

He bought a house in a small city called Kennedale, TX and he was going to make it work but after a year they both agreed it was not going as planned.

He was back seeing Jackie, who was now divorced and according to him, his wife knew about it. "We were two good friends trying to take care of each other but I never loved her more than friends." He told me. "I wanted to believe we both deserved more than that."

As much as it sounded crazy to me I didn't voice any disapproval after all, Tom had never been the kind of person who fit in normal behavioral standards anyway. Nothing about his life was normal. He was the living proof of contradictions and he seemed to enjoy that, like the *Joker* in *Steve Miller*'s song. He hated normal, he hated standards and he hated boring, just as much as he hated dress codes and I know for a fact many of his friends and girlfriends, including myself, will have more than one story about getting him to dress properly for an event. The years we were married alone we had countless arguments trying to get him to dress up for a dinner with my customers, a fundraiser event, Christmas party, our wedding day and even to the gym. He use to drive me crazy with his favorite line: *"I am not your doll! You're not dressing me up!"* Very few times did I succeeded using my fashion police card but those times never included a tie. It was extremely normal to see him wearing tennis shoes with dressy socks, cut off gym shirts or jeans to go to a restaurant or polo shirt with sweatpants.

However, anyone who was lucky enough to sit down for a conversation with him, would have his undivided attention and heart to heart time. He would never try to look over your shoulder for someone else to talk too or to agree with you just to please you. He was always truthful to his feelings. In a world of so many superficial people, it is safe to say he had a heart of gold.

As I mentioned, Tom's divorce with his sister in law went a little more complicated than he told me. Since he had mentioned more than one time their marriage was more like a convenience, I believed when they decided to go separate ways it was a mutual decision but only years later I learned it was not.

It was the end of December 2004 when he invited me to see his house as proof they were indeed separated and he was living by himself and I did. You know, once burned, twice shy. I went inside and saw most of the furniture gone and the empty closets.

"Everything is fine" he said and that's when we started our relationship.

I had plans to spend NYE night at church with my brother Carlos and Gigi but Tom declined the invite saying he didn't do the 'Jesus thing'. – those were his words, literally.

It was the first time we talked about religion and he let me know how angry he have lived with the "Guy upstairs" and the fact He had decided to give him diabetes when he was only 12, destroying all his dreams to become a professional football player. I didn't know what to say but understood his point, after all, I had my own envelope filled with unanswered questions myself. I went to church and prayed for the New Year arriving. I wrote down all of my intentions and put them in the envelope to be prayed upon during the Prayer's meetings every Friday. I was filled with hope for the first time after years of uncertainty.

I came back home to find Tom talking to Regina on the porch and he had a little surprise for me. A very nice bottle of Moet Chandon, something I had mentioned to him months ago as my favorite drink back on my American Airlines times, flying first class.

We spent the night talking, listening to music on the porch and drinking expensive champagne from coffee mugs, the only drinking container I had in my kitchen back then. I allowed him to sleep on the couch and explained the rules about my daughter not knowing we were a couple and he respected them. He had jeans on and nothing we had would fit him so I told him he had to sleep in his jeans.

Although we had been living in the USA since February, it was the first winter we were living in our own place and from not being used to that kind of cold, we had the heater running all the time at 95 degrees. Tom said he woke up in the middle of the night feeling like he was being burned alive and was dripping in sweat. He said he was so relieved when he saw Regina waking up, immediately asking almost without a voice, if she could bring him some water and she did. He asked why it was so hot in the house, we explained we were not used to that kind of cold being from Brazil and that was the only temperature to keep us from freezing. We were laughing at his red and sweaty face, and he was dying laughing at our explanation.

We offered him coffee and he started acting really hyper, swinging his arms and shaking his hands. "What is in this coffee??" He asked impatiently? "It's only Brazilian coffee, why?" "Oh my gosh, this is too strong!" We had another big laugh and I gave him plenty of water to calm him down.

I started cooking NYE lunch and he kept standing at the countertop watching. At one point he grabbed a piece of the bread brown bag and started writing something. At the end of lunch, he put his hand in his pocket and handed me the piece of the brown paper folded in four. I read the poem and tears came down my face. Unfortunately, the paper got lost after years of moving around but still I remember parts of it. He mentioned having feelings for this unknown girl who came to his land to give it a try, her skin so soft and gentle to touch and the peace he felt that warmed his heart. At the end he mentioned feeling scared while his heart was just saying, shut up Tom, just enjoy it." I had no idea about his writing skills but after reading the poem, it put me one step closer to him. It was a very good start for 2005 and I was happy, very happy.

The next week came with big decisions to make. We had to drive to Pensacola, FL and I was not happy with the fact I was going to leave Gigi behind. I didn't know enough about Tom and didn't want to put my daughter living with us in a hotel, with close to 50 men working with us. It was agreed he was going to fly me on the weekends to see her but as we got close to the moving day, doubts started rushing through my head. "What if he is a serial killer?" "What if he is a child molester?" "What if he went back to his crazy lifestyle?"

I did not know anyone who could give me any information about him other than Lorenza, our boss, so I got the phone and called him on an impulse: "Hi Lorenza, this is Angela. I don't know how to say this but I am trying to find any information about Tom before I move with him to Pensacola next week."

Lorenza sounded surprised but put my worries to rest saying: "Angela, all I can say is that Tom has a very good heart. He is a good man and he cares a lot about you."

That was all I had at that moment and at least it was something good. I also called my mom sharing my concerns and her words were: "Filha, why do you think God would put someone in your life to hurt you or your daughter? I don't believe God is mean like that." I decided to take a leap of faith again.

We left Dallas on January 9th, 2005 at 6pm towards Pensacola, FL, a 12 hours' drive. At one point we stopped at Subway for dinner and Tom was about to discover one of my struggles since I've moved to the USA. I ordered my sandwich and basically said yes to all the options offered by the server making my sandwich almost 4" tall. When we set down to eat, I went ahead and removed half of what was inside and he looked at me confused.

"Why the heck did you say yes to everything just to remove half of it?"

He asked. I explained to him I never understood anything they were saying because they spoke way too fast so I just nodded my head. He laughed so hard he was crying. I realize now that it was then when he started to work on my confidence without even knowing it. He said:

"Next time just tell them exactly what you want and if they start going too fast, you force them to slow down so they can understand you, ok? And if they don't get it right, you tell them to make another one. You are paying for it you need to get what you want. Our next stop to a restaurant I tried to make him order for me but he refused.

- Just tell them what you want."

I was so intimidated my voice was breaking.

- Say it aloud Angela, so they can hear you. He said firmly.

I remember a few times someone tried to rush me and Tom gave his dirty look to the person saying: "The lady is not done yet."

He always made me feel safe.

Pensacola was a small city with signs of severe damages from hurricane Ivan.

I had never been living in a city close to the ocean before and it was very exciting to know we could be at the beach in only 20 minutes. Although it was winter, the temperature was about 20 degrees higher than DFW, which made me feel much more confortable. Talking about this subject with Tom, I started to explain to him how excited I was for spring and summer time. I said I wanted to go to the beach all the time and get a *gold color,* as I was unfamiliar with the word *"tan"* and that's when we had our first argument. My line was:

"I can't wait for warmer temperatures in March and get a *gold* color!"

That word with my Brazilian accent translated to him as: "I can't wait to get a *goat* color!" He looks at me with a question mark face:

"Why the heck do you want to get a *goat* color for?"

"Because I think is very pretty! Why you no like?" I asked.

"It's not pretty! I don't think is a good idea!"

He responded with a very firm voice.

"You're a very rude! I responded making an angry face.

"Rude? How is it so? Why in the world someone would want to look like a goat?"

"Goat? What is that?"

He went ahead and drew something that looked like a dog with horns. I still looked confused. Then he did the noise:

"Goat, goat... like baa...baa... why the heck you want to look like a goat for?"

I then explained to him what I meant to say with the color gold was not goat! And we both had a good laugh. The language barrier adventure had started and we had no clue it was about to get more excited as the day passed by.

Tom insisted I attended the first meeting with Cox Communication about the audit project. It was the first time I had to dress up for work since my arrival in the USA working as an illegal immigrant. Again, I felt intimidate at the thought of sitting at a table filled with executive people and having no clue what they were talking about. Tom looked at me and said:

"Just start making notes on your notebook in Portuguese... nobody needs to know you don't understand. I will explain it to you later. Make faces like you do understand everything... half of the people here don't know what they are doing anyway. I will intercept any questions they try to throw at you. Gosh! I wasn't sure how to feel about all that. I always had to be the one taking care of myself, had to learn very early to stay on the safe side so people didn't hurt me, braving new territories – from jobs to countries – like I was a 10 foot tall woman. I went head to head with people so many times challenging them intellectually to raise their level to mine when they made fun of my height.

For someone like me who started working at 12, I can say I've got my fair share of work environment experiences and unfortunately some of them were very hard to cope with. We are talking about plain grown up bullies, lack of empathy with people's hardship, hurtful gossips and jokes, sexism, and hostile management due to lack of intellectual and leadership skills.

Not long ago I watched an interview with Jeff Weiner, Linkedin's CEO, about how compassion builds better companies and I cannot say how much I agreed with him and how much it gave me hope for the future of corporations. I believe companies should do a better job in hiring their management team. They should look for people with compassion and people skills because that is the mentality we must foster and build in people so they can grow strong as people - not tearing each other apart.

Thankfully, bigger than my bad experiences were my good experiences. I have had excellent bosses and along the years some of them became role models for their leadership skills based on knowledge and leading by example. They used my strengths as an asset and challenged my ambition to win as a team. They know who they are because I made sure to let them know how their integrity shaped me to be a better professional. Tom is for sure on top of this list. He was my boyfriend, true, but he was also a good professional;

his commitment to do the right thing (the Irish proud) was unquestionable.

To run a crew of 50 people where most of them were Brazilians was not the easiest task. There were many challenges and among these were getting them to be on time, a cultural trademark, then there was the language barrier, which Tom got minimized by hiring me as his assistant. Lastly was the trust to get the job done, which was the biggest challenge of all.

It was a daily chore for Tom to make sure everyone was on site doing the job. The crews were supposed to; check each individual house to make sure the cables were physically there and not blown away by the hurricane, check if they had cable connectors or needed new ones installed and disconnect the ones illegally connected. After they completed the job, they turned in their handhelds with the route done and Cox's Quality Control team would check their work. If the route had less than 95% approval rate, it had to be redone and our company got back charges for it. It was a daily struggle to get them to complete the route without the charges, some of them would not even show up at the route and returned their handheld as completed, jeopardizing everyone's opportunity to make money because Cox kept threatening to cancel the contract.

Tom and I decided to drive around and follow them to make sure they were doing the work. After a few times busting some of them at the hotel laying around in the middle of the day or not on the route, they finally got the message that Tom was serious about firing the ones not working. He was tough and he always spoke with authority but he never had to humiliate anyone to gain respect. I felt very lucky for the opportunity to be coached by him on a daily basis, actually 24/7 for many months to come.

I remember one night in Pensacola just sitting with him on the porch and talking until 3am and thinking: "Look at me here talking to him and trying to understand everything he is actually saying. I have no clue about most things but I sure appreciate the opportunity to learn. One day I will remember this day."

Indeed, I still think about that night remembering how far I've become with my language skills. Back than I was still struggling with just day to day normal conversation and it seemed he was having his problems with Portuguese too.

This one day driving to a route to check on the crew, some installers kept calling on the Nextel radio with software issues in their handhelds speaking Portuguese:

"Oi Angela tudo bem?" (Hi Angela, how are you?) ... and then described their issues and I helped them troubleshoot the unit. After five or six calls, Tom turns to me saying:

"Wow, these Brazilian people are very rich, uh?"

"Humm...what?" I didn't get it at all. He continued:

"They are going *"to the bank"* all the time!"

"I'm not sure I know what you're talking about"... I was still very confused.

"They call you on the radio all the time saying, Angela *"to the bank"*

It was my turn now to laugh at his language interpretation. I was laughing so hard! Then I explained to him they were not saying *"to the bank"* they were saying *"tudo bem"* which means, how are you in Portuguese.

The language struggle continued that same day when I met with Lorenza, the VP to tell him I had got Tom's cell phone working again.

"It's perfectly fine now, the problem was the *"ship"* I got a new *"ship"* and it is working fine." Lorenza keeps looking at me and biting his lip with a confusing expression. He has always been such a gentleman and his politeness was always admirable to a point as he kept trying to understand what I was saying.

"The *"ship"* was the problem...? I am not sure I understand..."

Tom had stepped away to answer a phone call and he comes back to find Lorenza and I looking at each other in silence. "What's wrong?" He asks. "Did you find out what was wrong with the phone?" I said I did and explained to him the *"ship"* was defective. "The *"ship"*?" what *ship*?" His voice was getting loud now. I answered impatiently: "Yes!!! The *"ship"* inside the phone!" He took the phone in his hand puzzled: "The *"ship"* inside the phone?..." and after investigating for a second he shouted: "Ah! The "chip" inside the phone!!! Lorenza walked away, probably to avoid laughing in front of me.

Tom spent some time explaining the difference and the proper pronunciation of CHIP, CHEAP, SHEEP, SHIP and CHIPS. It is 14 years later and I still struggle with them all, trust me!

Then we had the cherry on top for the day just a couple of hours afterwards.

We met Lorenza at his hotel to get new handhelds for the crew and he was explaining to us how the new ones were going to work as we had different software in place. He handed us the new units and while Tom was placing them in the car he tells me: "The *"manual"* is in the glove box." I was the one confused now. One of our crew members name was *"Manuel"*

"The *"Manuel"* is in the glove box?" I wasn't familiar with the pronunciation of the word "manual" He said;

"Yes, I put in there myself" I was thinking… something isn't right here…

Then I asked: "Why???"

Lorenza tilted his head:

"What do you mean, why?"

He then remembered what had happened earlier in the day with the language misinterpretation and just walked to the car to show me.

He grabbed the manual and showed me: "See, the manual is right here."

"Oh, manual!!! I understood you're saying "Manuel"!!!

"Why would I put Manuel in the glove box for?" He asked me.

"That's what I was trying to understand too!

Gigi had stayed with Carlos and Regina and I was supposed to come on the weekends but it only happened two weeks later due to delays on the project kickoff. Regina and Gigi drove down with our friend David another two weeks later and by the end of February I told Tom I had to go back because I could not live away from my daughter.

I was trying to let her finish at least one year in the same school and wait until May to move her with me but as much as life was getting better with the money situation, I could not wait for school to end. I needed her with me immediately. His answer was: "Then go get your daughter." I responded I would not move her to a hotel filled with construction men when I had no idea who they were. It was then that Tom showed me the kind of man he was. He left me working at the office and said he had some meetings.

By noon Tom comes back to the office saying he had rented an apartment in a good school area and it was for me to make the plans to go get Giovanna in Grapevine, TX. That same day he took me to Court Furniture to rent everything we needed for all the bedrooms. He bought me a ticket to DFW and rented me a big van to drive back with Gigi, Regina and the few things we owned. I was beyond happy! I was humbled that a man who barely knew me was doing such big and bold moves for my daughter and myself. I shared the news with Regina and Carlos and that same weekend I flew in to DFW to prepare the move.

Up until the last minute I was under the impression Carlos was going to be relieved with us moving out because we had our differences when it came to Christian living. He was much more conservative than I was and that sometimes created arguments between us. Regina's arrival in the house got him a little more over the edge as she was not raised in a Christian doctrine like we were and was a true free spirit.

When we were all packed in the minivan and about to leave the parking lot, Carlos hugged me and started crying. I was shocked and didn't know how to react to that. I had invited him to come live with us and Tom had promised to give him a job but he declined, another reason why I thought he would be happy to be living on his own now but it didn't seem to be the case. With tears in my eyes and a heavy heart I left DFW and Carlos behind.

The next 12 hours driving to Pensacola were filled with Gigi's giggles playing and singing in the backseat among the pile of clothes and few items I owned. She said she was happy for having me close to her again and I was happy I was going to be able to provide her much better living conditions. We arrived in Pensacola past 1am on a Monday and that same morning Tom helped me get her enrolled in school. The following weekend I took Gigi to pick her own bedding and for the first time she had a complete set, with matching pillows, shams and comforter.

I treated myself with a very nice one too and it felt good to finally be living in a decorated apartment with nice furniture.

The following Monday I got Gigi ready for school and Tom walked her to the bus stop while I finished breakfast for the rest of us. I watched that tall and strong man holding my little girls hand towards the condo's gate and my heart felt happy. I can still picture that moment in my mind like it was yesterday. Again, I felt safe and I knew my daughter was going to be safe too. That was the first time I felt I was falling for Tom.

There is an old saying in Portuguese that translated to English is something like: "He who wipes the child's nose kisses the mother's cheek." I can see the truth behind it. That was the beginning of a life transformation for my daughter and I and little did we know the magnitude of it, in every shape and form. I had never met such a generous person as Tom before. Never.

He was a kind man with a very kind heart. Of course he was doing all those nice things because he was in love with me but he did not have to do the same for Regina or even for his nephew Timothy, who was 18 years old. He also brought him to Pensacola later to help turn his life around after he was released from the juvenile facility for a misdemeanor of theft of property.

He gave Timothy a company car and made him one of our QC inspectors. Timothy lived with us [less than a month] until Tom got him set up in another apartment.

Tom also got Regina a partner to work with doing the street audits and when it didn't work he gave her another job doing QC inspections as well.

We didn't have to pay rent, all that me and Regina had to do was to split food and utility bills. I also had flexible hours and was able to bring Gigi to the office to hang out with us until end of my shift.

If anyone was wondering what happened to Paulo... I was still spending money on calling cards and speaking with him on a regular basis. However, he was starting to notice the difference on how short I was cutting the conversations. I told him about Tom but limited the truth to "he had offered me a good job and was helping me with Gigi." After some time, Paulo's suspicions started to increase and he asked if we were in a relationship but I denied it. I was not strong enough to say it was over although in my heart I knew it was.

In one of my endless conversations with Tom about my life and what had led me to end up in the USA with a six years old daughter, I gave him the short version of my affair with Paulo. Tom bluntly said he had had many girlfriends in his life and he would never let any of them just take off to another land with a little girl in a situation like mine. He said that both Roberto and Paulo had let me down in the most cowardly way. That got me thinking and reconsidering my feelings for Paulo after all, Tom was right. Today that point is even more clear to me.

Although I have always been an independent woman, going through a divorce, lack of jobs and even going to the extreme of moving to another country just so I could provide for my daughter, was a tremendous weight on my shoulder. After five years carrying on my own, I was ready to accept some help and Tom was providing me that. It was not only the financial help he was providing me... he really cared about me and I knew he was being truthful. I also enjoyed his company, we had a lot of fun together, we had very good chemistry and I cared about him too... I was falling for him and I knew it.

Paulo on the other hand was pushing me to answer his calls by sending emails and making me set up time to talk to him -I started to get annoyed. When he realized my stories were not making any more sense and he was losing control, he said he was coming to visit me in Pensacola and I freaked out. I told him half truths explaining me and Tom were living together because he was going to marry me to help with a green card. The more I talked to him, the more I realized how tangled in my lies I was getting and it felt awful.

Every time I planned to tell him the truth, he sounded desperate in the call, very sad, saying how much he missed me and he knew he was losing me - I felt bad. I had loved him so much I could never bare listening to him sad like that so I just came up with more and more lies to feed him some hope. I said after I married Tom and got my green card, I was going to get a divorce to be with him but all that were lies. I never meant that because I knew Tom was the one who I wanted to be with because his love for me went beyond what any man in my life ever did. Above all, I had fallen in love with him. Writing this here now sounds much easier… back then my mind was just a mess.

Gigi finished first grade and Tom helped me enroll her in summer camp at the YMCA doing gymnastic. I remember looking back just a year ago at how desperate I was when school was over with no place to leave Gigi and no money to pay for a daycare. What a disaster! Every day was a marathon to find someone to watch her while I was working.

What a difference a year can make! This time everything was nice and smooth, Gigi had lots of friends and lots of activities to do every day. On the weekends we had the beach, picnics, restaurants and movie theaters, always looking for some fun. On her 8th birthday I baked her a nice chocolate cake and Tom got her first bicycle as a gift. She was happy and she was safe now. That meant more than anything else.

Chapter 12
Hurricane season

Hurricane Dennis had formed in the Gulf of Mexico in the beginning of July 2005 and it was headed to Pensacola. After seeing hurricane Ivan's destruction less than a year ago in the islands, Tom decided to shut down the operation and head back to Dallas for a week until it had dissipated.

Regina decided to stay with Mike, her new boyfriend and Tom, Gigi and I drove to DFW. I was going to stay with my brother Carlos and Tom, with his mom.

What I did not know was that a much bigger hurricane had formed in Brazil and it was headed to DFW on a nonstop Boeing 777 and the damages were going to last much more than just a week. The forecast didn't make the headlines so I just got a 6am phone call breaking the news on July 12th, 2005:

"Happy birthday my love. Guess where am I right now?" Paulo asked me in Portuguese

Still half asleep I looked at the caller ID and saw the 817 area code reading DFW airport. I felt a very loud honk raping my ears and my eyes got wide open very quick.

"Shit! Shit! Shit!!! What I'm gonna do now?"

"Hmm…Hi…what a nice surprise…" but my voice rat me out.

"You don't sound very happy…" he said. What's wrong?

"I'm sorry, I'm still half sleep. Of course I am happy. I will be there to pick you up shortly."

The airport was less than 10 minutes away from the apartment in Grapevine. I kept looking for him outside the baggage claim where he said he was but couldn't find him. He walked toward the car and it took me a minute to recognize him. He had lost over 40 pounds and his face had very clear marks of lack of sleep. He got in the car and I could not hide my shocking face so he broke the ice: "I don't look too good, do I?" I said I didn't understand what was going on. Why the surprise? He said we had a lot to talk about. He unpacked and handed me a nice gift box with a card, the first one in five years. Gigi also got a gift. That was all new to me and I looked surprised.

I suggested we take Gigi to play at the pool because I didn't want her to listen to what we were going to talk about. While Gigi was playing we set down at the pool to talk. He looked at my pearl necklace, a gift from Tom for mother's day and asked: "That is a very nice jewelry, did he give you that?" I nodded affirmatively. "This is very expensive, I can't compete with that." The one he brought me as a gift was a nice silver one and I said that didn't have anything to do with decisions I had made. He knew me better than that. I never needed a man to buy me anything. It was never about a financial status, it was about the small things. I then explained to him that Tom and I were together.

He said he figured that out but he needed to tell me what brought him there. He explained his wife had asked him for a divorce months ago and he was working on finalizing things but he was being very precocious about how this was going to affect his daughter.

"I don't want to lose you" he continued. "and I am terrified to acknowledge this is already happening. I haven't been sleeping or eating, I have been depressed since I have figured out what is about to happen with Tom and you. I want to do what I can to stop that. Angela there are a lot of things I didn't tell you over the years and I should of.

I bought a piece of land years ago in the city you wanted to live in outside Sao Paulo, planning for our future. I had been planning all along. I always wanted you in my life forever. I want to take you back to Brazil, I want you to get your masters degree and put Giovanna in a good private school. I want to take care of you from now on. You have to come back with me. Please my love, forgive me for not ever recognizing how much you meant to me. I can't live without you. You are the woman of my life and I want to make you happy forever."

I listened to his words and I wanted to scream: "WHY NOW????" I was angry. I waited for that for years! I waited for signs, for hope, for any crumbs he was willing to throw on the floor for me to hold on to it and now that I had decided to move on, now that I had let somebody else in, he comes back knocking on the door offering me the world! The worst part was to hear he was planning our future all along - but I had no clue of any of it. I didn't say anything but through my eyes he read everything, like he always did. He knew me too well.

"Why are you not excited about this? My love, your eyes doesn't show the love you use to have for me anymore. They are not happy, you were not happy to see me like you did in the past. Please talk to me."

I lowered my head. I was avoiding looking at him so I could hide my true feelings. I could never hurt him.

"I don't know Paulo. It's complicated now. I don't know what to do."

"Please chose me, come back to Brazil with me. It's going to be different now."

I was happy to be interrupted by Gigi saying she was hungry and we went back to the apartment. I gave her something to eat and while she was watching TV he called me to talk on the porch.

"What do you say? Can we please give our story another try?" He asked again.

I finally let my frustration out and told him I couldn't believe he waited all this time, preserving his family while I struggled with my daughter, keeping me on the back burner and never making a decision until he was basically forced to.

I know I didn't have any rights. His commitment was with his family and I was just the whore on the side but I had singed up for that when I fell for a married man, didn't I? No one needs to judge me here, I did that to myself and lived with the guilt for years but was I the only wrong one in the whole situation? How about his wife for keeping a relationship only for the convenience when she was not in love with him anymore? How about him and his lack of decisions? Sounds like I am trying to find ways to justify my mistake and maybe it is easier for me if I look for heads to share the blame, but at that point it didn't matter anymore. I was about to find out later, the whore is the only one to blame.

My frustrations didn't stop him. He was on a mission to take me back. Before I even finished my arguments he got on his knee and holding my legs he begged me to please give him another chance.

I was so uncomfortable with the whole situation. Everything about it was bothering me and I felt pressured. It was easiest to just say yes, that I would go back with him. He was so happy. He hugged me and kissed me and hugged more... "You will not regret. We will be very happy, you will see."

"Why the hell did I do that for? I am not sure I want to go back. There are reasons why I left."

I go back inside and get a call from Tom. "Hey babe, happy birthday. I can't make it to Dallas today from Fort Worth but will you meet me to have lunch with my family tomorrow?"

All I wanted to do was to run away. I didn't want to make any decisions anymore. Paulo went to take a nap after the long flight and I called pastor Gabriel for help. After confessing to him my affair with a married man for years and feeling very ashamed for it, I explained to him the current situation and Paulo's plans to take me back to Brazil. He already knew about my relationship with Tom since beginning because Tom used to be his boss too. Pastor Gabriel and his wife Meire were my spiritual support for the longest time since I came to America and I respected his opinion. They are very dear people to me to this day. He listened to the story and without any judgment, told me to consider all the facts first: "Was Paulo already divorced? Was it really going to happen? If I went back to Brazil, I knew I could never come back since I had stayed over my six months tourist visa permit. How about the opportunities my daughter was going to miss out on by not getting educated here in the USA? And there was also the fact that here, she didn't have any contact with my father.

He was right but I was torn. The possibility of building a life with my soul mate, a man I adored for so many years and dreamed about waking up by his side everyday was very tempting and of course, I still loved him. I just didn't know how much of that love was still left.

Paulo took Gigi and I out for lunch in Southlake, a very nice area close to Grapevine. We spent the whole day together at the park and while Gigi played we talked about the past and made plans for the future. I avoided thinking about the future decisions I still had to make with Tom.

Tom had let me know he was going to spend the night at his ex-wife's and it didn't bother me. I was not in a moral position to make any judgments myself.

The following day I went to meet Tom's mom and dad for the first time for lunch. I was wearing a very nice green dress and high heels. Tom was wearing his regular T-shirt, jeans and sneakers so when his mom looked at me she couldn't hide the comment: "Oh Tom, she's beautiful." Then she whispered in my ears: "What do you want with my son?" in a jokily way, making a point about the differences in our dress code. I told her, I didn't care how he dressed. It was like that all the time and it didn't bother me.

I mentioned to Tom we needed to talk but the opportunity never happened. After lunch he took me to meet his best friend Bob Lockard and his wife Susan. While we were talking on his friend's porch, he answered a call from Lorenza saying he had to get back to Pensacola right away so he drove back that night.

He said we would talk when we made it back home.

I went back to my brother's apartment in Grapevine and told Paulo I didn't have a chance to talk to Tom and he was pushing me to just take off with him.

I said I had to do this the right way. Tom deserved that. I made my plans to go back to Pensacola and he freaked out. I tried to easy his feelings making promises that everything was going to be fine. I was going back to Pensacola, get my things packed and would meet him in Brazil but somehow he could feel there was a chance it was not going to happen. I bought a ticket to get back to Pensacola two days later because I had to go to the Brazilian Consulate in Houston while I was still in Dallas. I was going to try for a third time, to have Roberto sign divorce papers which he had denied for the past five years.

Paulo offered to come along. The drive to and from Houston felt like a happy family time although in front of Gigi we only behaved as friends. She was in the back seat, he was driving, I was helping with directions, he was making jokes and we were all having a good time. I remember looking at him and thinking how perfect we were together. I knew he was bringing his A game to impress me but I also knew his feelings were real. I knew what I had to do…at least until the morning came.

The following morning he took us to breakfast and from there he was going to drop me at the airport. I had spent the night thinking and overthinking and trying to justify my decision. The more I tried to convince myself I had to go back with him, the more I kept thinking about how Tom had took me under his wings without even knowing me. I also kept thinking about how safe I felt when I was with him and how I would be throwing away an opportunity to be truly happy - or going back to a relationship I had tried for four years that didn't work. After all Paulo was not divorced yet. These two options had me divided right down the middle and I could feel anxiety building by the minute inside my body.

I asked Paulo to drop the car off at the rental place for me while I was getting checked in. He agreed and told me to wait for him but I didn't. My heart was racing and my mind was tangled so I checked in as fast as I could and did what I did best. I ran away – this time was only to the gate to catch my flight. He tried to call but I turned off the phone. I wasn't sure about going back with him and I didn't want to tell him that because up to that morning, he was under the impression a decision had been made.

As soon as I landed and turned on the cell phone, his calls started nonstop and I finally answered with another lie: "hey… I am sorry, I didn't have any signal at the gate." He sounded desperate again. He kept asking me about my plans, when I was going to talk to Tom, when I was leaving there…if he needed to come pick me up…I told him to give me some time to resolve everything and that I would call him back when it was done. I know he was trying not to give up on me again. He was trying to redeem himself and prove he deserved a second chance but I was feeling suffocated. That afternoon I set down with Tom and told him about Paulo's plans to take me back and everything that had happened the past two days. That's how he handled:

"Do you love him?" He asked.

I said, yes.

"Do you love me?" he asked.

I said, yes.

"I don't' know what to do, I am so sorry." I continued.

"Do you see yourself being happy with him?"

I said, yes. Then he said something completely unexpected:

"Angela, I love you so much I want you to be happy, even if it is not with me. Go with him. And he left. I stayed there sitting and thinking: "How unselfish is that? What a man he is!" The answer was clear to me. I had made a decision.

He came back a couple of hours later with a CD from Cher (he knew I wanted) and wrote a message on the cover with a permanent marker: "From an American boy. I will always love you" Here's for you to listen when you think of me.

I was in tears and I jumped on his lap.

"I am not going anywhere. I want to stay with you. I never had anyone loving me so much he would rather just see me happy, even if it cost your own happiness"

I broke the news to Paulo and he went back to Brazil without me but that's when the winds from the hurricane really picked up. He wasn't ready to give up just yet. Which surprised me even more. He went to my mom's house, met my family and tried to get more people on his team to convince me to come back. Even his mother.

According to him, both his wife and daughter were supportive of him finding a new girlfriend and suggested for him to look for me while in DFW. It sounded to me they were both trying to push him out of the house, since he had shared in the past they had a lot of arguments due to his teenage daughter's behavior. He was the bad cop trying to keep her in line and this was causing tension.

His desperate behavior however, started rising suspicious on his wife and daughter. Together they hacked his computer while he was visiting his mom and they found all of our emails and intimate pictures from years ago. Just like that all the years of being a good father and husband were flushed down the toilet in a matter of minutes. All the hard work to protect his daughter, including losing the woman he loved were destroyed by gusty winds.

He had spent the day at his mom's house crying over her shoulders about my decision and came back home to find his clothes in a bag. His daughter was crying and screaming calling him a cheater, a pervert, among other sad name but they didn't stop there. They went full steam on a mission to destroy him, everything he worked for including his reputation. She called his work to let people know the cheater he was, she told the yoga group, which I was part of and shared my home wrecking abilities and also called my sister to ruin my reputation in my family. She also let my sister know she was going to call Roberto to get me and my daughter deported and that's when she crossed the line I had drawn. First, I took responsibility all on my own. I told them it was me who seduced him and I was the one who was going to suffer the consequences. Hurting my daughter was not part of the deal. If they tried to do anything to harm my 8 year old daughter in any shape or form, and if I ended up deported to Brazil, they should be prepared to fight head to head with me. I was going to spend every single penny I owned to sue them for invasion of privacy because I had sent those emails to a private account.

That stopped them from hurting me however Paulo was left to feed the angry wolves and they did eat him alive. They used his guilt feelings to get pretty much anything they wanted, including a very unreasonable child support. They humiliated him; and the relationship with his daughter, which he was trying so hard to protect, was forever compromised.

He didn't have a second chance like most criminals have. His sentence was set to a very high price from someone who was used to preaching peace and forgiveness in yoga classes. His daughter never talked to him again. The devastation left by our sin had just started and he was the first one hit. Mine was coming at a slower but much longer pace.

Chapter 13
The aftermath

Y ou know when you feel something is coming? You feel the
change in the air, you feel the strange calm before the tornado is
formed? Well… I didn't feel any of that.

In a matter of days damages could be seen everywhere. From my
years of an affair with the man I believed to be my soul mate. As far as
I was concerned, the destruction had stayed behind me when I made
the decision to stay with Tom. Paulo was left to clean his part of the
mess with his decisions just like I did when I left Roberto for him. It
was my turn to relax while he dealt with the mess but the
consequences were keeping up pace with me like a mudslide.

I decided to start a new chapter in my life and to start a family with
Tom. The project in Pensacola had come to an end. Tom had been
commanded for a project well done and passed with flying colors to
the next one, now in Philadelphia.

Katrina was the next hurricane coming towards the Gulf of Mexico
and although it was not supposed to hit us, we felt effects of it with
very powerful winds making us unable to leave the house because we
simply could not open the door.

After it passed we started packing for our next home. Regina was
staying behind again as her relationship with Mike had made more
progress. Tom, Timothy, Gigi and I drove in three separate cars to
Philadelphia. It was the beginning of September and the leaves were
already starting to turn as we drove up North. Gigi and I enjoyed the
beautiful scenic drive.

I still had thoughts of Paulo - mostly wondering what would've
been if I had decided to move back with him to Brazil. I couldn't help
but think about the storm I would still be riding after his wife and

daughter's discovery. "I did make the right decision." I kept telling myself. Those two would never allow him and me to be happy together. If they are doing this now, I could only imagine what they would be able to do if I was there and knowing myself, I would probably make it worse for him by trying to fight back.

I don't think the situation had to go unpunished but I didn't think it had to be to this extreme. I had gone through way worse with Roberto but I never had a personal vendetta to destroy him. First, he was the father of my daughter. Second, at one point I did love him and could never imagine anything bad happening to him just because I didn't love him as a husband anymore. Roberto had his issues as a husband but I would not harm him in any shape or form for that. To see someone like Paulo be punished like he was the worst criminal in history, was hurtful. I did try to write his daughter an email about how much he loved her and how much he tried to protect her during all those years but all it did was make matters worse.

I've got a call from his sister telling me to leave them alone, it wasn't helping to have me in the middle trying to easy things for him. With that, I took a huge step back and let the dirty water run its cycle. He tried to reach out back through emails, friends and even by mailing me a CD, highlighting a song from a Brazilian rock band called Paralamas do Sucesso, "Wherever I go."

"I close my eyes to find you... I am not by your side but I can dream about you...wherever I might go, I will take you with me inside my eyes."

Trying to get over someone I still loved was painful – literally. The heart ache was both a physical pain and an emotional stress I had to battle on a regular basis. Every good memory of our encounters, our endless talks and promises to endless love were tormenting. I went for walks when I felt I could not hold it inside anymore to let the tears out. I made up excuses for the times they just popped up unannounced. "I have to start concentrating on my relationship with Tom and put an end to this chapter." But it was hard not to think about him...I was falling apart silently. I started working out as a daily dose of a morphine injection to ease that pain.

Chapter 14
...and then Fall Season arrived...

to shed all my old leaves so new ones could grow - and geographically I was in the right place for the view. To watch the leaves changing with VIP seats in the city was one of the most beautiful natural experiences of my life. We were now living in Royersford, PA, a very small city nestled in the middle of the mountains just outside Philadelphia. I have to say it is the favorite place I have ever lived.

We picked that area because of the schools of course but ended up falling in love with everything about it: the small community, close to Valley Forge for my joggings, King of Prussia Mall for my shopping and the scenic drive included with the commute to work, or any place. Giovanna was enrolled in second grade and we finally saw and understood the school system differences from the South to the North, much more demanding like Tom always warned us.

From leaves, to school and lifestyle, everything was changing...we were also warned to buy warm clothes and be prepared for a whole other different level of cold weather. Tom told me to go shopping and I went for my first winter wardrobe makeover. He didn't know I didn't know what to get and I didn't know he didn't know I could not relate to what level cold he was talking about; so pretty much shopping was a fiasco. I got one jacket and only one pair of a closed toes stiletto. As I opened the two bags to show him he kept looking at me wondering where the rest of the stuff was.

"Where's the winter stuff?" He asked

"There, those two things I just showed you." I answered.

"You mean you are planning on walking through snow in white stilettos?"

145

"Well, you said I needed something to protect my feet, those are close toed shoes." He shook his head and called his mom.

"Hey mom, guess what? Angela just got herself some nice warm shoes for Pennsylvania winter. She got some close toed stilettos." He was crying laughing and I didn't quite get why. I told him he would never see me walking on flats because I simply hated them plus I wasn't known for my coordination walking without heels. I tripped too much.

He said he was going to take me shopping for proper winter clothes the next day to show me what I should be prepared for. He told me stories of one particular winter in Pittsburgh where the temperatures got to -50 degrees Fahrenheit and his father having to warm up the pipes because water got frozen inside. I just listened and still without relating to what he was saying, I agreed to go back shopping with him.

The next day he got me ski jackets, fur boots, hats, gloves, scarfs, snow boots and I left the stores feeling like I was ready to jump on Santa's sleigh on a trip to the North Pole. I thought it was a little bit too much and I would never wear all of that but it took less than a week to find out I was wrong.

He said it was going to snow and I imagined the only experience I had with snow back in Texas, about three inches. The next morning when I woke up, the level of cold he was trying to explain finally made sense... I had to shovel the driveway to get to my car and spent a long time trying to find my mustang in the parking lot as it was completely buried in snow.

"Aaaa...that's what he was talking about..."

Yes, the year of 2005 was marketed by milestones... so many significant life events. There is a particular one I have not mentioned as I consider this subject to be the heart of this book and I didn't want to lack the attention it deserves: Tom's health. I am going to retrospect to February of that year, where I was exposed to my first experience of his health condition.

It was Valentine's Day and he went to take a nap before dinner. I knew he had type one diabetes but again, I had never met anyone with this condition so I had no idea of all the care involved to keep blood levels at bay. I had seen him taking his insulin before meals since we moved in together and I was instructed to buy sugar free products. That was the extension of what I knew. The real history of his condition might had gotten lost in the translation because I had no idea of what to do when I was faced with the first crisis.

I was upset he didn't mention any plans for our first Valentine's Day so I didn't wake him up from his nap or cook dinner. I just sat down on the couch to watch TV. It was close to 8pm when I hear this loud scream coming from the bedroom and he started shaking convulsively. His eyes were opened and his head was hitting the headboard so my first impulse was to put a pillow in between but I had no idea what was going on as I had never seen a person seizing before in my life. I was shaking from head to toe, running from one side to the other and then started trying to call someone to help me.

I tried several people in the hotel from our crew before someone finally picked up and told me to call 911. An ambulance from the hospital across the street from the hotel was sent in minutes and a big scene was formed around our room. When the paramedics arrived, I explained to them he was diabetic, they tested his blood level and said it was down to 40, which was too low and he needed to have an emergency shot to bring him back. As soon as they put him inside the ambulance he woke up and started fighting the doctors saying he didn't want to go to the hospital because he was fine. The paramedics tried to force him by bringing the straps and in seconds he tore them apart and pushed them away, telling them to leave him alone... he was about to punch them when he saw me approaching the vehicle and yelled:

"Oh babe... I am sorry..." I got closer and hugged him..."

"It's ok...you're gonna be fine..."

"I didn't want you to see me this way... I am sorry..." He was crying.

They took him to the hospital across the street and gave him a shot and sent him back in less than a hour. He got a $1200 bill for the two minutes ambulance ride across the street and $2800 for the shot.

He than explained to me that next time a seizure happened, to test his blood level and he taught me how to use the test strips. If it was low, to pour orange juice down his throat. He explained that somehow the sugar in the orange juice was the only thing able to bring his sugar level up very quickly. If it wasn't low blood related, to just make sure he wasn't hurting himself while seizing and wait until he came back. He explained to not call 911 because all they did was to give him a shot and charge him $2800 for it without insurance, which he didn't have. He couldn't afford paying them this money every time he had a seizure, which usually happened once a month.

After that I started reading about diabetes and understanding a little more about it. I than went on a mission to keep his blood level at bay by cooking pretty much every day, twice a day, only healthy food and that schedule kept him seizure free for four months.

On his next episode I followed the steps to find out what was going on... his sugar was low so I started by opening his mouth to pour some orange juice and learned the hard way to never put your fingers inside a seizing person's mouth. He almost bit my finger off and I almost passed out with the pain. I learned when he came back from the seizure some time was required for him to be fully conscious again. A full cycle episode lasted about one hour, from the time he screamed and start shaking, about five minutes total than collapsing and snoring very loud for another 20 minutes. When he woke up, he wouldn't recognize anyone or where he was, and most of the time he could not control his bladder. The tension of the locked muscles also caused him headaches and body pain for at least two days and his tongue had holes from biting making it hard to eat for almost a week.

By the third episode I had had a full picture and developed a system trying to minimize his discomforts. Luckily, most of his seizures happened in the middle of the night so I always had a cloth on the lamp table to put in his mouth and keep him for biting his tongue, sometimes it didn't work so he would end up with blood on the pillow and his face. I would straighten his head pulling pillows around to avoid him from hitting the headboard and put towels underneath his bottom to avoid the urine from wetting his side of the mattress. Later I also got a mattress cover. As soon as he came back I would give him a Tylenol to avoid the body pain the following day.

The system to keep him comfortable was under control however, my emotions were also taking a toll. I would get very scared and cry, not knowing if he was going to came back from the seizures. Tom on the other hand seemed to be indestructible, like a iron man. He would wake up the next day and get ready for work. I could tell he was in pain sometimes chewing his food when he covered his mouth, or he moved slower due to his back and shoulder pain but never complaining.

Being the healthy person I have always been, thanks to the good Lord, I could never understand Tom's willpower to function after a seizure and I wanted so bad to fix him... but all I could do was cook him healthy meals and remind him to take his medicine as his seizure medications also slowed his memory down.

If we weren't together, I would call him to make sure he had something to eat and also timed our trips to restaurants in case the waiting time was too long, I had candies in my purse all the time. I wanted to avoid his seizures because it hurt me so much to see him in pain. Little by little all of these changes took place and before I realized it that was my everyday life.

The job had some changes too. This project was not the easy auditing we were doing in Pensacola anymore. It was a more technical operation installing Comcast phone systems to existing cable boxes. This time however we were short of help as all the cable people had migrated South to help with the aftermath of Hurricane Katrina in New Orleans. It was hard to compete with the money the government was paying for that project and the warmer weather conditions.

Tom was doing the best he could with what he had in hand. He asked Comcast upper management for the cable plant map to help out the crew. He arrived home with rolls of maps and taught me how to find the Standby Power Supplies on the map, write down the address and create an excel spreadsheet. He also asked me to separate the addresses by Nodes to make it easier for the crews to complete the route. Once the Node was done with the install, the night crew would do the next step of the job with the Line Sweep and Cert to check the quality of the transmission and the noise mitigation.

Comcast's Quality Control crew had established a protocol to follow in order for the route to be considered done and invoices to be paid and that's where all the conflict started. We had only a few guys to do the installation part of it and get the lines ready for the Sweep and Cert crew, basically double the number of install guys and the reason was simple: Due to the technicality involved to perform the sweep, the pay rate was almost three times more than doing the install and nobody wanted to do the dirty job.

When you work as a contractor, you only get paid after the job is done and approved by the company's Quality controller as I explained before. Tom was known in the industry for his high standards and 'no cheat' policy, which meant, he was really tough with the crew and did not tolerate excuses about the weather being too cold or the pole too hard to reach.

Everyone wanted to be paid, specially with the holidays being just around the corner. The crew wanted to make good money to be able to go home and see their families, which meant they were not going to get paid during that time. Everyone was running against the clock but they were not speaking the same language to find a solution. It was very frustrating for me to watch them arguing every single day over the same problem but never trying to find a solution. I tried once to offer some insights to help but my English was not good or loud enough to win an argument with the Northeastern guys. Most of them with a very aggressive Italian background.

Speaking of miscommunication, it was around that same time that Tom proposed and of course, the language barrier put our own spin on the occasion.

He took me to a romantic Italian restaurant close to the office in Conshohocken, and during dinner he decided to pop the question without any plans…just like anything in his life, living in the moment. We were having such a great time, talking and laughing and at one point we were just glazing into each other eyes and he asked, I said yes, we kissed… I was so excited! We started talking about wedding plans, dates, etc… and when he asked if I wanted a 'fancy wedding' I immediately said no, almost like a reflex with a very confusing tone to my voice:

"I don't want a 'fence' wedding…'

"Why you don't want a 'fancy' wedding? Every girl wants a fancy wedding! He responded.

"Well… I don't! – I answered firmly.

The argument went on and on…

"Is this a Texan thing? – I finally asked.

I was already imagining myself walking down a pasture dressed in a plaid dress and braided hair, and he would be waiting for me on the other side of the fence… I was going through every detail of my wedding outfit in my head and stopped at footwear options:

'Oh my gosh, I will have to wear flat cowboy boots too!!! Nope, never gonna happen!' Now he is the one looking confused and asking:

"What do you mean, a Texan thing??? Can you please write down what did you think I asked?"

I asked the waitress for a paper napkin and wrote. "No 'fence' wedding!'

He covered his mouth like he used to do for his hysterical laughs when he could not control it or stop… he tried to write down a word but he couldn't, he was crying laughing… the waitress came to the table to ask if we were ok… I just shrugged… I had to idea what he was laughing at this time. She answered that basic, ok than… He got the same napkin and wrote it down: Fancy wedding… not fence!"

I told him I didn't know what 'fancy' meant and he went back to laughing hysterically! Then he grabbed the napkin back and still laughing wrote: 'fashion' that's what that word means, he said it out loud.

I then understood his out of control laughter and joined him, making a scene…everyone was looking at us and we had no choice but leave the restaurant without finishing dinner for more than one reason. When the waitress came back with the bill, she fished for an answer: "I guess you're both ok now?..." Tom gave her the short version of the story: "My girlfriend is Brazilian and her vocabulary is still very limited. I proposed and asked if she wanted a 'fancy' wedding and she angrily replied she was NOT going to get married on a 'fence'."

As we walked towards the door we could still hear the waitress laughing, and sharing with others, who also joined her making our gran exit even louder. Tom was on the phone during the whole drive home, sharing both news with his family. I started to make some sort of plans but Tom seemed to be traumatized about the big wedding thing because of his first one, making me question why he even bothered to ask if I wanted a fancy wedding in the first place. He said he planned to make things clear about it but for obvious reasons he got side tracked.

I than suggested to get married in Vegas, just a quiet small ceremony but the answer was also no. No wedding dress either... I gave up on the planning, just told him to let me know what he wanted to do when he decided and that was the fastest route to get married I've ever seen.

He told me to jump in his car and we headed to the courthouse, got a marriage license and set up the date for ten days later. I got a long hippie white dress from Ross Dress for Less and was able to convince him to wear black long sleeves shirt and black jeans. Gigi was holding the rings, his nephew Timothy and his girlfriend Kristen were the witnesses. Looking back, it sounds so funny how unplanned and unprepared everything was but there is one thing that marked that moment forever... when I close my eyes, I can still see Tom's face and how emotional he got when the judge read the prepared vows they had for couples like us. They were big and beautiful words making big commitments and promises for a lifetime till death took us apart. It took me years to understand what I actually made vows to, simply because I did not understand the content but for Tom... he was looking at me and holding my hands so tight... and crying emotionally... saying was the first time he felt ready to commit to a relationship. Time felt right and the only memories we've got from that day were a couple of pictures taken from a flip phone. We finished celebrations with lunch at Texas Roadhouse, across the street from home. Sadly, the short celebration was about to be cut even shorter with bad news from the office.

We were told one of the company's directors wanted us out. The crew was complaining they were not making any money with the speed of the installers and Tom ended up being the one to be blamed. On our first day married we were both out of jobs and headed back to Texas.

Chapter 15
Newlyweds on Bitter Moon

We moved into the house Tom used to live in with his ex-wife and although it didn't feel right we were out of options. I didn't like the energy in the house especially after learning about all the spiritual threats from his ex. She wanted to hurt him for leaving her and there were rumors of a voodoo doll she had made of him. Being born in Brazil I was aware of what that meant and didn't take it as a joke like everyone else did. Truth or not, our lives just seemed to be going in the wrong direction as days went by. I got a part time job until my papers at immigration got finalized and I could find a better one. Just a couple of months later, I got a customer service job at a warranty company.

Tom on the other hand was having a hard time finding anything that paid the kind of money he was making as a Project Manager. He had to take a huge step back on his career to support our family and went back to work as an installer for Charter Communications in Fort Worth. The position was in Waxahachie, almost an hour commute from home. I could see he was very frustrated being an installer and his stress level kept going higher by the day increasing his number of seizures in a month. Gigi was only eight years old so I had made arrangements to fit our schedules and house routine. My shift at the warranty company was from 1pm to 10pm, he had to pick Gigi up from the babysitter's house and I usually left dinner prepared for them in the morning before I went to work.

We were new in the neighborhood but I had become closer to Cheryl, my neighbor next door when Gigi and her daughter Cierra became good friends. Tasha, her older daughter was Gigi's babysitter. About a month later working this schedule, I got a call from Cheryl saying I had to come home. I arrived home to find not only one ambulance but also 3 or 4 police cars at my door and I didn't' understand why so many cops. Before I entered the house, an officer met me at the door and explained Tom had a seizure and Gigi called 911.

I asked why there were so many cops involved, expecting bad news but he let me know they had tried to bring Tom back with an emergency insulin shot but he woke and started fighting the paramedics. They tried to strap him down but he got more violent and four men were not able to hold him down. They had to ask for back up. The moment I stepped in the house Tom recognized my voice and screamed: "Babe is that you? Please come here, I am afraid."

I angrily explained to the officers they should've known the protocols when a person comes back from a seizure; they are unaware of their surroundings and very confused. It was uncalled for them to strap him down like that. They just needed to give him some space. After that episode they got to know more about Tom's conditions and the good thing about living in small towns is, we get to know each other on a personal level. One of the officers gave Gigi his card so she could call him directly next time that happened.

Three months later Tom started working his way back to be a Headend Technician when he learned a position was opened. He was very excited and said things were going to finally get better. I also got a job offer as the operational coordinator in another company also making more money. The good news arrived the day after we went to see the Rolling Stones in concert at the Zilker Park in Austin with the tickets I had got for Tom as his birthday gift. The whole deal just felt like a big extended weekend celebration, even though we were both at work that Monday.

I was about to give my two weeks notice that day and felt extra inspired to leave dinner prepared for Tom and Gigi in the morning. I cooked chicken Alfredo left the table set for them with a cute note under their plates. I called Tom on his lunch break and we talked for a while, he was beyond happy with the possibility of going back to work as the headend with more technical people. I started my shift and gave him another call on my 5pm break when he was supposed to be driving back home but didn't get any answer after several attempts.

I went back to work and got a call around 8pm from Carol, Tom's mom saying he had got hurt in an accident and was hospitalized. Aaaa, that damn silver lining... it was so close but it moved again! I left work and called Cheryl, to let her know she would need to keep Gigi for the night as I was headed to the hospital. Tom was unconscious and intubated; his mom and his friend and boss Bob Lockard were waiting for me in the lobby. Tom had been admitted as John Doe because somebody stopped at the accident scene and stole his wallet with all of his ID's. The hospital was able to identify him through the company's truck, calling Charter to find who was driving that particular vehicle. Bob didn't have my number so he called his mom. The cause of the accident was unknown, the doctors suspected a minor stroke and the only information they had was that Tom had flew the truck out of the bridge on I-20, landing on someone's roof. Looking at the truck later, it was hard to believe someone had been left alive. His injuries were three broken ribs and some minor cuts at his head. The doctors had to sedate him after his attempts at pulling the tubes out and checking himself out of the hospital. When he woke up the next day I was by his side and was able to calm him down so he could keep the tubes in. I explained they needed to keep the tubes in until they were secure no other damage was caused to his internal organs.

I had to go home for a shower and some rest but after only 10 minutes inside the house I got a call from the hospital to come back. He was out of control again and they needed me to stay there to help him stay calm for the rest of the tests they had to run. They had questions about what led him to simply pass out while he was driving. The MRI showed signs of a stroke but for some reason they were not able to detect for sure. Tom was afraid they were going to say it was a seizure and if they did, his driver's license would be suspended and he would lose his job. That had happened before and only years later I was able to understand the consequences of it.

It is hard to see the logic behind having your driver's license suspended but not being eligible for disability benefits. To stop him from checking himself out, I promised to stay with him at the hospital for as long as it was needed. I spent 10 days and 10 nights on the chair next to him until he had enough. He said he had yet to find a doctor to decipher his health conditions and an explanation for his seizure disorders and he was not willing to lose his job again while they took their time looking for answers.

Tom went back to work and found that his promotion had been cancelled. The company was afraid to trust him again driving and put him to work at customer support, troubleshooting systems over the phone. For most people that would not be a problem but for someone like Tom, who chose to become a cable guy so he could have the freedom to work outdoors, it was a prison sentence, and he didn't have any reservations showing it.

His frustration was extended to our relationship. He threated to quit and I had to go over and over again about the financial reasons he could not afford that, including the insurance coverage to buy his medication. As his career was again going backwards, mine was making noticeable progress. I had been hired to work as the operational coordinator of a cold chain management company, a huge progress from the call center. The position required I travel to meet with my customers and that added even more steam to Tom's frustration, introducing me to a jealous side I had never met.

"I feel I am losing you..." he would say.

"But I can't afford to quit, we need both incomes to pay the bills. You need to trust I won't do anything wrong."

He didn't and going to work become a challenge I never knew could exist. He would call me several times a day, the fights were always scheduled to the week I had to go on a business trip and continued throughout my customer's visits to a point, I had to turn off my cell phone. That was our first year of marriage. The blissful harmony expected on the honeymoon ended before it even started with so many changes to manage.

Luckily, for both of us sake, Lorenza called to save the day and release Tom from his misery offering him a job managing an audit project in Houston. Lorenza explained how the owner of the company agreed firing Tom was a mistake and said how hard it was for them to get paid for the work we kept telling them we couldn't invoice because the crew had not completed.

I had my questions about Tom quitting a steady job to go on another seasonal job but he didn't care. He said he wanted to go do what he knew best, manage people. The 8 to 5 office job was not for him, and he quit the day after the call.

I thought it could be a good thing, maybe now he would leave me alone with my job but that was not the case... his agenda included making me quit as well to work with him in Houston and he didn't rest until he got me packed and moving again to be his office manager.

Our first year of marriage was marked by instability and little did I know that it was just the start. What looked so tumultuous in the beginning, was going to look like a walk in the park in the future.

The project ended only five months later, Tom tried to get the owner to commit to a long term one, after talking to an old friend who worked for Cox Communications in Pensacola. He had assured they could stay there for a long time, however the company we were working for was just interested in short term projects, quick in and out projects with high profits. That left both of us to start 2008, a year marked by a big economic crisis, without jobs.

By March, all of our savings were gone and all the credit cards maxed out. His medications alone without insurance were about $1800 monthly and we were not allowed to cash unemployment since we had not worked long enough. I swallowed my pride and against Tom's opinion applied for food stamps and Medicaid but got denied. Tom explained to me he was not surprised. He said he could only make comments based on his own experience with the government social programs. Every time he needed it, he was always turned down which was the reason why he had to hide his seizures episodes to avoid getting his driver's license suspended. Without work he could not afford his medicines to keep him alive. After many attempts proving we were completely broke, we got approved.

I talked to my brother Carlos about opening a handyman company. We were good working together, he had lots of experience fixing things and I had the legal documents to open a business. I printed some flyers and he went around the neighborhood delivering them. That same day we got calls to schedule jobs from fixing gutters to building, landscaping and fixing fences. It seemed we were on a good path and that kept me busy for about six months until Tom got a call from Lorenza to manage a project in Tulsa. Again he began the talk for me to move with him. I tried to convince him to let me stay in Dallas and keep my work with my brother but he was determined to take me with him, saying this time was going to be different. Lorenza gave him hints to leave me in Dallas until the project got bigger but he was not interested in leaving me behind and I knew I was not going to win. I broke the news to Carlos who understandably got very upset and I followed my husband to Tulsa.

It only took a week for him to get upset with management and quit and before I even had a chance to unpack, we were driving back to Dallas.

I told him I was going to retake the business with my brother but he said I needed to start looking for a real job. The arguments turned to constant fights and blaming games. Tom was frustrated with the lack of opportunities; he was used to walking from one job to another with his experience and credibility in the cable industry. People knew him for being a hard worker and very knowledgeable but since his last accident they started questioning his health and reliability and that was not all: Cable was becoming more and more digitalized, fiber optic was a reality and WIFI was the new name of the game.

All these required advanced training in technology of information and Tom was having a very hard time adjusting to that. A very bad economy and his mother's cancer diagnoses added even more winds to the storm. Carol was more than a mother to Tom. She was his best friend, his anchor, his confident and his mother. He tried his best to avoid her new condition and believed she would get better. "She will be alright." He kept repeating every time we came back from a hospital visit.

As for myself, I was also frustrated because our life had no stability whatsoever. I could not make one single plan or commitment of any sort because I didn't know when our next move could happen. He started to blame me for not finding a job and said I just wanted to live of side jobs with my brother. I felt hurt with this accusation and found the fuel to prove he was wrong just like when I was 13 years old confronting my father. I was determined to find another job and this time he was not going to convince me to quit. I dug myself in the internet for a week applying for every single job available in DFW until I got a call for an interview. The position was back in aviation working with a helicopter customization company who was very busy with the Brazilian booming market. Portuguese proficiency was the key to translate paperwork for the Brazilian Civil Aviation Authority and that put me ahead of the game. I bought a suit I could not afford for the interview costing his rage:

"Are you insane? We are broke and you spend $200 on a suit when you don't even know you will get the job!"

I knew I had to return it after the interview but for that moment I just felt like I had to start reacting so he could stop looking at me like just an immigrant who could not function without him so I said: "I will get this job! Watch me!"

Two days later HR called me saying I had the job. I told Tom he had to start looking for training at the Community College to recycle his knowledge and advance his cable career.

Tom wasn't comfortable with me taking the driver's seat and my "real job' started bothering him again. Part of my job was to entertain the Brazilian customers visiting our company, taking them out to dinner, some shopping and also on trade show trips. My income alone wasn't enough to pay the bills so I tried to convince Tom to get a temporary job just until he got his certificate and a better job at the cable industry but he refused. He said he was not going to just stay home making little money and going to school while I was living the executive career. That was too embarrassing for him and the Irish pride once again, got the best of him. He quit school and said was going to focus on a good paying job but that never happened and the stress involved started to affect his seizures which became unpredictable.

My 7am to 4pm shift required me to wake up at 5am, cook full breakfast for Tom and Gigi, get her school lunch packed and Tom's meals for the rest of the day to make sure he had enough to eat in order to keep his blood level normal. After that I had do my makeup and hair and leave the house by 6:30. At night I also cooked dinner and they helped with the cleanup. I had never considered myself to be a little *Suzie Homemaker* by any means but since I had divorced Roberto and married Tom, I was committed to fix my mistakes from the past to make this marriage work. My lack of "housewife skills" was pointed out many times as the reason why my marriage with Roberto didn't work so this time I was working around the clock to prove I could hold a marriage.

I did try to get Tom to help with responsibilities but the poor thing had two left hands and every time I asked for help I had to fix something he broke. I did my best to keep everything under control, cleaning, cooking, sending payments, keeping the lawn, fixing stuff around the house, getting Tom's medication, calling to remind him to take his medicines and eating during the day, Gigi's school programs and homework, groceries...etc. Saturday was the heavy cleaning day and that's how I spent most of them. Dinner was always a to go fix.

It was one of those Saturdays that we topped the "wedding on a fence" language confusion episode. I was cleaning the master bathroom and trying to find a space for the robes we got as Christmas gifts from Tom's mom. He was in the bedroom dusting off the furniture to help me. (I thought he could handle that part but to be safe I made sure to remove everything from the top of the dresser first.)

I shouted from the bathroom:

"Hey babe, do you think we can get a hooker?"

"I don't know, can we?" He answered.

"Yes, I think we will need it."

"Okaaaay..." He replied mysteriously from the other room.

"When do you think we can get it?" I asked

"I don't know... when do you want it?"

"How about tonight? Can we have two of them?"

He showed up at the bathroom door, still holding the cleaning rag and said:

"Before I call you the wife of the year, what exactly do you need?"

"Well, your mom gave us these robes and I don't have a place to hang them so we will need some 'hookers'!"

He covered his face with the cloth...

"Oh my gosh, Angela... hooks! You need hooks!"

"What's the difference, I asked?"

"Let's see... one of them are prostitutes! Which one do you want?"

"Oh, I see!"

Of course the calls to his family followed right after...

"Hey, guess what?! I have the coolest wife ever!!! She just asked me if we could get hookers for tonight.!

"She asked what?... She wants what now?....

"Hookers! But she needs them to hang robes!

"Oh, I see..."

I could hear his brother's laugh out loud from the phone.

Chapter 16
Unnoticed Grievance

T imothy Shriver's words about the "unspoken rules" of his childhood when it came to grief and loss was the wakeup call I needed to understand the trigger to Tom's major downfall. Unfortunately, that Super Soul Sunday was aired three weeks after Tom's death in 2014. Up until that moment I had been trying to pinpoint when did his health get so bad. I had major arguments with his neurosurgeons and psychiatrists, questioning the combination of the medications and its side effects but had never questioned what had changed inside him, Tom, that kept him from reacting or even making an effort.

On that Super Soul Sunday interview with Oprah, Timothy Shriver said "If you get grief wrong, you get a lot of things wrong." When I heard that, I made a note in my notebook like I usually do when I listen to her interviews, looking for the highlights and insights for me to brainstorm later with myself. I circled that note and kept repeating it to myself: "If you get grief wrong, you get a lot of things wrong....huh?!" That makes sense! I asked myself when did things go from a roller coaster to a rapid free fall? I went ahead and sketched in my journal something like this:

11/28/2014:
Feelings:
How did I get here? What were the lessons? The painful process:

- 2004: Met Tom: Was brokenhearted by Paulo inability to commit. Feeling powerless I decide to accept Tom's love. It was safer.

- 2005: Move in with Tom, life is good and much easier. I feel safe with Tom and I am in love with him.
- 2006: We get married but miscommunication becomes a challenge with language and cultural barriers. We fight a lot.
- 2007: Tom's mom is diagnosed with cancer.
- 2008: Tom can't keep a job and bills piles up to the roof.
- 2009: Carol passes away and Tom seems to grieve in silence.
- 2010: We lose everything.

I kept writing but to keep from spoiling the chapters ahead, I will skip to the part I highlighted: *Tom seems to grieve in silence.*

2009 is a year painful to remember. It was actually the year I bough my first adult journal to relieve my anguishes because I felt unable to voice what I was feeling in words. I tried many times to tell Tom how I was feeling and every single time became an argument. My first entry was:

4/26/2009 – In this crazy life of mine, nothing seems to be in control…like a roller coaster I feel my life going everyday in a different direction… I make plans but they change as the wind blows… (…)

I remember being frustrated a lot. Keeping a job was extremely hard, Tom was mad all the time with the lack of work combined with the lack of money. The stress caused his seizures to become more and more frequent. I was up most of the night taking care of him and getting up on time was a challenge not counting the times he had seizures when I was about to walk out the door to work, making me late.

He would get mad with my business trips and customer's dinners aggravating the situation and the fights escalated to physical aggression in a couple of episodes. One of them he threw me across the living room, I hit my head on the coffee table and ended up in the hospital. The doctors found a way to talk to me in private and asked if I wanted to press charges but I didn't. I just said I was going to leave him. My co-worker gave me a number of a place called Safe Heaven in Fort Worth. I went for an appointment but instead of talking all I did was cry. I remember asking myself, how did it get this bad? It was hard to acknowledge that the person who promised to love you and protect you was the one now hurting you in every shape and form. I started planning to leave Tom when I came back from my business trip to Brazil in August 2009.

During that trip, I met with Paulo. We had friends in common at American Airlines and he found out I was in town. He called the hotel and we met to have dinner in downtown Sao Paulo and we talked - a lot. We talked and it was nice to hear about what had happened in each others lives for the past years. He said he missed me a lot, and I did miss him too. I mentioned to him I was planning on leaving Tom without mentioning why. We never made plans to get back together but he wanted to come to my room. I sad no and he was not happy about it. I told him if there were any chance for us to be together in the future, we could not start of wrong again. I had to do the right thing and divorce Tom first. I didn't want to pay for any more pain inflicted by myself with wrong decisions. That was the plan until I came back to Dallas that week to find Carol was in the hospice.

I went straight from the airport to see her. She woke up and talked to me and Gigi. She complimented me on weight I had lost and said I looked real good. We chatted about the trip to Brazil for a while and she said she was tired and wanted to rest. Tom's dad was joking and saying she had to promise to live until their 50th anniversary, which was going to be June 2010.

We went home and I knew it was the last time seeing her but Tom did not seem to get what was happening. He was in denial and kept saying she was going to be alright. I remember sitting with him on the back porch that night and he was saying how strong she was. He talked about the time they were both sick but drove to the hospital together because there was no one available. He was still recovering from his amnesia in 2001 when they got a call from the doctors saying they had found out why her blood count was so low. She was bleeding internally and they wanted to see her immediately. Tom's memory was still weak but she convinced him to drive her saying she would give him directions to the hospital. Due to her low blood count she was having a hard time sitting up straight and kept falling towards him and they were both laughing hard the whole entire drive. "Look at us? "Said Carol. "Two fucked up people trying to get somewhere! How stupid is this!"

He told me that story laughing so hard he could barely finish. I was laughing at his laugh and we spent hours talking. When we were done he said: "she's gonna be just fine," and we went to sleep. In my mind I said: "No Tom, she's actually dying." But I could not repeat that to him. The following morning Tom's brother Tim flew in with his wife Sandy from South Carolina, we all had lunch together and headed back to the hospice. Carol was no longer lucid, barely opened her eyes, Tom's brothers and father were joking talking about random things but avoiding saying anything death related because that was the Irish way, don't talk about it.

They all seemed to be afraid to voice their feelings or fears or even shed any tears. It was hard for me to watch and hold everything inside. If the family wasn't showing any sad feelings, it would make me look like a fool if I started crying and I didn't want to create a scene. I went to the bathroom and cried by myself than washed my face and went back to the room. When the evening came we went back home, except for Tim and Sandy who spent the night with Carol. Tom's father also left to get some sleep but after watching her struggle throughout the day, he whispered in her ears it was okay for her to leave. She didn't have to make it to their 50th anniversary. He kissed her and left. We got a call that Sunday morning saying she had passed. We got to the hospice for the final goodbyes and found Terry and Tim fighting about the way she was going to be buried and Tom's father walking in circles in the parking lot.

"What the heck is going on?" Tom asked.

"Tim wants to call a priest and we all know mom is not religious! Terry said.

"Since they don't have any funeral arrangements, I just thought it would be nice to have some sort of prayers. Tim defended himself.

"Well, you can't just show up here now on the day she died thinking you can control how things is going to be handled!"

Attacked Tom who always disagreed with Tim's or anyone's religious beliefs. I was horrified, all these arguments happening around

Carol's lifeless body still on the bed. My first thought was to grab those three boys by the ears outside: "What the hell is wrong with you all?!" Can you act like an adult for a chance? "But instead I just told them they needed to respect whatever their father wanted to do. He lived with her for 49 years and I was pretty sure he would know what her final wishes would be. So I went outside and tried to speak with big Tom, who kept stroking his hands in his hair nervously: "I don't know...I don't know...I can't believe she is gone. My girl is dead."

"You need to say something Tom. They can't keep her just laying dead in the bed like that. I said.

"Well, I know she wanted to be cremated and our ashes spread together where the Three Rivers meet in Pittsburgh. He said.

"Okay, so we will call a funeral home for the cremation." I said.

Tim called and made the arrangements while the two other boys kept arguing. There was no service, just a goodbye at the hospital. During the drive home Tom said:

"My mom was absolutely right. She said that was going to happen the day she died."

"What do you mean?" I asked

"She said she knew Tim was going to be fighting to have a religious service and me and Terry would be going after him just to disagree with him. Tom said laughing.

"This is not funny! I said. - If she knew it, why didn't she make a will to state her wishes. It is not normal for people to be watching siblings fighting over their mother's dead body!"

"We are poor people Angela we don't have wills. He said."

"Well, a goddam piece of paper would suffice! This is not normal Tom. You Irish people are crazy!"

I spent the rest of the week trying to get hold of Tom's father but he was not answering the phone.

"Tom we need to check on your dad." I said.

"Angela, he needs space. He will call if he needs."

Finally, on a Sunday he answered the phone.

"Tom are you okay? I have been trying to talk to you for a week."

"I think I fell asleep on the floor. I just woke up." He said.

"Have you eaten?" I asked

"I am not hungry Angela."

I hung up and told Tom we were going to his dad and taking him food.

"I think it is a mistake, I am sure he wants to be alone." Tom said.

"I don't care, we're going." I said.

I cooked some seafood pasta and headed to his house in Joshua, about 40 minutes from our house, on the countryside of Fort Worth. I made him eat first than we started talking. He sat down with his hands on his head looking lost.

I finally looked him in the eye and said:

"It is okay to say you're sad. It is okay to say you miss her. She was your girl since you were 11 years old. She was your best friend and wife for 49 freakin' years! It is okay to cry! We are not going to judge you!" I hugged him and it was like opening the floodgates.

"Oh my gosh, I am so sorry, please don't think I am weak. I am so ashamed of crying in front of my son."

"Tom, cry all you want! I would be judging if you did not. After all, you said you loved her so much all the time.

I just wish I had done the same for my Tom. I don't know why I never did… and it never occurred to me to ask how he was feeling after losing his mother, his best friend. When I look back today I can see the signs were there all the time but he was raised to not talk about his pain and I was too busy trying to hold us financially together. There are many things I wish I had done differently if I had the chance. Maybe I would have helped him grieve better and if that had happened maybe he would have opened up and healed inside and that would have helped him stay alive. Some things however, you just don't get a second chance and that was only one thing on the long list of mistakes that followed after that. Like Timothy Shriver said: *"If you get grief wrong, you get a lot of things wrong."* - and that was no joke.

Me and Paulo didn't talk again or make any plans of a future together. I was too busy trying to keep a roof over our heads. All the balls I was trying to jiggle in the air eventually started to drop one by one. Only a month after Carol passed I was let go of my job. They said it was due to the company's downsizing as a result of the bad economy but my boss had made it clear to me in one of her outbursts that the only reason she kept me employed was because I spoke Portuguese. I had too many personal problems affecting my job and she was right. I had to drop Gigi at school first, make sure Tom had his medicines, leave him food for the day pre-prepared, and at least once a week I was running on two-three hours of sleep. I rarely punched my card at 7:00am sharp. Then there were the days when Gigi was sick like most kids get at that age and I had to leave work to pick her up at school.

Losing my job was the final straw and we have no other option but to file bankruptcy. We tried to apply to get disability for Tom but the first interview with the Social Security office in Fort Worth was humiliating. From the outside Tom looked like a perfectly normal and strong person so the agents thought he was trying to get a free handout to stay home. I tried to explain his seizure disorders and diabetic situation but they had a hard time connecting his diagnosis with the strong man in front of them.

"I don't think he qualifies for disability…" said the agent.

"So and so… does this guy look sick to you?" the lady asked her co-worker sitting next to her.

"No, he does not!" the other lady said laughing. They did not even want to look at the medical records folder I had with me.

"See, I think it is very unlikely for him to get approved. It is just easier if you help him to find a job. I am pretty sure you will find something he can do."

Tom's face was turning red. His Irish pride was beyond hurt. It had been so hard to actually convince him to go apply.

"I am not crippled, Angela." He said angrily when I suggested it.

"But you cannot keep a job either and it is hard for me to keep my job when I have to be your caregiver. We need some stability and you need your medications, which we cannot afford without insurance. How many things will we have to lose for you to accept you need to be on disability?"

That's when he agreed to go to the Social Security office and after the humiliating treatment he sworn to never go back.

He tried another cable job with John Carter's company, his good friend from long date, setting up cell phone towers. Shortly after a week I got a call from John asking what was wrong with Tom as he could not remember basic steps of cable installation. He said they were inside this location filled with electronics when Tom started to feel sick and very confused. I asked if his sugar level was low and he said they had just finished lunch so probably not. He said he was going to send him home. Later on I got a call from Tom, he sounded very confused.

"Babe, where are you?

"At home. I answered.

"No, you're not here. I don't see you. He continued

I went outside and didn't find his car.

I kept him on the phone and kept asking him to tell me what he sees around him.

"I see a yellow sign. He said.

"What does the sign say?

"There's a monkey in the sign.

"What else do you see?"

After a long time asking different questions I was finally able to figure out that he was 15 minutes down the road parked in front of a Mexican grocery store. I drove there with Giovanna to pick him up. I had to leave his car there and drive him home. He said he felt his head was hot and he was sweating a lot. His blood level was ok and there was no fever. I then remembered an article I read about Electromagnetic Field Sensitivity and the symptoms of people who got sick due to EMF exposure. They matched with Tom's. Ten years ago, this information was not widely spread, I had to dig very deep to find articles about it because I was determined to find the root of the unexplained seizures not low blood sugar related.

Today, there are a variety of articles proving the connection of seizures being trigged due to electromagnetic field acoustic vibrations. Tom has worked his whole adult life exposed to very high-power radio and television transmitters so I was convinced there was something else debilitating his brain. When I talked to his Neurologist about it, he looked at me like I was over reacting. "Your husband is epileptic, period."

Well, I was not arguing the diagnostic. I was arguing the fact that he went years without having a single seizure when he was a kid to having multiple ones when he became an adult working in the cable industry. According to his relations, things became even worse in 1999 when he was working as the Headend Technician for Charter's. The seizure occurrences became so frequent he almost got killed by them and finally lost his memory for almost a whole year. For that reason, I wanted to prove some people were indeed abnormally sensitive to electromagnetic fields. However, I didn't have the language skill to express myself properly and most of all, I didn't have the time required to fight for the cause. We were financially falling apart and had to file for bankruptcy just to get the creditors off our backs. Our cars had been repossessed and the house would be next.

In an attempt to save the few things we owned I took the driver's seat. I made the decision to put the house up for sale and start contacting every customer card I had in hand, personally asking for a job. I came across one with a note on the back: 'Coronel Wanderley's friend'. Coronel Wanderley was my mentor at Texas Aviation who molded me to be his eyes inspecting the Civil Aviation Authorities paperwork prepared to export aircrafts to Brazil. Throughout the years both him and his wife Maria Jose became very good friend of mine. After researching that friend's company's website, I found out they had a position opened which I was qualified for. I called Coronel Wanderley and asked if he could put a good word in for me if I applied, which he did. About a month later this company flew me in to Fort Lauderdale for an interview and in July of 2010 I officially took the driver's seat and started a plan for our relocation to Florida as I was offered the position.

Chapter 17
In charge but not in control

H ere is where I physically drove from North to South – literally speaking.

My goal was simple, take control of our finances making living a little less stressful. I did have a plan: I was going to be making enough money to pay our basic monthly bills and Tom was going to take a huge step back on his career, being a cable installer making very close to minimum age until something better came up. The company I was hired to work for was offering a good salary plus benefits, which was crucial to afford Tom's medications and keep him alive.

The first roadblock was to get approved for an apartment with bad credit so I rented two bedrooms until the transition happened. My good friend Marcia introduced me to a friend of hers who had a big house and was going to sublet the rooms.

The roadblocks that followed after that felt like bricks thrown to build my own underground grave. For every progress I thought I made, another one hit me in the head putting me on my knees but I was not ready to surrender yet. Over and over I got up, with bruises on my shoulders, my head, my back... until the bricks start hitting my face too and eventually, I could not even tell what direction they were coming from anymore. The plan in my head sounded like a perfect one but like we've heard before, the devil lies in the details and gosh, Limbo had me scheduled for a visit.

There was the things I failed to plan. Everything I didn't know...and you don't know how to plan the things you don't know you will need. I failed the basics of compactness, packing a 2800 square foot house in a two-bedroom space... okay, hang on... hold that judgmental comment, ok? Hear me out first... Although I did not grow up with Geometric Block toys I didn't skip that many classes in school, ok? I do have some problem solving skills under my belt.

I had a plan to rent a storage space until we moved in to an apartment but failed also to take into consideration the cost of living in Florida and that left me no choice but to accept the owner's offer to pay them a reduced price for storage by using their garage. This monetarily did help but also opened a door for another problem; access to family boxed stuff - and we felt entitled to access as needed. It eventually became hard to keep it organized getting the house owner very upset and that was not the only thing. Access to the common area like the kitchen and living room also became a problem. Tom lost his job just a few weeks after he got hired and his laying around watching TV in the living room was frowned upon. I did my best to keep things organized and keep up with the neatness of the house - they never had children so the house always looked like one of those display homes. I volunteered to clean the whole house every Saturday which eventually was not enough. To take care of a teenager girl and an epileptic person - to cope with all that while keeping a fulltime job was humanly impossible.

I failed to be prepared for the cultural shock which for Tom, Pittsburgh born and raised in Texas was hard to adapt to. Actually, we were all shocked, after getting used to the United States ways of doing things. I came to understand that South Florida was more like North of South America than South of North America, culturally speaking. Most people spoke Spanish, the traffic was chaotic, customer service was inexistent and people were angry all the time. This is my particular experience and I do believe they have their reasons... It is a touristic city with a gateway to Latin America and some other countries in Europe.

As a consequence, the city was always packed with tourists who were not used to the roads, making them lost and driving like they are lost too... the stores had to cope with a lot of foreign customers who didn't speak the language and although it was a huge incentive for the State's economy, it had to be hard dealing with it on a regular basis. Let's add the fact, for half of the year the snow-birds became regular residents and there was not enough asphalt for that many vehicles. I stopped feeling bad about my compactness shortcoming after my first winter in Florida.

Tom hated Florida so much. It was day one of his first job when he announced that, mastered with his usual sarcasm:

"Hey guess, what?" – It was his first words when he entered the house.

"Oh, hey honey how was your first day?" – I asked

- "Well, I found out I have a very strong heart and will not die from any heart decease." – He said, with his signature sarcastic smile, covering his mouth.
- "I guess that's good?..." I answered waiting for his next line to understand the joke.
- "I was doing my installation survey downtown holding the clip board for the notes when the honking competition started. I was so distracted when the first angry honk got me by surprise I dropped my clipboard on the floor. I moved away to the next cable pole then, bammm, another angry honk… than another one, and another one…I dropped the clip board again and again… my heart was racing so fast, I was shaking… so I had to get inside my car to calm down a little bit. What's up with all the honking??? Don't they understand it will not make the traffic move any faster?" – he sounded exhausted and was shaking his head frustrated.

I was laughing for his clumsy way to deal with the city… I wasn't happy either but I guess for someone who survived Sao Paulo traffic, that was a piece of cake.

Since that job didn't last much more than a month and my salary was barely making ends meet, I started to look for side jobs and opportunities using my network to make any extra money. The owner of the house used to work in real estate and told me the Brazilian good economy was attracting a lot of investors to South Florida. If we worked together it could be beneficial for both of us. I tried to convince Tom to get his Real Estate license, bought him the book to study but never succeeded in getting him focused enough. Every day was a different argument about how much he hated Florida and his daily focus was to bring a list of different reasons to justify it. I set down with him over and over again and like a broken record I repeated to him: "Tom, that's all we have right now, lets focus on ways to make this work please..." and the next day, as soon as I got home, it started all over again...

One day I came back home from work and told the house owner I had a Brazilian customer who was planning on buying a vacation apartment in Miami. The guy was a very rich person and since Tom had showed no interest in getting his license, I was going to find the business and be happy with a referral fee... again, any extra money was welcomed at that point. I told Tom I was going to meet this customer with the owner and didn't make any effort to invite him to come along. I was mad he was not making any effort to ease the weight on my shoulder. The meeting with this customer took way longer than we planned as Brazilians tend to have dinner very late at night. When we got home I found Tom walking up and down the street with a murders look. As soon as we stepped in the house he started yelling I was having an affair with the owner. I explained the meeting took longer than we thought but he kept throwing insults at me, insinuating I was in someone's car parked somewhere making out. The owner of the house was astonished with Tom's lack of control, demoralizing me in front of my daughter and of course added more pressure for me to find another place to live. We were living in Florida for only three months and I was feeling like I had been there forever because every day was a different challenge to deal with. I found out a co-worker's mother worked as the manager of an apartment complex in Weston and with her good heart and help, we moved to a townhouse, beginning of December 2010.

Around the same time, I learned another co-worker from my department wasn't happy with me. He was also my boss's best friend and that put me in a very delicate position. I tried to find out why so I could fix the problem, after all, I loved to work for that company and in particular my boss who I admired so much. As we know, in most corporate cultures, your work quality plays a very small role if you are friends with the boss. The "what you know versus who you know", will be most professionals either worst nightmare or paradise.

I was fast getting more and more tired as the days went by. Tired of trying to make my marriage work, tired of trying to make ends meet, tired of trying to get Tom to focus and help me, but all I could see was he was slipping further and further away. His seizures were back to twice a week and that led me to a lack of sleep. This time however, I didn't make the mistake of bringing my problems to work again. I tried at all cost to cover up my body's pain from holding Tom in the middle of the night, my constant migraines from lack of sleep and my emotional frustration. Everything was a mess and as much as I tried to hide it, my enemy at work had his eyes and ears wide opened looking for dirt on me.

We had a Chaplain at work who was supposed to help us with our emotional battles, a very kind gesture offered by the CEO of the company. I requested for personal sections on my lunch time to ask for some guidance on how to cope with my emotional exhaustion. My enemy found that to be enough reason to spread rumors around the company saying I was always complaining about life and was always being very negative.

From my experiences at my last job, I recognized the poison very quickly and start making an extra effort to always sound positive and counting on energy drinks to help me. I also made an effort to go talk directly with the person and ask if there was any way we could get along better but did not succeed. I realized the problem had something to do with the fact I spoke Portuguese and the Brazilian customers, which was his territory, felt comfortable talking to me. He was feeling threatened for his position.

Our first day at our new apartment Tom and I were at war and I told him I wanted a divorce. I looked at the unpacked boxes, no furniture, and collapsed at the corner... I grabbed my journal, I had to let it out...

December 24th 2010,

> "Today I just want to fall apart here, open all my heart and soul and pour out these bad feelings - out and loud. I feel hopeless, I hurt a lot inside... I feel in pieces, lost, sad and mad... I feel lonely... I miss my sisters, I miss my mom, I miss my dreams... My body is numb, my tears are dried... how many more times will I have to start from scratch? How many more homes will I lose? How many more times will my heart be broken? How could I be so hurtful to keep a family together? I guess I'll just have to feel the floor once again..."

We didn't get divorced and less than a month later, I was back journaling again.

> "(...) The problems are still here, the same old reasons why they started in the first place because they never got fixed. We don't evolve in this relationship and grow because we are stuck in the old problems. There is no communication..."

I felt I was hitting a dead end with Tom. He was frustrated, his pride was hurting with me being the only bread winner. He spent the whole day in the house, couldn't go anywhere because we didn't have any extra money, actually he did not have a car either and I was not able to convince him to accept just anything available to help me out. His common sense wasn't there... simple conversations become huge arguments and I was tired of fighting... I was crying all the time and my social smoking habit became an addiction. He wanted to talk when I got home from work but I was always exhausted from both lack of sleep and trying to fight politics to keep my job. I spent most of the time at the patio smoking, avoiding conversations which could turn into fights. I could tell he felt lonely and angry too, just like me, but at least I was able to get out of the house to work and he didn't.

Our arguments were nonstop insults from both sides. Tom was a master in mind games. He had admitted in the past to torture ex girlfriends with arguments and after learning more about them, he confessed most of them had drug addiction problems. He met his match when he met me, from day one he tried to play mind games with me, I let him know exactly how I got my PhD on mental abuse survival 1 on 1 by growing up with a pedophile and living with a Macho husband. I could smell mind games from miles away and if two men were not able to break me in thirty years, his chance of success was very slim.

When Tom felt overpowered by my statements, he would use his only weapon: language skills. He would make fun of my English and to fight back I would insult him in Portuguese. Almost every fight I would repeat - for his bad luck, unlike his ex-girlfriends, I never used any drugs so he could stop trying to play mind games with me. It was very aggravating to be the one paying all the bills, cooking, cleaning and getting his medications, taking care of his medical needs and being attacked every time I came home because he couldn't get over his hurt ego. I wanted a divorce. I was done but before I threw in the towel, I suggested counseling as a last resort. I guess deep inside I didn't want to be blamed for the disaster our lives had turned into.

Our first section with Dr. Bruce Forman, was a blame fight, we were both talking at the same time and no one was listening, including the doctor. He probably had many first sessions in his practice and knew the venting process. The second section, he asked us to show up on different days. Dr. Bruce Forman was also a Rabi and although he held a PhD in Psychology, his connection and commitment to find the root of the problem went above and beyond his counseling skills.

Around the same time Tom had an appointment with a Neurologist at Cleveland Clinic, Dr. Rodriguez to review the side effects of his seizure medication. Among other side effects, Trileptal was giving him rashes from his thighs up to his back. The rashes were so bad his skin was now developing necrosis. Dr. Rodriguez decided to change his seizure medication to Topomax and the side effects went from a physical form to a mental avalanche. During the first month the results sounded very positive. Tom's mood was more stable, his mind was clear and I saw some hope on the horizon. I remember mentioning to him how happy I was to have my husband back. I thought that between the right medication and counseling, we could turn things around and make our marriage work. That thought disappeared shortly over a month when the medications side-effects took a wrong turn on a road to disaster.

Chapter 18
Side-effects

I arrived home just after 5:30pm as usual, dropped my keys and kicked off my shoes, grabbed a cigarette and walked towards the porch for some minutes of silence and to deflate my mind. Tom and Gigi knew not to bother me until I came back inside, those were the only moments I had to myself.

The first exhale always came followed by a relief sigh. The traffic in Florida was an everyday real-life Super Mario Bros.-challenge level super hard. Between the aggressive driving and lack of asphalt for so many cars, it had me thinking of trading my car for a forklift truck many times. Other times, I would daydream about how fun it would be to have one of Inspector's Gadget bionic toys adapted to the hood of my car. For instance, an arm holding a giant speaker which would stretch all the way to the driver in the car in front of me to remind him to use his signal light next time. That way I wouldn't have to kiss my steering wheel to stop my car behind his... or a giant boot which would kick the car in front of me when the driver decided to move below the minimum speed limit because he was paying attention to his phone. I always wondered what were the real reasons behind so many bad drivers being concentrated in a single strip of land and why they were always so mad... including myself.

Simple facts are, it is a touristic area like I said before, most people are driving around in rented cars, following GPS's and not familiar with the area, like I mentioned before. It is also a state known by year long beautiful weather, beautiful beaches, a lot of retirees and super high cost of living... not exactly the perfect combination for your regular daily routine and commute. I needed at least 20 minutes to let that all out. The exhales after the relief one came filled by worries, which bills I would be able to pay that month and which ones I would have to skip so I could buy food, gas and Tom's medication. Day in and day out, those were my main thoughts. I walked back in the house and started preparing dinner. Tom was dying to start a conversation…

"How was your day?" He asked

"It was ok, just busy as usual, how was yours?"

"Boring as usual…"

I felt bad because I knew there was nothing for him to do, he had no car, no friends, no job… the people he would call were starting to get annoyed with his complains about life, about Florida and lack of jobs for him.

The side-effects of his medication were also taking a big toll on his body. He had lost 40 pounds in just over a month. His speech coordination made it really hard for people to stay interested in a conversation. It was common to hear that someone he was talking to on the phone hung up on him and I could see why when we set down to talk. It requires an extreme amount of compassion for you to deal with someone with a mental disability. Compassion is what lacks the most in today's society. It is hard not to judge or expect a normal rational logical thinking person. It is hard to listen with your heart and your soul - to find a connection… to understand what the person is trying to say when the person is fighting against his brain.

In his case, let's take into consideration he was on two different medications to control his seizures. That means these two medications (Topomax to control his actual seizures and Depakote to control his manic disorder) from two different manufacturers with two different chemical compositions were trying to be processed by his body. A successful outcome of these medications meant the meds would work on his hyperactive brain's electrical activity which is the cause of the seizure, and slow these down to prevent a sudden surge. The Depakote medication was working to stabilizer his Manic Disorder, which is also a brain dysfunction. Let's try to imagine someone trying to function on a daily basis with half brain capacity function if not less… how do you imagine this person talking, walking, cleaning...etc? Now, lets try to imagine that same person remembering to take his insulin four times a day, test his blood level that same amount of time while also feeling all the possible side-effects of those other medications? Have you heard of them?

According to the Epilepsy Foundation, the common side effects of seizure control medications are: Dizziness, blurred-vision, feeling tired, rashes, problems with the liver or pancreas (remember, he was diabetic), serious drop in the number of white cells and also serious drop in the number of platelets (which is needed to control bleeding). Is it a coincidence that the cause of his death was brain hemorrhage? I don't think so.

The side effects combined were by far much harder to deal with than the illnesses. He was able to hide and function for many years without showing any signs of it. He dealt with it his way, hiding behind a sarcastic personality, drugs, women and alcohol. It was his way to create a distraction from his debilitations and fragility and it worked. During his whole adult life, people labeled him as crazy, drug addict and irresponsible and failed to recognize the illness and the medications effect behind all of it, including his own doctors. Behind all of that combined, there was a highly intelligent and kind man. The man I fell in love with. I fell in love with his energy and his heart. That's how we connected from day one. His ability to talk about things on a whole different level, not trying to rationalize the obvious way but going beyond the reason, beyond what normal eyes could see. His mind was so wild and it was funny to watch him freak people out in a conversation. 95% of the people could never reach his reasoning.... Most would get so lost... "wait, what...?" and he would cover his mouth and laugh sarcastically. He had the talent of giving life to minor subjects and provoke your curiosity to go deeper and although this is what I loved about him it was also the reason many people didn't. That evening he was about to show me a whole other level of tripping...

"Hey guess what?" That was his favorite line to get my attention.

"What?..." I answered as I begin working on dinner preparations.

"I can feel the bottom of my feet moving like fish fins and it is making it hard for me to walk."

"Wait…what?..." I answered with a question mark expression.

"I am telling you, I can feel the bottom of my feet floating…" – and he went on and on giving me every little detail of how it felt when he was walking.

I couldn't reach what he was talking about and didn't have the energy to try to figure it out this time. The next day he called his dad to tell him, who later called me to tell me he thought Tom was nuts. That week he had an appointment with Dr. Forman to talk about our marriage. I got a call from the doctor in my office telling me Tom had signs of Manic Disorders and needed a psychiatrist evaluation as soon as possible.

I hung up the phone and thought: "Maybe we have found some answers now…"

When I got back home, Tom had more of his manic feelings to share…

"Hey, guess what?....I walked to Walgreens and explained to the pharmacist about my feet and he told me I was showing signs of dehydration and told me to buy some Pedialyte and I did! Oh man, you have no idea how good it felt! I could feel my brain expanding, electricity running through my body like I was being resuscitated! I don't feel my feet like fishtails anymore! I got so excited I called my dad to tell him but he told me to stop with all the nonsense, I sounded nuts and he hang up on me."

I start thinking maybe the Topomax was causing him to dehydrate and after googling, sure enough, one of the side effects was increasing body temperature causing dehydration. That was back then, today I have found a new update on the side effects on drugs.com saying that this could lead to life-threating dehydration. I explained to him what I had found and said he needed to do his best to keep himself hydrated and I was going to add pedialyte and Gatorade to our grocery list. I also explained about Dr. Forman's call and said we needed to set up an appointment with another doctor.

We went to see Dr. Mariana in Davie, FL and after a co-pay of $70 and a less than five minutes visit, she prescribed him Risperidone, ignoring all my efforts to talk about the drugs he was already taking and the side effects of all of them.

I was very upset but there was not much to be done, I filled his prescription, dropped him home and went to work, late again. The new medication of course came with a whole new set of side effects, according to drugs.com

More Common:
Aggressive behavior
agitation
anxiety
changes in vision, including blurred vision
difficulty concentrating
difficulty speaking or swallowing
inability to move the eyes
increase in amount of urine
loss of balance control
mask-like face
memory problems
muscle spasms of the face, neck, and back
problems with urination
restlessness or need to keep moving (severe)
shuffling walk
skin rash or itching
stiffness or weakness of the arms or legs
tic-like or twitching movements
trembling and shaking of the fingers and hands
trouble sleeping
twisting body movements

Less Common
Back pain
chest pain
speech or vision problems
sudden weakness or numbness in the face, arms, or legs

Rare
Confusion
dizziness
drowsiness
extreme thirst
fast, shallow breathing
fast, weak heartbeat
headache
increased thirst
lip smacking or puckering
loss of appetite
muscle cramps
pale, clammy skin
poor coordination
puffing of the cheeks
rapid or worm-like movements of the tongue
shivering
talking, feeling, and acting with excitement and activity that cannot be
controlled
uncontrolled chewing movements
uncontrolled twisting movements of neck, trunk, arms, or legs
unusual bleeding or bruising
unusual facial expressions or body positions

With the exception of the three highlighted ones, Tom experienced all of it with an aggravated episode on October 31st 2012 where for the first time, he had four seizures in a sequence. The first one came when I was outside on the porch talking to my good friend Jen Amudsen, a customer and a friend who came to visit the company I worked for and stayed with me for the weekend before heading to a tradeshow.

When she heard the first scream she jumped confused and scared... I was so used to his seizures I just went to the living room acting normal and said I had to make sure he was confortable so he wouldn't hurt himself. I ran to the bathroom, grabbed a small towel and put on the side of his mouth. Then moved his body to laydown on the couch and put the pillow on his side so he wouldn't hit his head.

Then I set down on the floor trying to hold his body as much as I could because the convulsing part always made his shoulder hurt the next day. Jen looked terrified but I told her he would be fine again in about an hour, just a little confused so just needed to restrain from making conversation.

He came back after 20 minutes as usual, I medicated him with his night insulin, the seizure medication and a last snack and took him to bed as it was already past 10pm. After he fell asleep I went back to the porch to talk to Jen, she said she had no idea what I was dealing with and I said I tried to keep to myself. I had many people judging me in the past, including losing a job for sharing my struggles at home with a couple of co-workers. It was not easy to deal with his disability and financial problems but it was much harder to deal with the lack of compassion from people. Most of the time I just wanted to vent my pain and hear from somebody that it was going to be okay... just someone to listen to without judging and what I found was people got very uncomfortable with that... this time at the new job, I just tried to keep myself busy as much as I could to hide my pain.

Little over an hour later, I hear Tom having the second seizure upstairs and this time I was actually scared because that had never happened before. I stormed to the bedroom and prepared him again with the same care and after the seizure passed, I went downstairs to get Jen confortable for the night because she had to drive to the convention in Orlando and I had Brazilian customers coming for a meeting at the office in the morning.

That night however was the mark of things going from bad to worse and it was going to make the years I thought were bad look like they were vacation days.

After Tom came back from the second seizure and urinating on the bed, I changed the bed sheets, got my suite outfit for work ready and laid down to sleep. It was almost 2am when another seizure came. It took another hour between the care and post cleaning, including new bed sheets, I laid down again to sleep but now I was too scared and with too much on my mind to relax. I just laid there starring at the ceiling. Right before five the fourth seizure happened and I realized it was going to be impossible to make it to work that day. Jen left at 6am and I started to get breakfast ready for Gigi and get Tom dressed to go to the hospital. I dropped Gigi at school and took him to the hospital. His neurologist Dr Rodriguez, suggested an overnight EEG to monitor his brain activity and we got that scheduled for a week later. I prayed for answers but just like the MRI, they came back normal.

Disillusioned by medicine and frustrated with side effects, I started to get used to two seizures in a sequence, two to three times a week. While he was dealing with the physical effect, I was suffering with the emotional effect but somebody had to pay the bills.

Chapter 19
The downfall

H ave you ever tried to step outside a situation, look at it as an outsider, without judgment and just observe? My first time trying this was 2013. What a year! The year I call today: Doomsday. I was too busy in the rat race, trapped like most humans just trying to keep a roof over our heads, for the second time in my life. The first time was in Brazil, and the reason why I ended up in the USA.

Aaa, the amazing human/rat race, repeated over and over again every single day at the same time at the same place. So predictable! So pathetic! Sometimes your heart tells you to get the hell out of it but then your brain says: "Who's gonna pay the bills?" You want to break free, your heart screams for life, for pleasure, for love... but who's gonna pay the bills? I had this dream of being a writer/ song writer, I hated the trap, I hate the wheel, but who's gonna pay the bills?

You see, at one point my dreams were like a steam for my life train, they were my motivation, they were my wings and I had no fear... I spread my wings and took off but the winds I faced were so goddam strong. They have knocked me down so many times, today there's only a few feathers left. Living on the bottom of the hill made it really hard to fly all the way up. I had to climb really high mountains without any proper equipment - just my daring attitude. And this last fall, I wasn't sure I was going to survive.

Our only hope was to get Tom's disability approved In March, I could no longer afford his medications and bills and he needed some sort of home care. He was an American Citizen who worked and contributed with Social Security since he was 14 years old. We had hundreds of pages of doctor's treatments and statements about his condition but that was not enough proof for the judge to decide in his favor. For the third time he was declined the benefit. I was irate with the decision especially because our next door neighbor, a 25 years old kid had just been approved alleging back pain. It made me think about double standards and how inefficient our system actually is. The lawyer appealed again but the problem was, we were running out of time.

The stress involved was becoming too much for me to handle, I was on the edge on a regular basis and falling into depression. My friend Isabel realized the signs and told me to go to a doctor and ask for some medication at least until things got more manageable and I did for lack of any option. I needed to keep my job but that actually backfired. The medication made me more energetic, and after offering to help other departments during my boss's absence for a business trip that was frowned upon (driving attention to my department as being slow), my position was "terminated".

Without a job and without insurance it was basically impossible to survive.

My first thought was to move back to Dallas but Giovanna was still in school and I wanted to try to wait until she graduated high school. It always amazed me how she was able to manage school and never let this affect her grades. She was doing so great with her AP curriculum and also enrolled in Harvard debate level, law club and had been recently appointed as the president of the club. That got the attention from some renowned universities and the invitation letters started to pile up. I also had promised her that for once, I would let her graduate from the school she started the grade in. I just needed to hang in there for 2 more years and find another job in Florida. She loved that school.

I needed to be strong because my husband's life and my daughter's future depended only on me but right after I cashed my first unemployment check I realized that wouldn't cover even the rent. Tom realized how desperate I was and made a couple of phone calls to some people in Dallas and an old friend offered him an opportunity to make some money there.

I called his friend back and explained Tom's health condition and asked him to please not entertain that idea, but Tom had made up his mind and by the next day he was gone. I tried to manage the trip until he made it safely to Dallas. I knew it was dangerous so I tried to do what I could. I called his nephew's ex girlfriend who lived in Pensacola and asked if she would mind taking him over to rest for the night but she said she couldn't, she was married now and it didn't sound like a good idea. Tom made it to Louisiana and I got a call from a local Subway saying he had a seizure in the store. I panicked but the guy said they had called 911 and he was fine now. I talked to Tom and tried once again to talk him out of it and make him turn around or wait for me there so I could come get him but his words were: "My family needs me, I have to try to do something."

The next problem was to try to find him a place to stay in Dallas. His first thought was his young brother but he had told me he was already helping his niece and her son and could not help Tom too. I explained he just needed a couple of weeks until he got his first paycheck and could pay for a place to stay but he declined. My brother Carlos who lived in an apartment with a roommate said he could stay there. He only had a couch for him to sleep on but they're going to make sure he was fed and had a place to stay. That eased my heart a little. The next day was a Monday and Tom went to meet his friend to start on the job but it would take about a week for the project to start. On day three I got a call from his friend John saying he had made a mistake:

"Angela, what happened to my friend?" – he said.

"John, I told you he was not well, he is under a lot of medication."

"You shouldn't have let him leave." – he continued

"You don't think I've tried??? Have you met Tom? – I responded with an upset voice

"What should I have done exactly? Tie him to the bed? I had a huge fight but he started to pack and left with just a few pieces of clothes. If you don't know, he has manic disorder too."

"You should get him institutionalized then!" – John sounded frustrated

"I don't even know what that means! Never heard of it!"

John explained to me that Tom didn't seemed to be in his right mind. He could not even remember how to perform the basics of cable installation. Something was very wrong and that meant he was not capable of making any decisions by himself and by institutionalizing him, I would be the one making all the decisions for him.

I called Tom and told him I was going to find a way to fly there to drive him back. As we start talking I realized he was not well at all, his voice sounded trembling. My brother was at work so I called his dad and asked him to drive to Arlington to take him to the hospital and after almost imploring him, he did.

Tom was admitted at Arlington's Memorial and was released three days later with the diagnosis of: Seizure disorder, Metabolic encephalopathy, possible secondary to underlying psychosis, hypertension and acute renal failure. He was told to follow up with his neurologist and psychiatrist once he arrived in Florida. Tom never mentioned we didn't have any insurance for that.

I started asking people to loan me money to buy the ticket to get him but without any promise of when I would be able to pay it back, I did not have any luck. I told Tom I would buy a bus ticket but before that happened he called me telling me he was on the road driving back - he didn't stop until he arrived home. He drove nonstop and made it from Dallas to Fort Lauderdale in only 18 hours – don't ask me how that happened.

I was able to find a side job as a secretary through a good friend which would've helped if it wasn't for Tom's medication cost without insurance, all of them combined the cost was $1800 a month. After several phone calls I found out that I would be able to get them through Jackson Memorial in Miami paying half price but still, it was a lot for my budget and the bills turned into an avalanche.

Gigi's sweet 16 was just days away and I let my soul crumb to pieces... I felt like a total failure. I had promised her a beautiful birthday party and told myself I had to stop making such promises to her because obviously I couldn't keep them. I wanted to change so bad... I didn't know why those things kept happening to me, I just wanted it all to make sense... I wanted a chance for a change. Things was changing for the worst... day after day was filled with bad news I cried myself to sleep that night knowing my daughter would not have the special celebration she deserved. I kept looking for jobs but no luck. A month later was my 40th birthday.

I woke up early morning with no electricity in the house. It had been shut off for no payment... I called FPL and explained I had a diabetic person in the house and his insulin needed to be refrigerated, I had lost my job and was doing what I could to make ends meet. The lady agreed to reconnect if I paid a portion of the bill and I did. Gigi tried to entertain me and took me for a walk at the mall, bought me a soup at my favorite place and made my day look much better than it was. She had saved money from her birthday gifts from her friends and bought me a small gift.

I woke up in the middle of that night with Tom sitting on the bed, having a conversation with someone while he pretended to manually wash the bed sheets and humming a little song.

I tried to talk to him but he seemed to be out of it like a sleepwalker and after about half hour he feel into a seizure on the bed, and another one right after. I drove him to Jackson Memorial, he was admitted and stayed there for 10 days. Exams after exams were done with no concrete results. I went to pick him up and when I got back home I found the eviction notice at my door.

I called a former AA colleague that I had reconnected with who was living in Fort Lauderdale too and she told me I could come stay with her until I found a job and a place to live. I got a UHaul truck to leave my things at a storage, Gigi was going to stay at her friend Sophia's for a while and I would stay with Tom and my dog at this former AA colleague.

Tom was very sick so it was basically Gigi and me packing, including bringing all the heavy furniture down from two sets of stairs. That took the whole night. At first I was very thankful that at least I would have a place to stay but less than a week later I realized this colleague had an alcoholic problem. Every night she came back home from work under the influence, she would preach to me about my poor decisions in life and how wrong I was about everything. I felt so humiliated... but I could not justify myself for two reasons, first – it is very stupid to argue with someone drunk and second – she did not know anything about my life. All she knew was a chapter and unfortunately not a good one but that was not my whole entire life so I just kept quiet knowing I didn't have anywhere else to go. Ten days later I found myself locked outside the house because she got mad. I took her 14 years old nephew to run some errands with Tom and I and didn't make the 9pm curfew.

It is August of 2013 and I am jobless/ homeless/ hopeless and feeling worthless.

My Earth Angel Spiritist friend Elizabeth who lives in Rio de Janeiro had been trying to keep me emotionally strong with prayers and after reading the cards for me she explained that I had a lot of Karma to overcome not only created by me but also my ancestors.

"Well, this is just great!!!" I thought to myself after reading her message. I was so mad! So much effort to make it right and I still find myself vulnerable to bad energies. Are you freakin' kidding me?!!! I looked up angrily and I shouted: "Hey, I am trying to make this shit right so give me a goddamn chance, will you?" Stop throwing these stones my way for a little bit at least until I get to stand up ok?!!! Go spook somebody else for a change! How come You can allow people with bad intentions to hurt others when they are already down? Where is justice?? Your systems sound pathetic to me. I see people who have done much worse getting away with it but the fact that I had an affair is gonna hunt me for life? That's ridiculous!" I was in a huge argument with God and like every spoiled kid, I left stopping my feet. I was going to give God the silent treatment.

There was not much to be said anyway… I was living in my car with my sick husband and my dog and my cat. Tom had a seizure in the car the third night and I started looking for help, calling everybody I knew who could offer a hand. My brother Carlos came to the rescue again and said he would charge his credit card with a week at Inn Town suites and I could pay him back when I got a job. The problem was to hide the animals as it was not allowed so we hid them in the middle of the clothes basket and sneaked in the room.

A week later my friend Marcia in Dallas reached out to an old friend called Miriam who lived in the area and basically begged her to help me. Miriam took us all to her house and said she would help us with the deposit to get a place to live. A thread of hope was lit… I don't think she will ever know what that meant to us. When you're broke from inside out, hurting in every possible layer of your being and someone you never met before puts their arms on your shoulders and says, "Let me see how can I help you." ....

She didn't ask for anything in return, she just took us in with opened arms.

She also invited us to a service at her church and I was reluctant. Church people had never been my friend, they judged too much and their God was very intimidating. I had too much baggage and I already knew He had left me hanging high and dry for a reason. Also, I would never be able to convince Tom to go to a church, he didn't believe in God and I didn't know if he was ready for a visit with the Guy Upstairs.

I felt however, as a courtesy we should attend and surprisingly Tom agreed.

The service was beautiful, the pastor had a different and talented way to connect to people. I felt a shift in my energy, I felt loved and I felt hope again. I stood up at the end of the service and reconciled with God. To my surprise, Tom followed me to the altar. Slowly things started to move in the right direction, we finally got approved for a house after a long time trying because of our credit and the eviction notice. We moved in October of 2013. As we were unpacking my daughter told me she would never take a roof over her head for granted ever again. We hugged and we cried with gratitude together.

The next step was to find a job to have an income to pay the bills, otherwise this would be gone again very soon. We had a house but I didn't have a dime in my bank account. My friend Isabel sent me $40 and I bought groceries for the week. If you try to connect the dots here, you will realize I was living every single day by faith.

The very next morning I locked myself in the bedroom to pray and told God. "I don't mean to be ungrateful but You need to understand I need a job otherwise we will be on the streets again and actually owning lots of money to Miriam. Please, I don't want to live in the car again." That prayer had my heart and soul in it and I decided to just stay there on my knees in silence... in His presence. My phone rang and I felt like it was an answer to my prayers and it was, a job interview for a Sales Manager Position got me working in less than a week.

Chapter 20
A Near Death Experience

I was standing again after almost a year fighting in the eye of the hurricane. I felt stronger, or at least I though I did. I looked at the last scars I had collected, I touched them and acknowledged the missing feathers, there were more stories to tell, survival stories. At this moment, I told myself, I do not have a dime to my name – financially. However, I got tools, I got experience and I feel it is time to "queue the eagle and go run with the horses" (Jeremiah, 12:5). Raise like a Phoenix and take my final flight. I felt something inside was ready to explode, I was ready to conquer and ready to take my prize.

Although I was still having daily arguments with God and being clear about how disappointed I was He had never sent me a miracle - and me having to conquer everything with my bare hands. I also told him I was not going to let that hold me back. I was going to keep moving forward not waiting for a miracle to happen. I just asked Him to stay there by my side, every step of the way just so I would have a safe place to fall in case I got tired again. This time I at least had money coming in and Gigi had her first job at Chick-Fil-A, which was some sort of help.

Only 10 days at my job and I was asked to go to a tradeshow in Las Vegas for a business meeting, flying on a private jet. One of my customers was selling a plane and I had another customer who wanted to buy it so I had to go and make sure they would meet and get the deal closed. My boss got very excited about the possibilities of the business and I started preparations for the trip, booking hotels, scheduling meetings and dinners with potential customers. The private jet would leave the following Sunday and the show started the Monday after.

Friday arrived and I had everything arranged, I called Tom on my lunch hour as usual to make sure he had eaten and taken his medication. He answers the phone saying he had been looking for the bathroom but could not find it… he sounded very confused. I told him to go take his insulin and eat than go rest and waited on the phone until he did. I went back to work imagining what had happened that he couldn't find the bathroom… what did that mean? I texted Gigi to find out what time she would be home to check on Tom and she let me know she was going straight to work after school and she wouldn't have time to come back home. My shift was from 10am to 7pm so I arrived home around 7:45pm to a scene that to this date cause me chills to think about.

As I opened the door, I find Tom passed out in a pool of blood. I was terrified and as I screamed he woke up. He asked me to help him find the bathroom and still in shock, I did. I told him I was going to clean him up and take him to the doctor but he said he was fine he just wanted to take a shower and eat. I helped him shower and realized he had a cut on his forehead. I figured he had a seizure and hit the coffee table.

After helping him dress I cooked him dinner than went to clean the blood on the floor… it was a lot of blood although the cut wasn't that big. It was past midnight, he was sleeping and the bleeding had stopped so I went to bed. Around 2am I see Tom wake up, get off the bed and stop in front of the window. "What are you doing there? Do you need anything?" I asked.

"I need to go to the bathroom but I can't find it." He repeated.

I grabbed him by the hand… "here, let me take you there."

After he was done, I guided him back to bed.

"Try to get some sleep, you look tired." I said.

At 6am I woke up with someone trying to open the door and found Tom trying to leave the house.

"Where are you going?" I asked.

"I need to go to the bathroom but I can't find it." He said for the third time.

I helped him to the bathroom again, got him in bed and locked the door. I needed at least another hour of sleep I was beat. Gigi woke up at 7am and went to work, Saturdays she worked double shifts to make some extra money but around 7:30am she was back and woke me up:

"Mom, what's going on??? Dad is walking down the street in his underwear!!!"

"What???"

"Yes, I just saw him. I wore the wrong shoes and my boss said it wasn't safe to walk in the kitchen with these so I came back to switch and found him. He didn't want to get in the car so you need to come with me. Let's go!"

I put on some shorts and we both went down the street to bring him back.

Gigi looked at me and said: "Something isn't right!"

I told her I understood that and that I had tried to take him to the doctor but he refused and actually got really upset with the idea. I was hoping he would calm down. Gigi decided not to go to work and said she would try to talk him into going. He said he wanted to take a nap and went to bed so I got started with my day. He woke up around 11am, I had breakfast ready and told him I needed to test his blood level to give him his insulin shot, as I usually did when I was home. When I got the test kit he started arguing with me, saying I was trying to kill him.

"I need to test your blood levels I am sure it is very high because I can smell the acetone breath in your mouth." – I said.

As I got his hand to get his finger he hit my hand causing the test kit to fly away across the room.

"Tom, please stop! This is not a joke, I need to give you your shot!" By now, I was almost screaming.

Gigi was doing homework in her room and heard the arguments. "What is going on?" She asked.

"He won't let me give him the shot, his blood level is very high." I said with a hopeless look.

"Dad, you need to take this shot, do you want me to help you instead?"

"No!!!" He screamed. "You both are trying to kill me, I know it! I need to get out of here!" He ran to the door and I told Gigi, call 911.

They arrived and we explained the whole situation, showed the marks of blood still on the floor from the night before. I explained I haven't called them earlier because I had been battling doctors for the past years and every time I took him in all I got was a huge medical bill, including the ambulance rides and this time I didn't have insurance or ways to pay for it. The cut wasn't bleeding anymore so I thought he was going to be fine but something wasn't right this time.

The paramedics tried to talk him into getting in the ambulance but he was fighting them. They finally said if he didn't cooperate they were going to Baker Act him (a Florida law that allows the involuntary institutionalization of an individual) and after hearing that, Tom took off running to the door but was stopped by the policemen standing outside. They carried him back inside and strapped him down. I collapsed to the ground crying, seeing Tom in that stage was devastating.

They told me I would not be able to contact him for another 72 hours, according to Baker's Act law so I would not have any news until Tuesday. I called his family and let his brothers and father know what had happened. I told his father I was going to need help, I had an extra room and maybe he could come spend some time with us and help me watch over Tom while I was working. It was too dangerous to leave him by himself but he said he had his life there in Texas and that he was too old to move around.

I had to consider something else but I wasn't sure what else could been done so I asked God for guidance. At least for now I was going to be able to work in peace knowing he was in the hospital, being cared for by professionals. I called the hospital to get an update but all they could tell me was he was sedated. On Tuesday I get a call from the hospital at work saying Tom was awake and he wanted to talk to me.

"Babe, o babe, how are you? I have been so afflicted not being able to know anything about you." – I said almost crying.

"Hey…" he answered with a weak voice. "guess what?..."

"What is it babe?..."

"Heaven exists!..." he said with a firm voice.

"What do you mean?" I wasn't sure what he was talking about.

"I went there, I was there for the past days…" he continued. "I saw myself on the table and then my soul left my body. I watched the doctors deciding if they were going to operate on my brain as I was floating above them then my soul was pulled up like a magnet. As I kept going up the colors around me started to get very bright! Babe, they were so bright, so beautiful, I had never seen those kinds of colors before! I felt so good, my body had no pain, I felt very healthy, very light and in peace. I finally got somewhere and I felt my mom's presence. I couldn't see her but I could feel her. We were able to talk with our minds. Then I was taken somewhere else and I felt a much bigger presence. It seems it was the Guy in charge, or something. I asked him what had happened and he said my time had come. I panicked and asked how about you and Gigi… "If I am here, did I do something to them? Did I hurt them?" He answered you guys were fine but I begged Him to let me come back, I just needed to make sure you guys were fine… so I came back this morning and told the nurse I had to talk to you immediately. Are you ok?"

On the other side? My voice was cracking with a mix of feelings and emotions too hard to try to control:

"I don't know what to say… this is so powerful… I am speechless. What a beautiful experience babe. I am so happy you're back. I missed you. I am coming to visit you after I leave work. Get some rest and we can talk more later ok?"

I hang up the phone and stayed there trying to control the tears so I could go back inside the office. I was new at work and didn't want to show any personal problems again. No one knew what had happened and I intended to keep it that way because I didn't want to lose my job again.

I went to the hospital straight from work, I talked to the nurses and they said it was a psychotic episode but they were still running a lot of tests and he would have to stay in for at least two weeks. So that would be right when I was back from my business trip. Again, I felt relieved that at least he would be cared for and I would be able to concentrate on my client's meetings.

I visited him throughout the week and on Sunday I boarded a plane to Las Vegas. Since Gigi didn't have to work until the following weekend, I decided to take her with me, after all, she deserved a little break too and while I was going to be working she could enjoy the hotel.

While I was on that private jet I couldn't help but think on the extreme of my reality. Who was I to be there? Sitting on such a glamorous plane like I was someone important when my reality was so far from that... I wanted to enjoy it but I actually felt like my body wasn't even there. Everything about that experience felt surreal... I looked at Gigi's face taking thousands of pictures with a smile and smiled... at least she was having a good time.

In Vegas both her and I felt amazed. It was so beautiful, so many lights, so much to do, but I had to work and we didn't have a dime to spend at the stores. The money I had was to have dinner with the customers since my employer didn't have enough time to get me a corporate card.

On Tuesday evening I got a call from the hospital saying they were going to release Tom. I explained to them that I was out of town on a business trip and wouldn't be back until Thursday. I didn't have any family in town to pick him up. The lady on the other side had a very judgmental tone in her voice and said it wasn't her problem. I explained they had told me he wouldn't be released until Friday and that's why I didn't make any arrangements. I couldn't fly back either because my plane ride didn't leave until Thursday. She said she was going to just send him home and needed an address to send him to. My head was spinning, I had reservations that night for the most important meeting of that trip and I couldn't afford the risk of not showing up. In the lobby of the hotel I bumped into some former colleagues from my last job, including my boss who seemed to be very proud of my new position and career progress. He shared he had recently lost his son which was devastating news to me so I tried to keep the conversation on his side of the court, avoiding the disturbing news I had just received. I felt he was also trying to avoid too many details, I knew his son was his best friend and I could feel the pain in his eyes but didn't want to make him uncomfortable in front of his clients. He diverted the conversation saying he had won some money at the casino and handed me a $100 bill saying, here use this to gamble and have some fun. Little did he know that money bought me a week of groceries. It was the "rainbow on my cloud" for my hectic day.

I met my customers for dinner at one of Aria's most expensive restaurant. We drank $500 bottles of wine and had $100 entrees and again, it felt surreal. I tried to entertain them with my party stories and they seemed to be having fun. We resumed the night and headed to the hotel, I still had one last meeting the following day at the convention center.

I called the hospital in the morning and found out they had put Tom in a car in the middle of the night and drove him home. I was infuriated, so hurt, so mad... I could not believe they were so heartless, so irresponsible in doing such a thing but again, that was the Florida way. I called Miriam and asked if she could do me a favor and go check on Tom, I was going to be back the following day and she did. She later reported to me she found Tom home just sitting there in the house with no electricity. That had been shut off again because I was waiting on my first paycheck to pay it. She said she bought him a Subway and left because she had things to do.

I called my brother Carlos and asked if he could please pay my electric bill on his credit card and I would pay him back when I got my paycheck and he did.

When I got back that Thursday, Tom hugged me and told me he though Gigi and I had abandoned him there. I told him I would never abandon him, no matter what. He was my husband and I was going to do my best to take care of him.

Chapter 21
Let go and let God – bootcamp

January 2014 started with a schedule full of visits to my customers in Brazil. It would be almost two weeks and one of my bosses would be with me for the first round in Sao Paulo and Rio de Janeiro. The rest of the visits were North of Brazil in Recife and Natal, where my sister Alzeni lives.

This time Gigi was going to be home watching over Tom after school and her friends told her they would make rounds to check on him the days she had to work. After visiting with my family in Natal and after they learned about my struggles with Tom, they encourage me to think about coming back to Brazil. That way they would be able to help me - actually there was some sense in that. I began to work on a plan to go back to Brazil to keep my husband alive.

I was afraid, planning, calculating there were tons of uncertainty but I was trying to keep my eyes on the prize... praying for guidance and trusting God's plans. I kept thinking even if I didn't see His presence manifested, I knew He would be watching me from a distance because I knew He wanted the best for me. I need something to hold on to so I chose to believe He is in charge. I knew He could do much more if He wanted because His Majesty is so Great - but His wish was for me to learn on my own. Those were the trials which would make me stronger. Sometimes it felt He gave me too many obstacles to face, like a sick husband, no financial status, no help from family - and actually sometimes this made me resentful, however I kept going for obedience.

I remember for so many years I judged my family for being so dependent on religion to survive and believed they had to master and excel their own fears and not rely on God to hold them up all the time.

I take that back as I come to realize that our soul needs to be fed to hold the body and you can't rely on regular food for that... you need to feed your soul regularly with spiritual food...so I prayed:

"Dear Lord, let's do this again, please be with me. Let me know you're gonna be there for me everyday. I am not asking for miracles anymore... I know there is a chance this move will not work, maybe this is going to be just another mistake and "what if's" keeps coming to mind. I look in the mirrow and I see fear in my eyes, I feel butterflies in my stomach, my mind is lost in ten thousands thoughts an hour... I just need to hear this voice in my mind saying "it is time" – but... what "ifs" follows that voice, I have to admit I am scared... what if my family doesn't take me back? What if the support expected is not going to be the one they can afford? What if they judge how I raised my daughter? After all, the culture is so different. What if they try to tell me what to do all the time? What if I am not prepared to have family around me anymore? What if I don't get my boss to agree to keep me employed? Is this really the time to go or this is just another trap and <u>how do I know for sure</u>???? (I had that underlined in my journal when I wrote that) *Please Lord guide me on this. I am willing to go if I can count on You."*

For the very first time in my life I was afraid to make a decision and by now you probably figured why. I don't even know where to start... I would have to sell my furniture and surrender the cars.

It was around that time I watched my very first episode of Super Soul Sunday. I understood it as God's answer, like an extra shot of soul vitamins. I start making notes in my journal about every episode I watched. The interview with Maya Angelou and Eckhart Tolle had endless A'ha moments. "Let the Ego go... Let God flow! Let Him manifest! Wow! I never thought about that before?! Be the vessel..."

It was only the start and exactly what I needed to understand how the situation was going to unfold next. I understood this as the answer to my prayers. I was still struggling with my arguments with God though... I would write in my journal:

"Dear Diary, this weekend I am mad at God. We're not speaking. I told him I don't think He has been fair with me. I am mad with the fact that I am going to leave this country bare hands, just like when I arrived 10 years ago. I have worked so hard in my life, why He won't let me keep anything? I am going back to Brazil so I can breathe a little but I will not be surprised if it doesn't work because I am just used to losing... my expectations always fail me..."

The next morning, I would write: "Dear God... I am so sorry I misbehaved yesterday...please be patient with me... I am learning a lot you know. Today the guest on Super Soul was Phill Jackson and I finally begin to understand what it means to kill the ego and feel You - and when I got it, what that meant, my heart felt it and tears came to my eyes... "I feel You!"

"So, God, how can I serve? It has never been about me. I feel it and it is so overwhelming! So many times, I was afraid of letting it go, afraid of giving up control because I thought if I gave up control of my future I would lose my dreams. Now, I come to realize it doesn't matter anymore. Even if I lose everything, one thing from now on, will always remain: this feeling right now, which is for sure mine because my heart is filled with your love and I will never lose it because it comes from you. I am just the vessel."

The final breakthrough was still far from happening. A week after I wrote this in my journal, Tom was back in the hospital. It happened to be my birthday, and again I was running low in faith. Roberto called but not to wish me happy birthday but to tell me how bad I had raised Giovanna. She went to Brazil first to spend some time with him and he called to let me know she was embarrassing his family with her spoiled behavior and I was a horrible mother. I didn't have any fight in me left. I let him vent and hung up.

The date to leave arrived, I got the day off and started the final touches to get all ready. I got all the boxes closed for the freight forwarder company to take and started cleaning the house to give the key to the homeowner scheduled at 5pm.

In the middle of all the craziness, I forgot to tell Tom to eat something as I can go hours and hours without eating. I went to take a shower to get ready to go to the airport and came back to find Tom passed out on the floor. I had to call 911 as he was not coming back from his seizure after two hours. When the ambulance came, his sugar level was down to 20. They all looked at me and asked why I didn't call them earlier as he could've been dead in two more minutes. I was numb and all I answered was he always came back from his seizures.

The trip to the airport was now diverted to the hospital. I had to ask the landlord lady to allow me to stay for the night as I had nowhere to go and she agreed. In the morning I went to the hospital and was informed they were not allowing Tom to leave as they wanted to make more exams. I just looked at them and almost yelling said that they had years to try to find what was wrong with him and the bills could be used as proof of that so now, I didn't care what they had to say. Tom was leaving the country with me that night!

Against doctors advise I signed him out and headed to the airport. I had six gigantic pieces of luggage with all our clothes, a wheelchair and two dogs to push. Miriam dropped me at the airport. I gave a bellboy my last $20 bill to help however he dropped me at the check in and left. The check in agent took so much time preparing the paperwork for the dogs it caused us to miss the flight. So now here I am at the airport, with six pieces of luggage, a wheelchair with Tom barely keeping his head straight and two dogs to push somewhere to spend the night. The next flight would leave the next night. I had no money to go anywhere so in a very irresponsible impulse, I used the company's credit card to pay for a night at the hotel inside the airport. I was afraid Tom was going to have seizures in the middle of the airport lounge and get hurt. I remember going to sleep that night and crying asking God "why" he was putting a tiny person like me through all that physical pain when I was already beat to death emotionally and financially. My whole body was sore for days. But, we did make to Brazil.

As soon as I arrived I got help from all over. My mom's friend from church was also a nurse at the community doctor's facility so she got his insulin for free. She used her knowledge of people to get

208

him a doctor's appointment on the same week to get his schizophrenia medication and I found a very affordable Neurologist to prescribe his seizures medication. I also got him new glasses; he had been using a broken pair with tape to hold the lenses for over a year. Then I got him to a dentist too. Some of his teeth were coming loose from falling on the floor during the seizures and he had been dealing with teeth pain for months but I did not have the money to get them removed in the USA.

We had a weekly schedule rotation, me, my mom, dad and Gigi had times of the day to watch over him. Gigi went to doctor's appointments to help with the translation while I was at work. He would mention how loved he felt by my family although they couldn't even communicate with each other. Even my father had been supporting and caring with a most compassionate heart, to my surprise. That went on for months but all the help came too late. His health was damaged beyond repair. We could tell just by looking at him.

This one morning, I was doing my meditation before turning on my computer at home to begin working. I bowed my head at my desk and prayed. I decided to look for a song online to help me connect with that energy. The song was "Oceans, Where Feet May Fail" from Hillsong United. It was my very first time listening to the song and I was overwhelmed by the lyrics. I got on my knees and I told God I was surrendering to His will and His plans for Tom's life.

In that very moment I felt a very powerful energy surrounding me in a big hug. That love energy was so intense I begin crying uncontrollably like it never had happened to me before. I fell on the floor in total surrender. In my mind I was throwing the towel, defeated. I was not going to be able to save his life. In Jesus' love He was saying, I will take it from here, rest in Love. I didn't know what that meant back then. Tom passed away two days later, on October 31st, 2014. Of course he had to leave on Halloween.

"Goodbye my love.

Today you left and I feel so painfully sad. How are you? How do you feel now" Are they taking good care of you? How was it to meet with your mom? I am not sure how to feel...there are so many different emotions. I can't figure out this pain quite yet. I just feel sad, very sad, disconnected. I know I shouldn't... I know you are so much better now. Your back home, you are free from the physical pain.

I know we had a very challenging relationship, so many fights...but I wanted you to know, one thing I have never doubted is your love for me. For years I loved you back in return with a passionate kind of love but the past few years was a different kind of love. You know you were not someone easy to love and I admit you were the most challenging one but I never left because I cared so much for you. I keep asking have I done enough, but I don't think I will ever have that answer because now you're gone. I wasn't able to save you.

Tom, you changed my life forever! You saw me when I was invisible... you saw the potential and pushed me outside my shell to fight my insecurities. You made me who I am today and because it's you, you did in a very unfashionable way.

For ten years I felt everything good and bad and nothing in between. You woke up every emotion including the pain of losing someone I loved so much. My heart aches. You asked for a second chance to come back and make sure Gigi and I were taken care of and your wish was granted... I am with family. I will never forget you and I will forever love you, in so many different ways. Rest in health and peace now."

Chapter 22
Turning the Pages

The months following Tom's death were an empty search... I wasn't sure what I was looking for so I allowed myself to feel everything - ups and downs. One day I would get mad at him: "How could you bail on me like that?" Other days I would just cry... and of course there were the days I blamed it all on God... My mom would be horrified with my comments as any good protestant would.

"How can you talk to God like this?!

"Well, He can take it... He's God." Would be my grumpy answer.

I took care of Tom for years and I lost count of how many times I went to work looking like a zombie from lack of sleep. Why did He decide to take Tom the night I wasn't beside him? To make me feel guilty?

My friend Elizabeth tried to console me saying maybe if I was by his side that night, he would've fought a little longer to stay but it was time for him to rest.

My mom was there every step of the way trying to keep my pieces together while I was trying to understand my pain for months.

My mom and I developed a special bond. We would spend hours talking about everything. Months later during one of our long talks, she asked if I ever wondered what happened to Paulo and I said no. "Do you think he is still single?" she asked. I don't know... I don't think we were meant to be together, besides, his daughter never forgave him and in order to be with me, he would have to give up on any hope of reconciliation with her forever. I didn't want to cause more damage than I already did. He didn't deserve that.

Curiosity however, killed the cat but not my abilities to investigate his abouts which was extremely hard as he does not have any social pages so there I was, googling his existence.... And I did eventually find something: A note on a newspaper stating his wedding day with a British flight attendant. I wasn't expecting that, it hit me hard like the universe screaming at me: IT WAS NOT MEANT TO BE!!!! LET GO!

My sisters and my mom picked up what was left of me and my feelings not knowing exactly what I was crying about that night.... I finally broke down and explained what I was crying for and actually felt a little ashamed. Was it too soon? How much longer should I have to grieve? How long is it considered normal? I had been a caregiver for years and I was actually missing romance. You know what, it had been over four months, people were going to judge no matter what but I know I did what I could when he was alive.

In Brazil things weren't working quite as planned... The schools there didn't want to accept Giovanna to finish high school as she had started first grade in the United States. She didn't know much about Brazilian Geography, History, Portuguese and so on... I had endless fights with the Board of Education, as they wanted to move her back to 9th grade. I kept explaining, they could accept her as a foreign student as it was the rule in many states but it didn't work. I had to hire a lawyer to sue the board of education and Giovanna lost a whole year waiting, which was devastating for an A student like her. I also had lost my job a month after Tom passed because I could not cope with the loss and was fighting depression.

I decided to move back to the USA in March 2015 and again, restart from zero... I was supposed to stay with my brother Carlos but when I landed in Dallas I was informed he was now married and had started his paperwork for naturalization. This had been kept a secret because the official wedding was going to happen in July and for religious purposes they didn't' want anyone to know. That meant I was not going to be able to stay long and I needed a plan, which at that stage was hard to figure out. Tom's disability hearing appeal was scheduled for May 5th and I had to be in Florida by then but that's all I had. Other than that, I was applying for jobs day in and day out but I didn't have a car and unemployment was about to end too. In order to keep the peace, I accepted to live with an old "friend" who offered for a place to stay as long as I needed it.

Giovanna had been going through a lot of changes and losses and one way for her to cope with it was working out - and a lot. She was also bulimic, which I didn't find out until months later. She was hurting but she is not like me, a person who cries and falls apart. She does not talk about it and just tries to deal with it her way. She wasn't in school and she was devastated to see all of her friends from Kennedale getting ready for prom. I was still trying to figure out a way to get her in school but it was already the end of the school year. She was going to have to wait until August but she was very upset saying she didn't want to be behind. It was so unfair after all the efforts she made all those years. Her pain however was seen as a teenager being out of control, and this 'friend' asked us to move out giving me 48 hours to find a new place. I could not move back with my brother as he was starting a new life and after all he went through, he deserved to have me out of the way.

Luckily, I had reconnected with some of Tom's old friends when I landed in Dallas. I told them I had brought his ashes for us to decide what to do with them. One of them was Rick Rodriguez who also told me to call him if I ever need anything, so I did. That same day him and his wife Hope showed up and took us to his house. He said Tom was a good soul and a good friend and when they first met, Tom used to give him and his wife a ride to work because they didn't have a vehicle. Rick said he felt very sad when he heard about Tom's passing and he also felt bad he was never able to help when we were in Florida. This time he was going to make sure Gigi and I were taken care of until I got back on my feet.

I felt overwhelmed receiving that kind of love from a stranger again. Just like Miriam in Florida, he knew nothing about me but was willing to help my daughter and I. It was then I found strength again and decided it was time to rewrite my story. If God was giving me a second chance through the love of a stranger, I was going to take it and I was going to be a winner. I had nothing else to lose and I translated that as a clean sheet and an opportunity to make it right. Deconstruct and Reconstruct! I grabbed a pen and wrote:

"I am putting an end to this old journal. It has been a very long winter, and I walked through a valley of pain, sorrow, losses and tears. I was proved but now I've been approved by God and He is going to write me a new story. I am excited and I thank Him for this second chance. I bless this journal for being my place to fall apart for years and I am giving it a Grand Finale, all lessons were learned. I know He has something special and I am ready to receive it. Thank you."

I then bought a new notebook and named it: A champion's journal

On the first page: *"If I surrender, will you be there for me? If I fall, will you catch me? It takes a lot of courage to write the first page of a new life with nothing left but faith. I hope it is enough."*

Chapter 23
A rainbow over my cloud

S pring finally came. IT ALWAYS DOES.

I had to name this chapter in honor of Maya Angelou because it was her speeches that kept me looking for rainbows on my cloudy days. I start putting actions behind my faith and write in my gratitude journal on a regular basis thanking God and the Universe for things I needed in my life like they had already happened.

I thanked him for a job, I thanked him for a restored financial life, for being healthy, for being happy, even for the pounds I wanted to lose and for a good man - here I put all the good qualities he should have. I was ready for romance. During my meditations I had a smile on my face and I felt like it had already happened. Then I would ask for guidance to get there… "future me, leads the way…" The next step was to act and look for the opportunities trusting God's guidance. I applied for the jobs and I exercised…

Tom's disability was finally approved. He had to lose his life for the Disability Administration judge to recognize that indeed, he was not healthy enough to keep a job. There was a doctor on a video call during the hearing who went through his medical records and stated his condition was way too severe and that he should never have been denied, causing us so much pain. As I heard his speech about the consequences of his illness I couldn't control my tears.

The judge apologized several times and left the room with her head down. She was also tearing up. I was awarded the years we were waiting and that money was enough to put my life back together. Until the money was released, Rick and Hope did everything in their power to support us. He got Gigi a part time job at a gym with a friend he knew at Texas Family Fitness in The Colony, TX and the little money she made, paid for our phone bills and extra groceries.

When I got a job, Hope let me use her car until the money was released for me to buy one. The days she had to go to the office, either Rick or myself would drive her there. Two months later when the money was finally released we were able to move to our own apartment and although there were challenges since my credit was not good, Gigi turned 18 and we were able to have the apartment under her name.

By July, we were moved into a nice apartment and with the money we were able to get it furnished. I found a self-paced on-line private school and Gigi was able to finish High School that semester, studying day and night to graduate before August and she did with flying colors. I was so proud of her.

I had signed up for eHarmony. I was ready to be with someone. I figured I didn't want to waste time in bars and places looking for a good guy and I also was too old for that. I knew what I wanted and I knew it would be easier to let the computer do the legwork, matching me with someone who was looking for someone like me too.

I got a message from James from Tulsa. He skipped all the website quizzes and sent a direct message to me: "I think you're pretty and I want to meet you."

Although I wasn't feeling beautiful by any means, that compliment felt good. Those years of pain had added signs of age but I guess the picture he saw on my profile had a good filter. I hoped he wouldn't be disappointed when he saw me in person but I wanted to give it a try. He sounded like someone who knew what he wanted… my kind of guy!

I was also texting three other guys who had showed interested, two of them I met in person and I didn't feel the connection but this one… there was something about him… he was cute, and he was funny… his texts made me laugh and most of all… it gave me peace. We set up to meet about three weeks later as he was from Tulsa and I was in Dallas. He had vacation plans to be in Costa Rica so we set up a date for when he came back.

After two days in Costa Rica he decided to head back, he texted me and said his mind was somewhere else and he wanted to come meet me. The day before I was very excited and kept thinking: "I hope we have this same chemistry when we meet in person..." but I told myself to be prepared if we didn't. He booked a hotel close to where I was staying and asked me to meet him for lunch. I wore a red dress and he met me in the lobby. He grabbed my hand, making me turn around: "wow! You're prettier in person!" That made me smile. I didn't feel pretty but again, it felt good.

He brought Gigi and I little souvenirs from Costa Rica, I thought it was the most adorable gesture ever! He had my attention right there... "the little things, I thought..."

He gave me a hug and I could feel his strong muscles, he likes to workout too...very nice. He smelled good, and he was so charming... the chemistry was even stronger in person. We had lunch and talked for hours...he was a well-travelled man who also loved wine and coffee and had a wonderful way of connecting so our conversation was simply flowing. Good company just like I told the universe I wanted... "You manifested him..." My friend Marcia joked later and I think I did...

James come in to my life when I was ready to receive love and everything else fell into place right after.

"He brings so much peace", was my daily thought.

That very thought is what makes it so difficult to write about James. How can you write about peace? It was easier to write about Paulo because our story was supposed to be about soul mates, love and joy but it turned out to be filled with sin, forbidden encounters, lies, shame and painful goodbyes with a sad ending.

With Tom our story was supposed to be about feeling safe but it turned out to be a heck of a roller coaster ride with no seatbelt, barely holding me in, causing so many different levels of pains, lack of hope and grievance with a sad ending.

How can I write about James, a combination of love, chemistry, passion, joy, hope, safety and all those extra things you were supposed to feel with a classic definition of a soul mate? It is either indeed harder to write about peace or I am better at writing drama, which wouldn't surprise me. The truth is, with him everything just fell into place. Did that happen because I had finally figured out what I wanted and decided to place an order as a combo? It is a possibility… actually a lesson I have learned and I believe both God and the universe cheered with relief! "Phew, she's finally going to make our jobs much easier!"

James Weldon Moses was born in Paris, Arkansas. His dad left when he was still a small kid and his mom remarried when he was around 12. He has an older sister Rita and a young half-brother Jay Asbill. His grew up poor like me but without the drama, a subject he seemed to have mastered. At age 18 he joined the Army National Guard then he transferred at active duty the Coast Guard and it was a smart move. He walked away from the chronic problems associated with teenage dating. When he was 21 years old he was stationed in Sturgeon Bay, Wisconsin. He says he didn't have much planned other than the desire to save lives and that's how he ended up on a Search and Rescue Mission in the Coast Guard in Sturgeon Bay then transferred to Corpus Christi, TX in 1979.

He knew his father lived in South Texas as well and one day with his address in hand he decided to drive to his house to reconnect. He says he got close by but then decided to drive to the beach instead. When I asked why, he just said there was nothing his father could add to his life at that point. He was already a grown man. If there is something I admire most about James is his ability to focus on just what is in front of him and get things done.

He learned how to be centered after leaving the military and understanding how bad he was with the unknowing, having to deal with 9-15 feet waves on a boat with zero experience. Fear and Anxiety became real post traumas and he was living with chest pain on a regular basis. Karate lessons were the key to help him cope with those emotions. Once he mastered that, he had his life all planed out to avoid surprises, which is what eventually adds the drama. The very opposite of me (or Tom), who took chances and jumped head first. We can all agree it is one lesson I had to learn to avoid - repeating the mistakes I've made in the past.

He got a job as a bartender until he got his Airframe and Powerplant License to go work for American Airlines in Tulsa, where he's about to retire from.

When he was ready for his next step, he married his then girlfriend Angela who he was in love with. She had a six months old boy when they met, who James registered as his own and later they had a daughter, Jordyn. James told me he wanted to have a family and be the father he never had. His actions speak more than the words I am writing here.

His son Cole validated what I perceived about him. He let all the 50 guests of our wedding know the kind of man his father was with his best man toast/speech. He told us the story of how James reacted when him and his mom had to tell him the truth about his biological existence. According to Cole, James had to leave the room unable to control his tears. Later, he told Cole to feel free to find more about his father but he admitted he never had the desire to. His real father was someone who had never let their family down in any shape or form, according to Cole's words in his speech. Him and his sister Jordyn grew up having love, stability and support from both parents. Their bickering was mostly handled behind closed doors and together they raised wonderful kids.

Cole Moses civilian and military education includes one year at the university of Oklahoma as an Army ROTC cadet, a Bachelor of Science degree from the United States Military Academy at West Point, Basic Officer Leader Course II, Infantry Basic Officer Leader Course, Ranger School & Airborne School. He resumed his studies getting his MBA in Business in Stanford, CA in 2017. Cole is a loving son and father to his baby girl Lennon and two stepdaughters, Miah and Asher, a true reflection of his upbringing. He is married to Ashley Moses and they live in Seattle, WA.

Jordyn is also a loving daughter; a real daddy's girl and you can tell by the kind of relationship they have even living apart after she moved to Hawaii and become an independent adult when she was only 22 years old. She is now married to Nick Gresko who is also a military guy and the parents of little baby Parker.

When I first met James I have to confess I was not ready for a full commitment. After all, I had been a widower for less than a year. I told him I wanted to take it slow but before I realized it I was in love with him simply because it was hard not to be. From the beginning our talks were easy, different subjects from religion to aircraft engines, were had something in common. He was pretty happy with God and how his life turned out but he didn't believe in hell. Unlike me, he didn't have the desire to go on a deep search for enlightenment neither did he have big questions about the unknown.

However, for every deep question I presented him with - dragging him on mind trips, he would come along and listen with interest, then watch while my soul took off with my brain. Sometimes he would joke "come back to me Brazilian, I'm losing ya..." We would laugh and I would ask if he thought I was crazy... 80% of the times the answer would be "I never thought about these things this way...tell me more..." The other 20% he would engage and unleash his wisdom "we just have to be good humans, that's what we are here for... and from there he would give his final thoughts on how simple it should be if as human, we wouldn't be so busy tearing each other apart."

I never felt intimidated or afraid to flush my mind around him – I wasn't afraid of an argument. It feels good when you don't have to tiptoe around someone, when you don't have to reformulate subjects or look for the right moment to ask for something. Peace feels good... a simple life feels good. We get so much more accomplished that way. We don't actually agree about everything in life but when we're not trying to be right all the time, we have extra time to focus and learn more about the other person. We learn how to listen to their personal reasons or pains which led them to be who they are. Sometimes it even helps to simply point out the fact their opinion could've been formed out of pain and maybe they should have taken a better look. I believe an observation done that way will cause more impact with positive growth than to try to measure strengths by arm wrestling. That's how we build any kind of mature relationship.

To my benefit, James had learned some important lessons after ending his marriage of 27 years. He admitted although he was a good provider, he had not been a good husband for the past years which showed me a lot about his character. Some people say you know a person for real when you marry her. I say you actually know a person for real when you divorce her. James made sure his ex-wife was taken care of, giving her everything she deserved by law and never once, complaining to me about it. He says:

"I was mostly the one working but she was the one there caring for my children and giving me the peace I needed to be a good professional, knowing they were safe."

A kind of statement I believe anyone would appreciate when ending a cycle which had reached its course, skipping the drama and going straight to moving on. James never had anything negative to say about his ex-wife and I admire him so much for that. It was very comforting to know I was entering a drama free family zone and that was something I had been very careful with when I went back to the dating game. I was done with actually anything that could cost my peace. I had determined I wanted to build a future structured solely on LOVE so all the decisions moving forward had to come from a place LOVE as well. I had to be more conscious of what kind of energy I was inviting in and for that to happen I had to listen to how I felt.

For instance, one of the guys I met before James had a young daughter and he mentioned on the first date he was constantly fighting over custody with his ex. He was a very good man but just the thought of picking up what was left of a nasty divorce made me decline the second date. I figured I have had my fair share of days living between *Inferno* and *Purgatorio* and I was due for some days of freedom in *Paradiso*, as Dante Alighieri structured so well in his epic poem Divine Comedy. It was my time but it was also the choices moving forward that would lead me there.

When James mentioned to me he had plans for July 4th in Seattle for his son's wedding celebration and asked me to come along to be his date, I was a little nervous. I didn't know if I was ready for family exposure yet and let him know I would think about it. Realizing how reluctant I was to give him an answer he didn't mention the subject again. It had been a year since his divorce and he didn't feel ready to show up alone and face his ex-in-laws yet so he decided to change plans.

Closer to the date he flew me into Tulsa for a 4th of July Celebration at a rooftop hotel downtown. It would be my first time attending an Independence Day Celebration and I dressed accordingly for the occasion. It was a lovely afternoon.

There was a live band playing, drinks and finger foods service. As we watched the sun setting, the fireworks started to spark the sky around downtown Tulsa creating an Oscar winning view for best picture. James was holding me from behind as we both delighted in the magical beauty in front of us. At some point he held me closer and whispered in my ear: "I love you so much…"

I pulled his arms close to my chest and kissed his hand. I felt I was falling for him too but didn't say it back, I don't know why…maybe I was afraid of missing that silver lining again. "What if something goes wrong like it always does?" I had asked God and the Universe for someone like him but couldn't help to keep thinking: "What's the catch now?" I was having a hard time believing it was indeed a miracle… that something good had actually happened; "Will you hold me if I fall into faith?… if I let go of control, will you be there to guide me?…" What a hard lesson to master! How about following the rules you've set for yourself about your new future? "How do you feel right now?" That one was easy to answer: "My heart and soul were smiling."

A week later he flew in for my 42nd birthday, booked us a room at the Gaylord Texan and bought me a beautiful dress to wear for our special dinner, a necklace and earrings to go with it. He prepared every little detail including reservations for a romantic dinner at the Italian restaurant inside the resort.

"A Cinderella deal??? for real?…" I was still having a hard time believing all that could be actually happening while he helped me with the necklace. When he was done, I turned around and hugged him, whispering in his ears: "I love you so much…"

I remember looking back to my past birthdays and felt so grateful and so blessed… I drove him to the airport the next day, and after I dropped him off I cried happy tear the whole drive home. My mom and dad were in town for my brother's wedding so when I got home, I had a cake, which my mom baked from scratch, my brother and his wife were also there and along with Gigi, they sang happy birthday to me. People don't realize how genuine care can actually humble you. "The dog days are over." I thought and I was genuinely happy.

I don't believe James had any idea what his gentle and kind soul meant for my healing. To be arriving in my life like that after I had been crossing the valley of shadows for so long. He had so much love to give and all I had to do was accept so I did. I let myself embark on a journey many would warn me was too soon but have you met Angela? She suffers from a chronic decease called optimism. In the past that attitude had got in the way causing a good deal of pain but since she realized she survived, it could be possible she now thinks she has become bulletproof. My only compass this time was to make decisions more consciously listening to how I felt. I was not desperate for someone. I could take all the time I wanted without being committed to a single person but every day for the following months, I chose to be with just James.

What a difference a year can make! "There's a rainbow before me. Skies above can't be stormy, since that moment of bliss…" Dinah Washington's song became top of my playlist. I made a point of keeping this grateful feeling as long as I could so I read about gratitude and the power of intention – a lot! I wanted that kind of energy to resonate with me all the time. Learning how to transmute bad thoughts and raising my vibrations with the power of LOVE and sending it out to every living being or even the food I would eat was amazing. I became very aware of the type of energy I was putting out there by stopping to take things personal and to avoid arguments. This helped me understand we are all on different paths and exactly where we need to be. There's a time for everything and for everyone. It is important to respect the flow each one creates in their lives. I was allowing my new reality to manifest based on LOVE and GRATITUDE.

Speaking of Gratitude, that November of 2015 James had invited Gigi and I over for Thanksgiving and we got to meet his son Cole, with his new wife Ashley the new baby Lennon and his wife's daughters Asher and Miah. Up to that point I had met the single James. He had such a young spirit and we had so much fun together. That Thanksgiving I got to see his family side. He had got a gingerbread house to build with the girls and some other games to keep them busy.

He begin sharing with me the trips he made with his family in the past and the many memories they built together. Thanksgiving has always been my favorite holiday of the year and it would be the first time I was going to have a chance to cook the whole menu by myself which I delightfully enjoyed every single detail of. I think it is the most soul satisfying time when you can come together as a nation to simply say THANK YOU. That specific Thanksgiving time, if I was given the chance, I would be pilgrimaging around Tulsa announcing over a loudspeaker my long gratitude list. I was deeply grateful for my second chance and I celebrated that with a long table filled with family and good food.

As the International Sales Manager at my new job, I was travelling all over the world – just like I told God I wanted and James was very supportive of my career. It was a new side of aviation working with avionics, an area I knew nothing about but James spent some time teaching me about flight controls to give me a big picture of how the cockpit of an airplane worked. Those insights coupled with my curiosity for learning new things helped me approach my past customers, presenting the products I was now selling. I met more customers from that side of the industry across the globe, expanding my network considerably. I was in charge in South & Central America, Africa, Asia & Europe.

Working in a male-dominant industry can be very challenging, double whamming for a Latin who dresses differently and speaks with a strong accent. It can take much more than hard work to succeed. However, I used my strength as a good listener to get my customers to share their needs and I presented them with a solution. My customers loved my commitment to help them figure out the best solutions and due to the time zone difference on the continents I was over, there were days I worked from 7a to 1am, in order to cover all the territories I managed. I also had an extensive travel schedule for the first year and it wasn't easy to manage a long distance relationship, getting us both frustrated at times. James found a way of letting me know about his intentions by surprising me one weekend with a commitment ring, after almost a year we were together. I was extremely surprised and of course happy but I asked what made him make that decision.

"I want your clients to know you're taken!" – he said.

"You're not gonna pee on my leg too to mark your territory, are you?" I asked jokingly and laughed.

I wasn't expecting a serious relationship like I said before but that showed me we were headed somewhere in the future. I did want him in my life. He was by far the most charming, mature, intellectual and emotionally <u>available</u> man I ever met. I knew he wasn't perfect just like I am not either, and it would have been a matter of time before we found something we disagree on, but he had the attitude I was looking for in a man. There is no such thing as perfection but with the right attitude we can figure things out, ya know? Sometimes you just need a man that is more man than you are! I didn't need a prince to rescue me, a needed a man who would show love, safety and also gave me peace. No more rollercoasters.

In 2016 Gigi let me know she was ready to live on her own when our lease ended. My Brazilian mom's heart made me ask her almost crying: "What have I done to you? Why do you want to leave me?"

"Mom, you raised me to be an independent woman. You've done your job, I am going to college and I am ready to be on my own." - she said.

"Wow, I've created a monster!" I thought – "she's indeed her mother's daughter."

When I mentioned that to James he told me to come live with him at his house. There would be no need for me to pay rent somewhere when I traveled so much for work and I accepted. With tears in my eyes I packed my apartment in Grapevine, TX, July of 2016. Happy tears, bittersweet tears. That apartment had memories of a comeback stage. A place where I spent my days of healing after my long winter. A place where I rose from the ashes and spent a lot of alone time with Divine Life, feeling my blood being pumped inside my veins and getting stronger. My journal since that time has only gratitude moments registered. Intimate talks with God and guess what? No more fights. Even on the not so great days, the extension of my notes would be:

"He says He finishes what He starts so I am waiting on His words..." and I would go in silence telling myself: "Let what is being created be formed. Let go." Or sometimes I would only write. "Help."

And rest all my worries on the Great Mind of Love. He is always creating something new and good. That is His Divine force. If we only learn how to connect and let Him do what He does best, we would experience nothing but joy, even on days it doesn't look so bright. With that in mind I left my daughter in Dallas and headed to Tulsa, OK the end of July of 2016.

A new chapter had started.

I have asked myself many times what makes this relationship so different from the ones I had. Could it be possible that I simply manifested him like my friend Marcia joked so many times? Could it be that I had finally decided what I wanted in a person and asked God to bring me the right package this time? What makes me think it would be just about myself and what I wanted? How about James's feelings?

I also had to reflect what I wanted to receive in return. I could not be the real -life version of the extraterrestrial cartoon creature Stich. Lilo's best friend like my friend Regina would call me sometimes when I came unglued and expect nothing but love in return. It doesn't work that way. It is a two-way road. When you are with a person with the right attitude, you will realize the more you give, the more you receive – I am talking about love, companionship, partnership and constantly a little spoiling... the little things. A feet massage, his/her favorite drinks, small notes or texts, ask about his/her bucket list, be genuinely interested in what makes him/her happy. If you are with the right person, he/she will do the same in return when you least expect it. You have to be what you want to receive. Like I've mentioned before, James is someone easy to love and I think it is because happiness is already part of him just like peace.

When we met I had decided to start a clean chapter remember? I had decided to deconstruct the old habits and construct new ones, filled with intention and consciousness. That meant I had to make peace with my past and through out my relationship with James I openly spoke about them and the lessons I had learned with each one of them. I asked James to do the same and open up about his past, the goal was not to have secrets which could compromise our relationship in the future. At first he gave me half stories, remember, he is someone who lives in the present and doesn't like to talk or to create drama but eventually he felt comfortable sharing more details.

I was kind of disappointed there were no juicy, dark secrets to be shared... no where near the dirty secrets I had and no skeletons to compete with the ones hidden in my family's closet, not even for a tennis match. All conversations about the past were handled with a mature understanding, no judgment zone and no blaming games. As for myself, I believe if James had come into my life earlier, I probably would not be mature enough to make it work. Back then I was fighting too many battles within myself. I had spent half of my life letting my ego ride me like wild horse, looking for fulfillment, for somebody to rescue me and make me happy.

Church didn't save me, I treated God like a big bully picking on me. Marriage didn't save me either, poor Roberto had no idea how to tame a wild horse haunted by a traumatic childhood. Then I gave Paulo the mission to rescue me from the castle of horror I had locked myself in and used his family as the human sacrifice to accomplish the task. I am sure Tom could've been up to making all that go away, if it wasn't for his fragile health. Looking back now I can see clearly why none of them could have worked. It wasn't them. It was me who needed some serious work.

I had to be the one willing to make it right by taking responsibility for the choices I had made. I had to be the one picking up the pieces and face my fears, being the person I was meant to be all along. A strong version of myself already existed somewhere but it had been suffocated by ego. Whenever I decided to take charge back in 2015, she emerged like a loving mother. "We're gonna do this together this time. Let's set some ground rules first..." And that's when transformation took place. This True Version of me was already whole, beautiful and vibrant inside. Her faith wasn't depending on a person but a Higher Power and that's why it worked with James. We met and we didn't have to complete each other. We were already complete. We were just sharing the experience and this is what made such an easy transition. Marriage made sense for both of us two years after living together.

Chapter 24
How did I actually get here?.

When I started to write the first pages of this book trying to understand what I was feeling I had never written a book before, I wasn't sure what this was about. Every once and a while I would get this tap on my shoulder, words whispered in my ears, sometimes I woke up in the middle of the night with a subject in mind and added notes in my phone until I realized I had to give form to this story and honor my journey.

During a business trip last year in Europe, a hurt ankle cut my meetings a day shorter and I had to kick off vacation plans for my daughter's 21st birthday celebration earlier, as it was already planed and prepaid. We stopped for a day in Paris to have dinner with her high school friend Dani from Florida before I headed to our celebration destination in Ibiza. I asked her to stop at "Shakespeare & Company" bookstore to get one of my bucket list items checked and she agreed.

As I entered the store, the whispers became overwhelming. I felt at home, I felt honored to be in a place where so many great minds were inspired. I lost track of time - I could stay there for days. I grabbed a napkin in my purse and wrote: "I am working on a dream...send creativity my way. Much gratitude. Angela McCluskey from Tulsa, OK" and I posted that note on the board where hundreds of other notes were. My guess is that the universe said: "Okay, I will give you the push you need."

I left my job in the end of July 2018 and started focusing on our wedding plans (which were in October 2018). I found myself with extra time to finish this book. On August 4th 2018 I wrote on my creative journal:

"Hello you gorgeous writer! Look at you all sassy and once again getting ready to explore new horizons. It has been a long time since you tried something so big but I understand why... the last flight was a tough one, wasn't it? But look at the person you've become in the process... wow... Really! Look at you, even with some missing feathers exposing your scars, there you are... you don't care! You just stand there, nice and tall... welcome back. I love you so much."

There, although this book wasn't yet finished, at that moment I sent a clear message to the universe and I knew it was taking form somewhere. I just needed time to channel the message but I kept telling myself, it was going to be done one day. I acknowledge James as a blessing in my life because he simply allows me to be myself again, and that's how this book was able to be finalized. It is easier to see your true reflection when the mind is calm.

This past year was another milestone for me. I took one year off from the business world. I had my beautiful wedding in October of 2018 and watched my family grow from just Gigi and myself to a stepdaughter, stepson and their spouses and four step granddaughters. Our family gatherings now are a full house filled with a lot of love and joy and this is priceless. Little things we only learn how to appreciate when we have been in a battlefield alone.

This year also allowed me time for some volunteer work within the Hispanic Community and with that, came a new crowd of friends giving my social life a very pleasant sparkle. Another thing this down time allowed was time to regroup and rethink where I want to spend my energies making a living, until I can make a living as a writer. Within this one year I have been able to spend a lot of time with myself and to analyze the many lives I've lived; from the dreamer child to the rebel teenager, and from the frustrated adult to The Real me, which I call the "Beloved I AM."

I believe what delayed my awakening the most was my desire to fix everything.

I wanted to fix my poor childhood so I developed skills to take me out of it, getting better jobs. I wanted to fix parenting so I decided to start a family very early in life determined to be a better one. I wanted to fix my first husband when he was not broken, he was following his own path. I wanted to fix my Cinderella dream believing my Prince Charming had kissed the wrong princess and I had to force him to understand the awful mistake he had made. I wanted to fix Tom after all it wasn't fair to let the man who was suppose to be my warrior fall apart. I even wanted to fix God harassing Him with threatening dialogs trying to manipulate him to give me the outcome I think I deserved. Everything took a completely different course when I realized one simple thing: I did not have any more fight left in me and Surrender is a beautiful prayer.

It happened before when I had given up living, right before my big move to the United States - but a lesson not learned which will always have to be learned again. No exceptions. The second time around, ironically enough, I was back in Brazil, the starting point. Like a big circle. It was October 29th, 2014 in Natal, Brazil

I had a long day at work then helped my mom cook dinner. That morning my parents had taken Tom to see the neurologist as his headaches had intensified with the out of control seizures, which were happening through out the day now. I had conference calls the whole morning so Gigi had accompanied them to help with the translation explaining the symptoms.

During dinner they were explaining to me the doctor had scheduled an MRI for a week later. We lived in a fourth floor walkup apartment and after we watched the novella I went downstairs for my evening cigarette. My mom always came along for our night chats, talking about family and life in general. I always enjoyed my talks with her and this bond became stronger after I become an adult. This particular time I shared how tired I was of trying to save Tom.

"Maybe I have to accept he will always be ill. I am ready to accept I will have to take care of him the rest of my life. If that's what God wants me to do, it is okay. I will stop praying for healing and tell him to do His will and just keep me strong so I can help him."

That statement came from the heart. I meant every word I said. I went to sleep, Tom had two seizures that night and it was going to be just like any other day, start my conference calls running on three hours of sleep. I got ready as usual but before I started the calls, I bowed my head to pray on my desk. Afraid I was going to fall sleep with the lack of sleep, I put my headsets on and looked for my favorite song to keep me focused: "Praise you in the storm" by Casting Crowns." The next song came next without a particular selection based on the subject, I believe. The next song was "Oceans – where feet may fail" by Hillsong United. Every word of that song was felt in my soul with love, and tears were rolling down my face, "When oceans rise, my soul will rest in Your embrace…"

When the song finished my face was on the floor, my sign of surrender. My only prayer this time was: Do Your Will for my husband's life. His answer this time was clear – and powerful. Like I mentioned in the first pages: "I will take it from here."

Surrender is indeed a powerful prayer but not an easy decision. It means you will have to walk with blindfolds, with no idea where your next step will take you. "If I let go, will YOU hold me if I fall?..."

The next day I was going to have a very important call with my boss in Australia so I had to get some sleep. First I took Tom and my mom to meet with a couple from church. The husband spoke some English and I wanted Tom to feel he was making some friends in Brazil. During dinner I looked at Tom's pale face, very unusual, and asked if he was doing ok, he smiled and said yes. On the drive home I asked if he wanted something else to eat, he said he wanted some French fries from McDonalds so I passed by the drive thru to get him some. He looked like a kid enjoying a treat. It was past 10pm when we made back home, I gave him his nocturnal insulin, he gave my mom a goodnight hug and told her in Portuguese, te amo mãe! Mother says she remembers this like it was yesterday.

We went to bed and one hour later the first seizure came, then the second one… I got him comfortable with pillows around him and a towel on his neck and moved to Gigi's room around 2am.

I woke up the next morning and went to check on him. A scream followed as I opened my bedroom door. His face was turning blue and his eyes were opened but still breathing. We called the SAMU, equivalent of 911 there and they instructed me to move him from the bed to the floor to perform CPR, which both my nephew Rodrigo and I tried with no success for several minutes until the ambulance arrived. They showed up 30 minutes later just to announce he was dead. I dropped to my knees in desperation, hugging Tom's lifeless body on the floor and stayed there for a long time until my brother-in-law Isaias lovingly removed me with a hug.

"We have to take care of some things now Angela. You have to be strong."

Both him and my sister Alzeni got on the phone trying to get arrangements with a funeral home and a doctor to get a death certificate as he had passed at home, getting all the details needed. I also had to contact the American Embassy to get approval for the cremation. My family took care of every detail with love and compassion because I was numb.

I started a blaming game inside my head. It was my fault he was dead. There I embarked on a painful guilt-tripping journey. I felt everything, from the pain of the disconnection to the pain of defeat, I took it all in. I felt empty and dark inside.

During my evening cigarettes breaks with mom she was mostly the only one talking. I would just glaze at the sky with a painful look...my small talks were mostly angry statements to both Tom and God. "That midnight move was not cool, ya know?..."

I thought I was going to die from a broken heart. I was diagnosed with depression and introduced to my new drugs forced by my mother, which I took for a couple of months. My family and my journal were helping balance the rest. I had to force myself to react. That's when I began to start looking around me and the dark place I had been sitting in for the past few months. I wanted to understand those feelings. I didn't want to ignore them. Little by little I started to recognize each one of them. Layers and layers of pain inflicted by ego were peeled as I reveled my beloved I AM.

Those dark winters shed so many layers from me... it revealed my true self, my true strength and my true worth. Nobody will ever be able to take that experience and revelation from me because now, like a tree, I stand. My awakening wasn't pretty. It was messy and painful but I have made some good progress, while keeping my heart opened for some more light to come in, forever improving, forever searching...

We are all in a "never ending loving act", because we are human BEINGs not a human DONE, I heard that somewhere and it made sense. Every new negative energy surfaced is an opportunity to practice new healing. That's how we ascend in our vibrating frequency and get closer to Him as He created us to be. It is yours and mine decision to let GOD be magnified through our lives and that starts with a beautiful prayer of surrender.

He created you and I perfectly like his own, and deep inside of us there is a perfect version. The vision we were born with - to be a piece of His Great Art. We need to be the vessel to hear His guidance, to live the life we were meant to live. I am sure it is a life of fulfillment, abundance and grace because like I said, He is always creating something beautiful.

Look at a flower for instance: when a seed is planted, you don't have to keep telling it to be a flower. Same goes with a tree...or a cactus... they know what they were born to be. They trust a process that never fails.

I understand my calling and I am ready to help people do the same, one soul at a time and I do it often, every time I see someone in pain. I share my story and I offer insights that can help them to overcome pains. I am ready to help more people to connect with their Divine Love and shed all the layers that society, pain, judgment, shame and losses have put upon them.

I want more people to find the power supplied by Conscious Life and realize that Source is always available. All you need is an opened heart to receive it.

"Be still and KNOW (experience) that I AM God." (Psalms 46:10) it is the lesson I've learned with my quest and through surrender and resilience, I am here.

The End

There is a fable in the forest
Whispered by the branches, as they blow.
A tale about the truth of leaving
Things that no longer help you grow.
For on the surface it looks simple,
Like you only need lace your boots,
But there is nothing quite as painful
As untangling your roots.
And proof is found in tree stumps
Of the price some pay to flee,
That they would cut their lives in half
To cut the time before they're free.
Yet from the little left behind
Life has been known to grow again,
For unless you take your roots
A part of you will still remain."
— **Erin Hanson**

"Ora (direis) ouvir estrelas"
A poem by Olavo Bilac

Ora (direis) ouvir estrelas! Certo
Perdeste o senso!" E eu vos direi, no entanto,
Que, para ouvi-las, muita vez desperto
E abro as janelas, pálido de espanto...

E conversamos toda a noite, enquanto
A via-láctea, como um pálio aberto,
Cintila. E, ao vir do sol, saudoso e em pranto,
Inda as procuro pelo céu deserto.

Direis agora: "Tresloucado amigo!
Que conversas com elas? Que sentido
Tem o que dizem, quando estão contigo?"

E eu vos direi: "Amai para entendê-las!
Pois só quem ama pode ter ouvido

Capaz de ouvir e de entender estrelas.

"Now (you will say) Hearing Stars" is sonnet number XIII of the Milky Way sonnet collection by the Brazilian Parnassian Poet, Olavo Bilac

Now (you say) you hear stars! Right
You have lost your sense! "And I will tell you, however,
That, to hear them, I often wake up
And I open the windows, pale with astonishment ...

And we talk all night while
The milky way, like an open canopy twinkle.
And when the sun came, longing and weeping,
Still looking for them through the desert sky.

You will say now: "Crazy friend!
What do you converse with them? What sense?
Do you have what they say when they are with you? "

And I will tell you, "You have to love them so you can understand!"
For only those who love may have the ears
Able to hear and understand stars.

About The Author

Angela McCluskey-Moses was born Angela Cordeiro da Silva in Brazil in1973. She grew up in *Vila Verde*, a poor city on the East Side of Sao Paulo. She attended University Cruzeiro do Sul where she studied Business Administration and was an Aerospace Professional for 22 years.

She moved to the United States in 2005 and after overcoming significant obstacles, she decided to take some time off the corporate world to invest on her dream, writing her first book about her life story.

CPSIA information can be obtained
at www.ICGtesting.com
Printed in the USA
LVHW041709060220
646086LV00011B/878